RIVERSIDE COMMUNITY COLLEGE
1916

P9-CJR-296

DATE DUE

JA 6'82	FE 1'82	
MR 19'70	NO 22'85	MY 25'87
AP 8'77	MR 6'87	
	MR 31'80	JA 20'93
		MY 7'93
DE 6'73		MR 15'94
JE 10'86		
OC 31'80	OC 29'96	FE 15'97
FE 20'81	JA 18'91	AG 5'04
OC 30'81		AP 10'08

PS3515
I713B57

RIVERSIDE CITY COLLEGE
LIBRARY

Riverside, California

DEMCO—FRESNO

BLACK ON BLACK

By Chester Himes

BLACK ON BLACK

BABY SISTER
and selected writings

CHESTER HIMES

1973

Doubleday & Company, Inc., Garden City, New York

Riverside Community College
Library
4800 Magnolia Avenue
Riverside, CA 92506

PS3515.I713 B57 1973
Himes, Chester B., 1909-
Black on Black; Baby sister
and selected writings

Grateful acknowledgment is made to the following for permission to reprint material copyrighted or controlled by them:

Lyrics from "What Did I Do to Be So Alone and Blue," music by Thomas Waller and Harry Brooks, words by Andy Razaf. Copyright 1929 by Mills Music, Inc. Used with permission.

"All God's Chillun Got Pride," June 1944, "All He Needs Is Feet," 1945, "Mama's Missionary Money," November 1949, "Negro Martyrs Are Needed," May 1944, "Zoot Riots Are Race Riots," July 1943, "Lunching at the Ritz-more," October 1942, "Heaven Has Changed," March 1943. All articles appeared in *The Crisis* and are reprinted by permission of the publisher.

"The Night's for Cryin'," first published in January 1937 issue of *Esquire* magazine. Copyright 1936 by Esquire, Inc. Reprinted with permission.

"Now Is the Time! Here Is the Place!," March 1943 issue of *Opportunity*. Reprinted by permission of the National Urban League, Inc.

"One More Way to Die," published in 1946 issue of *Negro Story*.

ISBN: 0-385-02526-2
Library of Congress Catalog Card Number 72-76169
Copyright © 1942, 1943, 1944, 1945, 1949, 1973 by Chester Himes
All Rights Reserved
Printed in the United States of America
First Edition

CONTENTS

These writings are admittedly chauvinistic. You will conclude if you read them that BLACK PROTEST and BLACK HETEROSEXUALITY are my two chief obsessions.

And you will be right. I am a sensualist, I love beautiful people, I have SOUL. At the same time I am extremely sensitive to all the humiliations and preconceptions Black Americans are heir to. But I think my talent is sufficient to render these chauvinistic writings interesting, or at least provoking.

I wrote the scenario, *Baby Sister*, at the instigation of European producers who thought the American film *Raisin in the Sun* was a failure. French critics who read the scenario termed it a "Greek tragedy."

I wrote it in 1961 while living in a one-room penthouse atop a five-floor walk-up overlooking the *Ramparts* in the "old town" of Antibes. As the story of Baby Sister unfolded in my mind I was moved to tears. When not crying I was singing at the top of my voice: *What did I do to be so black and blue?*

During the writing the Côte d'Azur was assaulted by one of the worst hurricanes in its history, and at the height of its violence I envisioned the irrefutable ending.

With the exception of "Tang," which I wrote in Alicante in 1967 when my thoughts had concentrated on a BLACK REVOLUTION, I wrote the first nine short stories during the Depression of the nineteen thirties and the first years of the Second World War.

I wrote the four furious essays during the war while employed in Jim Crow war industries in Los Angeles.

Five of the last eight short stories were written after the publication of my first novel (*If He Hollers Let Him Go*) in 1945 and before I went to Europe in 1953, while living in Harlem and various New England states.

I wrote the last short story, "Prediction," in Alicante in 1969 after I had become firmly convinced that the only chance Black

Americans had of attaining justice and equality in the United States of America was by violence.

Chester Himes
Spain, 1971

BLACK ON BLACK

The camera moves over the slum streets, over the violent scenes, over the frenetic jazz clubs and the frantic bars of a Saturday night, over the filling churches of a Sunday morning, over the harsh contradictions, the squalid hovels and the swank apartments, over the fat smug faces of the prosperous and the lean lonely faces of the hungry.

A lone drum plays softly.

A voice speaks in all languages.

VOICE

This is Harlem, U.S.A., a city of contradictions. A city of Negroes isolated in the center of New York City. A city of incredible poverty and huge sums of cash. A city of the meek and the violent. A city of brothels, bars and churches. Here is the part called Sugar Hill, where the prosperous live—the leaders, the professionals, the numbers barons. Here is the part called The Valley, where the hungry eke out an existence and prey upon one another. The Valley is like a sea filled with cannibal fish. Put in your hand, draw out a stub. This is the story of a good-looking, healthy, voluptuous, seventeen-year-old black girl, called BABY SISTER LOUIS, who lives in The Valley. She lives with her family: her mother, MAMA LOUIS, and her three brothers: SUSIE, twenty-two years old, BUDDY, twenty years old, and PIGMEAT, fourteen years old. Her elder sister, LIL, a blues singer, lives with her man on Sugar Hill. BABY SISTER is a juicy, tasty lamb in a jungle of hungry wolves. And in The Valley there is no good shepherd. Only the *will* of the community can save her from the wolves. But the inhabitants of this community, restricted, exploited, prostituted, violated and violent, timid and vicious, living in their rat-ridden, hotbox, stinking flats, are either the hungry wolves themselves, or are struggling desperately to save themselves from the hungry wolves. And it is perfectly reasonable and natural these people should be hungry, the wolves and the sheep alike. If your own food—food for the soul and food for the spirit as well as food for the stomach—had been held just out of your reach for three hundred years, or longer, you would be hungry too. And one way to keep from starving in this land of plenty when you have no food is to eat your baby sister.

EXTERIOR.   STREETS OF HARLEM   DAY

The drum gives way to hot jumping jazz coming from an auto radio as the camera focuses on BABY SISTER LOUIS doing a slow motion twist beside a shiny convertible parked on Seventh Avenue near 123rd Street in the late morning sunshine. BABY SISTER is a hot-bodied, curly-haired, high-breasted, brown-skin girl exuding an effluvium of sex urgency. Her hips are doing a hard, slow, suggestive shake in her skintight skirt. Her bedroom eyes are taunting and her big hard breasts molded in a tight sweater are haunting. Pearly teeth peep between big cushion-soft red-painted lips.

This is BABY SISTER, Sing Sing quail, a lecher's dream, enough to make a preacher lay his Bible down.

Men are staring from the windows of Sugar Ray's bar, from the windows of the barbershop up the street. The crowd of flashy men in front of the Theresa Hotel at 125th Street have paused in their talk of whores and horses to watch her. A blind man with a white stick pauses to stare; Nubby, a legless beggar, squats on his leather pads to drool; self-righteous women, the saved sisters and the daughters of Jesus, pause in front of the church across the street to glare disapprovingly at the "brazen hussy."

And here comes SLICK COLLINS, out of the door of Sugar Ray's bar, doing a version of the stalking twist toward the waiting girl. You can see he is a wolf by the size of his teeth, a wolf in a white flannel sports jacket and green silk slacks, with shiny conked hair and heavy gold jewelry. You can see he is proud of his little hot piece, of his big shiny car, of his fine figure and his fine clothes. He is narcissistic about his smooth black self; he's got the world in a jug and the stopper in his hand.

What more can a second-rate pimp want? His little side piece has got everyone's attention and he's the envy of the block.

BABY SISTER faces him, shaking her body enticingly, tantalizingly.

He stalks toward her, keeping time with the rhythm, backing and filling, closing in like a stallion on a mare. The air is electric with suggestion.

Suddenly there is the loud sound of a stone striking metal:

BANG!

It comes from the other side of the car. Something has struck SLICK's fine big car. But what?

SLICK and BABY SISTER freeze in attitudes of suspended motion. SLICK frowns with sudden anxiety, exhibiting a ludicrous concern for his property. He could not have looked more anxious had BABY SISTER dropped dead. On BABY SISTER's face appears an expression of apprehension, of sudden fear. Hot jazz continues to come from the car radio, jeering at the tableau.

The spectators pour from the bar, from the barbershop, from up the street in front of the hotel. What's going on? What's this? They draw near in silent curiosity.

Again the sinister sound of a stone striking metal:

BANG!

But this time everyone sees it. They see the stone swinging through the air from the other side of the street and strike the side of SLICK's fine car. They do a double take. They see a skinny teen-age boy in a gray sweat shirt and blue jeans, bearing a strong resemblance to BABY SISTER, standing on the other side of the broad avenue, draw his arm back and throw another stone at the big fine car. This time the stone goes over the car, narrowly missing SLICK's frozen head and causing the blind man to duck.

This is BABY SISTER's little brother, PIGMEAT, throwing stones at SLICK's fine car.

From among the spectators a laugh breaks out.

But SLICK's eyes seem to pop from his head as though he can't believe the sight of some ragged punk throwing stones at his car.

BABY SISTER gives her little brother a look of fury.

Suddenly a look of insensate rage, a killing rage, contorts SLICK's face. He curses viciously.

The scene erupts into motion. SLICK draws his knife, snaps open the blade with a loud click and starts running across the street toward PIGMEAT.

Behind him runs BABY SISTER, her tight skirt drawn up to her garter belt, exposing long brown legs, running hard and fast in her high heels, her hard buttocks jiggling.

Seventh Avenue has two traffic lanes, one northbound and the other southbound, with an unkempt park in the center. It is a warm day and traffic is moving.

SLICK runs through the traffic as though he doesn't see it. Brakes squeal, drivers curse. BABY SISTER is just behind him.

PIGMEAT turns east on 123rd Street, a half-slum residential street, runs past old stone steps, grubby little shops, the dirty façades of cold-water flats, running fast in his canvas sneakers; SLICK in pursuit, puffing and panting, knife blade flashing, like a harlequin gone berserk; BABY SISTER bringing up the rear, hard breasts bouncing, buttocks fanning, brown legs straining, as though wading through air.

Housewives peer from open windows, children look with wide eyes, pedestrians stop and stare.

VOICES

(*following the running trio*) Chase 'em, baby.
Give 'em hell . . . Do you see what I see . . .
No one interferes.

PIGMEAT turns south on Lenox Avenue, a business street of bars, butchers, grocery stores, radio and television stores; dodges past pedestrians and turns quickly into an areaway between two buildings. He comes out into the courtyard behind, strewn with garbage cans and refuse thrown from the windows of the apartments above—whiskey bottles, beer cans, bedsprings, old mattresses, a dead cat. He has gained on SLICK. As he leaps through the refuse toward a faded green door in the opposite wall, it appears as though he will escape. It is obvious that he is familiar with this escape route; that he expects to find the door unlocked. He slams against the door without slowing down; but it is closed and locked from within. He bounces back; surprised and stricken he turns back toward the areaway through which he has entered, only to find SLICK heave suddenly into view. Desperately he searches about for a weapon to protect himself, picks up a length of rusty iron pipe and backs against the wall. Seeing that he has his victim cornered, SLICK slows down to catch his breath, an evil smile on his face, waving the knife like a riding crop.

SLICK

I'm going to teach you to throw rocks at my car, little motherfucker. I'm gonna waste you.

PIGMEAT

(*looking panic-stricken*) I told you to leave my sister alone.

SLICK

(*jeeringly*) I didn't listen and now I'm gonna mark you like you marked my car.

PIGMEAT

I ain't scared of you; I just ain't got no knife.

SLICK

Now ain't that too bad.

SLICK moves slowly toward his victim, as though relishing the situation. PIGMEAT grips his weapon, looking terrified. Windows in the apartments above are opened, black faces peer down with expectancy.

WOMAN'S VOICE

Shame on you, wanting to cut that little boy.

MAN'S VOICE

Tend to your own business, what you got to do with it.

ANOTHER WOMAN'S VOICE

I'm gonna call the police.

EXTERIOR.   CHURCH OF THE REDEEMED SINNER   DAY

BABY SISTER continues running down Lenox Avenue in the direction of a crowd of black people assembled on the sidewalk. A funeral is taking place in a storefront church. Parked in front of the church are two limousines and a big black shiny hearse. The plate glass front of the converted store is painted black up to the height of a man's head, bearing a white painted inscription: *Church of the Redeemed Sinner*. Stretched across the front is a white cloth banner with the crudely lettered announcement: *TODAY AT 10 O'CLOCK THE FUNERAL OF BROTHER JOHN LOUIS, MURDERED PROTECTING HIS DAUGHTER'S VIRTUE, REVEREND CONVERTED SINNER PRESIDING . . .*

Black people are milling about the entrance, drinking whiskey and beer from bottles, talking, laughing, weeping, waiting, enjoying a brief respite in the bright sunshine. Inside the church is crowded.

Without pausing, BABY SISTER pushes through the milling people and enters the church.

INTERIOR.   CHURCH OF THE REDEEMED SINNER   DAY

BABY SISTER runs down the aisle to the front pew, which is occupied by her family. MAMA LOUIS, a light-complected woman dressed completely in black, dull-faced, big-bodied, sits in the center, sobbing into a black handkerchief. Beside her, on the aisle, sits BUDDY LOUIS, twenty years old, slight of build, dressed in a dark green suit and black tie, his expression blank. On the other side sits SUSIE LOUIS, twenty-two years old, broad shoulders stretching the seams of a blue serge suit, strong lumpy face looking rock-hard with a smoldering rage, eyes glued on the preacher as though he'd like to knock out his teeth. Beyond him sits LIL LOUIS, high yellow with red-dyed hair, bright lipstick, smooth creamy skin, big-bosomed body of a blues singer but not yet fat, tears trickling unheeded down her face, wearing an expensive dark purple summer dress with a black lace shawl. Beyond her sits UNCLE PIE, member of the family by personal choice, a round-faced black man with slightly bulging eyes and short-cropped hair; he is the chauffeur of the hearse waiting to take BROTHER LOUIS to the grave and a bachelor living at the funeral home.

BROTHER JOHN LOUIS rests in an open coffin on wooden horses between two white plaster pillars with electric candles at head and foot. A white floral wreath behind the coffin bears the banner: REST IN PEACE, BROTHER LOUIS. His black face has a tranquil expression. It is silhouetted against the white satin lining of the raised coffin lid.

In the background stands REVEREND CONVERTED SINNER, a tall, lean, hungry-looking black man with a mournful expression, dressed in a faded black frock coat. He is preaching the funeral sermon, looking upward, intoning in a loud, sorrowful voice.

REVEREND CONVERTED SINNER

From the rimbone of the world to the dark streets of Harlem

is these sinful, murderous men, corrupting young women, young girls with hot tails who have not yet got the spirit.

CONGREGATION

(*in a mourning litany, rhythmic, harmonious*) Young girls, lawd, with trouble in their tails, lawd, and nothing in their heads, lawd, give 'em the spirit, lawd, send them salvation.

At that moment BABY SISTER skids to a stop at the end of the front pew, leans over BUDDY and MAMA and calls to SUSIE.

BABY SISTER

SLICK's trying to kill PIGMEAT.

Like two automatons, the brothers come to their feet in one swift hard motion. MAMA LOUIS screams. LIL gasps. UNCLE PIE doesn't hear. REVEREND CONVERTED SINNER breaks off in the middle of a word.

Pandemonium breaks out in the crowded church.

Without another word, BABY SISTER wheels, dress still pulled high, exposing her legs to her garter belt, runs back down the aisle, her high, iron-capped heels rapping in the suddenly buzzing church. Behind her comes BUDDY, face contorted in alarm. Behind BUDDY, pushing him aside to get past, comes SUSIE, his big hard body in the tight blue suit moving like a football player's, his face swollen in a brutal rage.

EXTERIOR.   HARLEM STREETS

The three of them push out onto the sidewalk, like fragments from a bomb explosion, plow through the suddenly converging crowd, BABY SISTER in front, striking out to clear a path, SUSIE behind her pushing her through, BUDDY following. BABY SISTER comes to the areaway through which PIGMEAT went, stops and points. Without a loss of motion SUSIE goes through, BUDDY following.

As they come into the courtyard, PIGMEAT swings his iron pipe with both hands, misses as SLICK steps back and falls to one side from the force of his swing. There is a cut on the right sleeve of his sweat shirt through which blood is seeping. People are hanging from all the windows on the courtyard. Some are trying to stop the fight; others egging them on. A woman is saying she has called the police. Two white men who have come from the store backing onto the courtyard are standing cautiously to one side, pleading with SLICK to stop.

Suddenly there are the sharp, clear, unmistakable clicks of springblade knives being opened.

SLICK freezes in the act of reaching down to slash PIGMEAT across the back, slowly turns his head. The brothers are standing in the courtyard, some distance apart, open knives in their hands, tense but motionless, almost without expression. A sudden expression of nausea appears on SLICK's smooth black face.

Wordlessly, the brothers close in. SLICK manages a quick smile, spreads his hands, lets the knife drop to the ground.

SLICK

(*in a whining voice*) You got the best go and the mojo.

Seeing his brothers closing in, PIGMEAT scrambles to his feet and seizes his iron pipe in both hands and swings at SLICK's head. SLICK ducks.

SUSIE

(*in a blurred, tight-throated, cotton-dry voice*) Let's get the story.

His voice sounds so dangerous the spectators are silenced. PIG-MEAT starts to make another attempt to hit SLICK, but is frozen by the expression on SUSIE's face.

SLICK

(*taking quick advantage of the pause*) He threw rocks at my car, knocked holes in the side.

PIGMEAT

He was going to take BABY SISTER for a ride, even going to keep her way from our pa's funeral.

BABY SISTER has slipped into the courtyard and is standing near the exit, watching the scene with an avid, impersonal, slightly cruel expression.

SLICK

I was only going to drive her to the church.

PIGMEAT

That's a lie. (*appealing to* SUSIE) He's trying to make a whore out of her.

SLICK

This little punk's crazy. Denting my new car like that. I wasn't gonna hurt him, though, just wanted to teach him a lesson.

The spectators stare with puzzled curiosity.

PIGMEAT

(*frantically*) I told him and I told him he better stay away from BABY SISTER.

SUSIE

(*in his dangerous-sounding voice*) What'd he say?

PIGMEAT

He didn't pay any attention.

SLICK

(*half laughing*) Listen to him.

Deliberately SUSIE closes his knife and puts it into his pocket. Without a word or a change of expression or any type of warning, he hooks a left into SLICK's stomach. When SLICK doubles over he lands a short left uppercut to the face, straightening him up, then kicks his feet out from under him with his left foot; and as SLICK goes down like a felled ox, SUSIE pivots with the same flow of motion and kicks him viciously on the jaw. There is a hard bone-popping sound as the jaw goes two inches out of place and SLICK lets out a grunting groan. Gasps of terror and dismay come from the spectators. Without a change of expression on his tight brutal face, SUSIE kicks the prostrate body in the ribs until it turns onto its back, then he reaches down and straightens out the head, stands back and kicks the jaw back into place. SLICK has swallowed his tongue. SUSIE reaches into his mouth with his handkerchief, pulls his tongue back into place, yanks him to his knees and lets him bleed.

SUSIE

(*without change of voice*) Can you hear me, daddy-o?

SLICK

(*in a muffled painful voice*) I can hear you.

SUSIE

(*to* PIGMEAT *who is looking on bug-eyed*) Tell him once more. For a moment PIGMEAT doesn't understand.

SUSIE

Tell him.

PIGMEAT

Now are you going to leave BABY SISTER alone?

SLICK

(*painfully spitting blood*) I swear I ain't never going to look at her again.

SUSIE

(*to* PIGMEAT) Let that be a lesson to you. You got to get this pimp's attention before you tell him anything.

Some of the spectators laugh. BABY SISTER stares from SUSIE to SLICK in horrified fascination. BUDDY appears slightly sick. PIGMEAT looks triumphant.

At that moment two plainclothes detectives dressed in expensive summer suits walk casually onto the scene, their .38-caliber police positives swinging loosely in their hands.

LIEUTENANT (TIMME) FISCHER of the Harlem precinct station, the younger of the two, is a white man and handsome enough to be a movie actor. He is tall and slender with a lean face and a tiny flickering smile, blue eyes, dark brown eyebrows, light blond hair with a slight wave. His official chauffeur, CORPORAL JOHNNY BROWN, is a light-complected black man with a dissipated face, hairline moustache, muddy eyes, straight black hair beginning to recede from the forehead and brushed flat to the skull, and an expression of cynical detachment.

LIEUTENANT FISCHER gives BABY SISTER a long intimate look, part reproachfully, part questioningly, but does not speak to her. She returns his look with a bold challenging stare. Then he turns to stare speculatively at her three brothers standing over SLICK who begins to groan loudly and theatrically.

CORPORAL BROWN gives BABY SISTER a knowing wink from his offside eye, then surveys the quartet of males with a slight snicker. It is obvious that both detectives know them all.

LIEUTENANT FISCHER

What's the trouble here?

SUSIE

There ain't no trouble.

SLICK

(*groaning loudly*) Take me to the hospital.

WOMAN IN A WINDOW

(*volunteering*) The man what's beat up was cutting the little boy when his brothers came.

CORPORAL BROWN

(*taking out a notebook*) What's your name, lady?

WOMAN

(*alarmed*) I don't want to go to court.

CORPORAL BROWN

Then shut up.

LIEUTENANT FISCHER

(*looking at* SUSIE) Who beat up this man?

SUSIE

(*returning his stare deadpan*) Beat up what man?

LIEUTENANT FISCHER

(*frowning angrily*) Don't get too cute or I'll take you, son.

SUSIE

Ask him who beat him up.

The LIEUTENANT looks down at SLICK questioningly. CORPORAL BROWN is looking at BABY SISTER cynically.

SLICK

(*lisping slightly*) Ain't nobody beat me up. We was just playing.

CORPORAL BROWN

(*to* LIEUTENANT) What did I tell you? I seen a joker with his throat cut saying he was just playing.

LIEUTENANT FISCHER

(*face tight with anger*) If that's the way you boys want it, go to it. Just don't let the other one turn up dead. It's not playing after that.

BUDDY

We got to get back to Pa's funeral.

The detectives stand back. The three brothers file out with BABY SISTER between them. Groaning painfully, SLICK tries to stand. The detectives watch him dispassionately.

LIEUTENANT FISCHER

A buck says he'll make it.

CORPORAL BROWN

What kind of bet is that? He's got to make it. Ain't no one going to help him.

INTERIOR.   CHURCH OF THE REDEEMED SINNER   DAY

The mourners make room for SUSIE, BUDDY and BABY SISTER as they file back into the church. REVEREND CONVERTED SINNER is awaiting them, reading the Twenty-third Psalm. MAMA looks at them with a face of dread.

SUSIE

He just scratched; he gone home to change clothes.

LIL and UNCLE PIE sigh in unison.

MAMA

Thank God.

UNCLE PIE signals the undertaker, who comes forward and takes MAMA by the arm and leads her past the open coffin for a last look at the face of BROTHER LOUIS. LIL takes her other arm. She looks down at the face and begins crying hysterically. The preacher signals the organist, who begins playing the old-fashioned organ and singing in a high tenor voice.

ORGANIST

This world is long, this world is wide, but the longest road I ever walked is the one I walked and cried.

The crying is contagious. SUSIE and BUDDY shake off help as they follow their mother and sister down the aisle. The congregation stands, wet-eyed and wailing, and forms a ragged procession past the open coffin.

EXTERIOR.   LENOX AVENUE   DAY

Outside MAMA is helped into the limousine behind the hearse. SUSIE and BUDDY sit flanking her. LIL sits in a jump seat. PIGMEAT comes up wearing a coat and clean shirt and takes the other jump seat. All of them look around for BABY SISTER who has not appeared.

Inside the church the coffin is closed by the undertaker's assistants. Six pallbearers, brother lodge members of the deceased, shoulder it and bring it out.

The chimes in the hearse begin playing "Swing Low, Sweet Chariot." The lodge band, resplendent in uniform, lines up in the street, begins rendering a Dixieland version of "When the Saints Go Marching In," drowning out the chimes. The coffin is eased into the hearse.

MAMA LOUIS

(*screaming*) Where is BABY SISTER?

BABY SISTER

(*appearing from behind the car*) Here I is, Ma.

MAMA

Get inside here.

BABY SISTER

(*in a sudden fit of hysterics*) Ma, don't make me go to the graveyard. Ma, I beg you, Ma. Please, Ma.

MAMA

You hear me, you get inside here, girl. You the cause he get killed, fanning 'round those weedheads.

BABY SISTER

(*crying hysterically*) Ma, I didn't know them men, I swear, Ma. They is always fooling with me. And I didn't know Pa was anywhere near. I didn't know he were gonna fight 'em.

MAMA

(*bitterly*) You hussy, I hope the Lord will punish you.

BABY SISTER

(*falling to her knees in the street*) Ma, I tried to stop 'em. Please, Ma, don't curse me, Ma.

SUSIE comes out of the car in one swift movement, grabs her by the hair, jerks her to her feet and slaps her sprawling on the pavement.

LIL comes out of the car with an open knife, puts the blade on SUSIE's neck.

LIL

(*choking with rage*) Try to hit her once more and I'll cut your throat.

MAMA sits still, looking frightened. Members of the congregation crowd about. PIGMEAT jumps from the other side of the car and runs to help BABY SISTER up. The preacher rushes from the church.

REVEREND CONVERTED SINNER

Lord A'mighty, you can't go fighting to the grave.

SUSIE pushes LIL's knife from his throat, turns without another look toward BABY SISTER and gets back into the limousine. LIL follows. PIGMEAT and UNCLE PIE between them lift BABY SISTER to her feet. She is limping slightly.

UNCLE PIE

(*looking at* SUSIE *reproachfully*) You shouldn't have hit BABY SISTER. She's a good girl. She ain't done nothing wrong. (*as though to himself*) I bet she's the only virgin her age in Harlem.

LIL

(*to* BABY SISTER) Get in the next car, baby. You don't have to look at it.

BABY SISTER

Forgive me, Ma.

MAMA LOUIS looks straight ahead without replying.

BABY SISTER limps to the following limousine. Her knees are skinned, her stocking torn, her hands are bruised. Her face is streaked with tears.

UNCLE PIE goes back to the hearse. The band is waiting impatiently for the saints to begin marching. Order is restored. Half-drunk mourners begin marching about in the street, some going one way, some going another, slapping hands together when they pass.

BABY SISTER stops beside the following limousine, puts her hand on the door handle, looks in at the other four passengers, whom she doesn't know, looks around toward the limousine ahead. She sees LIL watching her through the rear window. PIGMEAT has his head stuck out the side window, looking back at her also. But MAMA, BUDDY and SUSIE are staring straight ahead.

She turns quickly and keeps on down the street.

LIL and PIGMEAT watch her, their expressions unchanging.

EXTERIOR.   HARLEM STREETS   DAY

LIEUTENANT FISCHER and CORPORAL BROWN are parked in an unofficial two-tone sedan on 116th Street midway between Lenox and Seventh Avenues. They are watching the entrance of a poolroom several doors down, which has a curtained plate glass front. The people in the poolroom know they're being watched and every now and then a dark face appears in the clear glass above the curtains and eyes roll in their direction.

116th Street is a main crosstown artery in Harlem, second only to 125th Street in importance, and is lined by all types of stores, restaurants, movie theaters, hairdressers, fortunetellers, tobacco shops, bars and whiskey stores. Farther down, across from the poolroom, is the Temple of Grace. Daddy Grace was formerly one of Harlem's greatest prophets.

The people are shabbier than on 125th Street, louder, rougher;

the automobiles parked along the curb are older, the goods for sale are inferior. Up and down the wide sidewalk people come and go, looking at the white man out of the corners of their eyes.

CORPORAL BROWN

Everybody on the street has made us by now. What do you expect to get?

LIEUTENANT FISCHER

Everybody around here knows the two hoodlums who killed old man LOUIS.

CORPORAL BROWN

So what? You think they are going to come up and tell us?

LIEUTENANT FISCHER

If we keep putting down enough pressure, somebody is bound to give. The dope pushers are scared to show up at the poolroom, the weedheads are scared to smoke their pot, the number writers are scared to operate, the pickup men don't dare show themselves. If we sit here long enough somebody's going to finger them just so business can go on as usual.

CORPORAL BROWN

How long do you think that's going to take?

LIEUTENANT FISCHER

Who knows? Maybe a day, maybe a week, maybe a month. However long it takes to get them.

CORPORAL BROWN

You got it bad, ain't you?

LIEUTENANT FISCHER

(*in a cold, hard voice*) Johnny, keep out of my personal affairs and I will keep out of yours.

CORPORAL BROWN

(*looking into the rearview mirror*) Oh-oh-oh, speaking of affairs . . .

BABY SISTER is approaching from Lenox Avenue. She has regained her switching, sexy, tantalizing walk and heads turn in her direction. Obviously she doesn't know the car and doesn't see the detectives until she comes abreast. LIEUTENANT FISCHER whistles softly. She turns her customary disdainful look, but gives a start when she sees him.

CORPORAL BROWN

(*opening the streetside door and climbing out from beneath the wheel*) This where I get off, conductor.

He cuts through the traffic and enters a bar across the street.

Without being asked, BABY SISTER gets into the car from the sidewalk. LIEUTENANT FISCHER moves over beneath the wheel and looks at her intently.

LIEUTENANT FISCHER

Why aren't you at the funeral?

BABY SISTER

It was right up there where he was killed, in front of that dirty poolroom.

Involuntarily they both glance toward it. Now a line of heads shows above the curtains as though side by side on a shelf. All eyes are watching the two of them.

BABY SISTER

(*with threads of hysteria in her voice*) It was two weedheads just like them who come out and grabbed me by the arms.

LIEUTENANT FISCHER

(*dryly*) I know, you told me all this before. We're working on it now.

BABY SISTER suddenly bows over and claps her hands to her face, a shudder wracks her body.

BABY SISTER

It was awful. Pa came up and grabbed them and they began stabbing him.

LIEUTENANT FISCHER

(*harshly*) Don't think about it, I tell you. I will get them.

BABY SISTER

(*looking up in sudden alarm*) You keep out of this; let SUSIE get them.

LIEUTENANT FISCHER

(*seriously*) Tell SUSIE to keep out. It's my job, and personal too. If he gets them I'll have to get him and look what that will do to us.

BABY SISTER

(*adoringly*) You're sweet.

LIEUTENANT FISCHER

(*scrutinizing her tear-stained face, skinned hands and bruised knees*) What happened to you?

BABY SISTER

(*without rancor*) SUSIE knocked me down.

LIEUTENANT FISCHER

For what?

BABY SISTER

I didn't want to go to the graveyard.

LIEUTENANT FISCHER

Go home and clean up.

BABY SISTER

No, take me away from here. Everybody is gawking at us and I don't want SUSIE to come back and find me talking to you.

LIEUTENANT FISCHER

You have to change your stockings. I'll wait for you at the corner.

BABY SISTER

No, you buy me some stockings somewhere and I'll wash up in some lavatory.

LIEUTENANT FISCHER's expression portrays forbearance as he

starts the car and drives toward Seventh Avenue. Faces peer from the poolroom as they pass; other people from stores, doorways and windows glance at them furtively.

He turns south on Seventh Avenue and continues past 110th Street into Central Park, where he stops beside the road.

LIEUTENANT FISCHER

What were you doing with that pimp?

BABY SISTER

I just didn't want to go to the funeral and he was going to take me for a ride in the country.

LIEUTENANT FISCHER

(*angrily*) Keep away from him. He'll get you into serious trouble.

BABY SISTER

(*just as angrily*) You're always talking about me getting into trouble and warning me against this man and that man as if I'd hop into bed with any man I see. And here you are the only one who has got me into trouble.

LIEUTENANT FISCHER

(*defensively*) It was an accident.

BABY SISTER

(*furiously*) An accident! Is that all it means to you? Just don't have an accident?

Suddenly she begins to cry, tears streaming down her face and her body shaking convulsively almost the same as when she was doing the twist. He puts his arm about her and draws her body close, feeling its convulsive movement against his own.

LIEUTENANT FISCHER

Darling, darling. You know I don't mean it like that.

She moves closer into his arms and runs her fingers along the back of his neck, into his hair, and lifts her tear-stained face. He kisses her tenderly, then with increasing passion.

LIEUTENANT FISCHER

(*whispering in her ear*) Come go with me now.

She jerks from his arms so suddenly her head bangs him in the face.

BABY SISTER

I'm already in trouble enough.

LIEUTENANT FISCHER

(*gritting his teeth*) Who taught you the facts of life?

BABY SISTER

If you knew so much why'd you get me into trouble?

LIEUTENANT FISCHER

(*jaw muscles tightening*) All right, I'm going to get you out of trouble. I'm taking you to a doctor tomorrow.

BABY SISTER

(*suddenly terrified*) Oh Lord, I sure hope SUSIE won't find out. He'd kill me and try to kill you too.

LIEUTENANT FISCHER

(*starting his car to drive off*) Never mind your brothers, no one is going to find out.

He drives through the park to 86th Street and turns east past Fifth Avenue.

BABY SISTER

Where you taking me?

LIEUTENANT FISCHER

To get some lunch. It's the lunch hour.

BABY SISTER

(*petulantly*) I ain't hungry.

LIEUTENANT FISCHER

Well, I am.

BABY SISTER

I need some stockings.

He keeps on over Lexington Avenue, stops in front of a super-drugstore and gives her a five-dollar bill.

LIEUTENANT FISCHER

Get some stockings and some alcohol and cotton to clean your knees.

When she returns he watches silently as she changes stockings and cleans her knees, exposing her naked legs as naturally as an animal.

They drive to a restaurant with Jewish cuisine on 88th Street.

INTERIOR.   RESTAURANT   DAY

Their entrance attracts some attention but little. BABY SISTER attracts more attention when she goes to the lounge to wash.

The main course is over. The white waitress is removing the dishes, looking at BABY SISTER with deep sympathy. BABY SISTER is sitting upright at the table, crying inconsolably like a child. LIEUTENANT FISCHER is looking at her with a mixture of irritation, embarrassment and concern.

LIEUTENANT FISCHER

What is it now, darling? What did I say wrong?

BABY SISTER

(sobbingly) You ain't said nothing.

LIEUTENANT FISCHER

What do you want, darling? You must want something to make you cry.

BABY SISTER

(sobbingly) I just want to be treated like a woman with some clothes on sometimes instead of like some naked savage.

LIEUTENANT FISCHER

(earnestly, defensively) Don't I try always to treat you nice and with respect? It's just one of those bad breaks that you're in trouble; that might happen to anyone, no matter how careful they are. I did everything to keep it from happening. And I promise you it will be taken care of tomorrow without anyone knowing.

BABY SISTER

(*sobbingly*) It isn't that.

He looks at her with a tender, loving, anxious expression, reaching across the table to cover her small brown hand with his.

LIEUTENANT FISCHER

What is it then, darling? What's troubling you?

BABY SISTER

(*sobbingly*) I want a yellow dress.

EXTERIOR.   125th STREET   DAY

The car pulls to a stop before Blumstein's Department Store on 125th Street, abutting the Theresa Hotel, Harlem's largest and most famous hotel, where Khrushchev visited Castro. This is the heart of Harlem, both day and night, the main shopping center, the greatest congestion of the bars, the famous spots, the Palm Cafe, Apollo Theatre, Apollo Bar, Loew's Theater, Baby Grand night club, shoe stores, hat stores, drugstores, food stores, big cars, sharp cats and second-story windows bearing the names of doctors, lawyers, dentists, insurance companies.

Blumstein's show windows, extending down 125th Street, are crammed with bedroom furniture, kitchen equipment, stoves, refrigerators, electrical equipment, lawn mowers, automobile accessories, men's and women's underwear. One window contains an assemblage of colored plaster mannequins draped in bright colored dresses.

A black nun is sitting on a campstool beside the entrance, begging for the poor. A veritable stream of colored shoppers are passing in and out.

LIEUTENANT FISCHER

I would have taken you to one of the nice women's shops on Madison Avenue.

BABY SISTER

(*hurriedly getting out of the car as though he might change his mind*) They got the things I like here. Blumstein's just caters to us colored people.

LIEUTENANT FISCHER

All right, get your dress and go home like a good girl.

BABY SISTER

(*bitchily*) You old hypocrite, you wouldn't know me if I was a good girl.

LIEUTENANT FISCHER watches her hips switch as she plows through the crowd and enters Blumstein's.

INTERIOR.   LIL'S APARTMENT   DAY

LIL opens the door of a kitchenette apartment on the third floor of a house at the corner of St. Nicholas Avenue and 149th Street. She is wearing a red silk housecoat with a deep décolleté, showing the dark seams between her luscious yellow breasts, and smoking a cigarette in a very long ivory holder.

The apartment consists of one room with a window overlooking St. Nicholas Avenue, a studio bed along one wall, cocktail table, low armchair; in the corner a combination radio, television and record player. A platter of Lester Young solos is playing.

At sight of BABY SISTER a look of surprised annoyance mars LIL's expression.

LIL

Oh! And where the hell have you been?

BABY SISTER

(*pushing into the room*) Home in bed. SUSIE hurt me.

LIL

(*slamming the door shut*) If you don't think of a better lie, he's going to hurt you sure enough. We all went back looking for you.

BABY SISTER clings tightly to a package in her arms and fawns on LIL as though trying to win her approval.

BABY SISTER

I was invited downtown to lunch.

LIL

(*furiously*) You little bitch. That's what I get for trying to save you from a beating.

BABY SISTER

(*defiantly*) You can have DICKIE come here anytime you want. I ain't got anyplace to entertain a man.

LIL

(*with hands on hips*) Listen to you! Entertain a man! DICKIE's my man. I don't spread my legs for anybody.

BABY SISTER

(*leering*) Is he all that good?

LIL

(*misunderstanding*) Good? Naturally he's good to me.

BABY SISTER

I mean so good you don't want anybody else.

LIL

(*outraged*) You little jailbait! If I catch you ever looking at DICKIE—(*she breaks off startled as* BABY SISTER *begins hurriedly undressing*) What are you doing?

BABY SISTER

I got a new dress.
She throws her sweater and skirt on the couch, looking ripe and ready in her black bra and garter belt.

LIL

(*disgustedly*) Don't you ever wear any pants?
Without replying BABY SISTER unfastens the package, pulls the yellow dress down over her head, shakes it into place and turns her back to LIL.

BABY SISTER

Zip me.

LIL

(*bitterly as she zips up the dress*) And what Sing Sing sucker gave you this?

BABY SISTER

(*twisting in time with Lester Young's solo*) Like it?
LIL stares at her mutely.

BABY SISTER

Timme. You can't call him a Sing Sing sucker.
LIL's face becomes pinched in the grip of terror; her shoulders droop; her body seems to shrink. BABY SISTER twists to the beat of the music in her new yellow dress, unaware.

LIL

(*in the whining voice of great fear*) Don't make us no more trouble. SUSIE would kill you if he knew. BUDDY too. And him too.

BABY SISTER

(*with defiant disdain*) He don't mean nothing to me. He just likes me.

LIL

Don't tell me nothing about these white detectives here in Harlem. They all like hot young colored stuff. (*asking suddenly*) You're using those things I gave you, aren't you?

BABY SISTER

(*offhandedly*) Of course. You think I want to get into trouble? (*suddenly a look of consternation sweeps her face*)

LIL

(*noticing it*) Oh Lord, you're not already in trouble, are you?

BABY SISTER

(*patently lying*) Of course not. What makes you ask that?

LIL

(*shaking her head*) When one of these stingy white cops starts giving colored girls dresses—

BABY SISTER

(*interrupting*) He's always giving me something.

LIL

(*pleadingly, serious, almost in tears*) Baby, listen, I beg you on bended knees, don't let SUSIE find out.

BABY SISTER

(*taking off the dress, guilty and afraid*) He ain't going to never know, besides which it's finished.

LIL

Well, for heaven's sake don't take this dress home. Ma and everybody is upset enough as it is 'cause you didn't go to Pa's funeral.

BABY SISTER

(*putting the dress in an old shopping bag*) I'm going to say you gave it to me.

LIL

(*greatly alarmed*) Leave it here, you little fool.

BABY SISTER is pulling down her skintight skirt when a key is stuck in the door lock. She gives her sister a swift, intimate, confidential look as the door opens inward.

DICKIE, a well-dressed, good-looking brown-skinned man carrying a saxophone case, comes into the room, shuts the door behind him and looks delightedly surprised at the sight of BABY SISTER.

DICKIE

(*laying his saxophone on the bed*) Oh, company, and the cutest little girl in town.

BABY SISTER

(*throwing him an arch smile*) Oh, DICKIE, darling, give me some lips.

She steps forward and offers her pouting lips. Half laughingly, DICKIE gives her a brotherly kiss.

DICKIE

What a girl you're going to be when you grow up.

LIL

(*sourly*) God stay the day.

BABY SISTER takes the bag containing her new dress and turns toward the door.

DICKIE

Listen, don't leave on account of me.

LIL

Baby, I beg you—

BABY SISTER

(*maliciously*) You want me to go, don't you?

DICKIE looks from one to the other, puzzled.

LIL

They're waiting for her at home.

For an instant BABY SISTER looks frightened.

DICKIE

(*jokingly*) Is that new?

BABY SISTER tosses her head and puts on her indifferent smile.

LIL

Baby, be careful, please be careful.

EXTERIOR.   116TH STREET   DAY

It is past six o'clock when BABY SISTER alights from the crowded Seventh Avenue bus at 116th Street and turns east on 116th Street toward her home, swinging the shopping bag containing her dress with forced abandon. From this direction she does not have to pass the poolroom in front of which her father was killed, but she has to pass all manner of other shops where she is known.

She is celebrated on this crowded vicious street, but unprotected, fair game for all the hoodlums who wish to accost her. As she goes past in her switching walk, high heels tapping, loiterers whistle, speak to her, ask for dates, walk along beside her. She ignores them theatrically, which increases their boldness. She greets elderly acquaintances, friends of the family, many of whom have attended the funeral, with affected politeness in return to their scowling disapproval. Several elderly women turn about to stare at her sexy walk, shaking their heads in indignation. This is obviously a common occurrence.

INTERIOR.   TENEMENT ON 116TH STREET   DAY

She turns into the narrow shabby entrance of a walk-up tenement across the street from a movie theater. A big middle-aged man coming from a ground-floor apartment at the rear attempts to block her way.

MAN

(*flashing a handful of money*) Hey, hot baby, how about it?

A door is jerked open at the rear of the dark hallway and a woman is limned in the lighted doorway, arms akimbo. The man hurries out.

BABY SISTER hurries up the stairs, passing numerous people. Every man she passes accosts her, tries to proposition her or rubs against her. She fends them off, some angrily, some laughingly, some flirtingly. The women avoid contact with her as though she is contaminated.

On the fourth floor she pushes a bell button at the door of the apartment.

INTERIOR.   LOUISES' FLAT   NIGHT

The door flies open revealing a front room containing a round dining room table and a double bed in one corner.

SUSIE, sitting nearest the door, has his hand on the knob. Seated about the table are MAMA, UNCLE PIE, BUDDY and PIGMEAT. They all stare at her wordlessly.

SUSIE leaps to his feet, grabs her by the arm and jerks her into the room, slamming the door shut with the same motion. His hand is drawn back to slap her when he catches sight of the package. He jerks it out of her grasp, slams it onto the table, rips the shopping bag apart and holds up the new yellow dress by its

sleeves in the manner of a Puritan exposing a witch. Slowly he
turns his head and gives her such a baleful look she begins to
tremble.

BABY SISTER

(*quavering*) LIL gave it to me. I swear 'fore God. You can ask
her.

SUSIE's face gives a spasmodic tic. Erupting into such explosive
violence she doesn't see the motion of his hand, he slaps her face-
about into the closed door.

Her hands fly up to break the impact, then, instinctively, she
fumbles for the knob, jerks open the door, dashes into the corridor
and begins running without looking back.

Shoulders hunched, face swollen, SUSIE starts after her. PIGMEAT
extends a leg and trips him. SUSIE flies across the corridor and
crashes into the staircase. He bounces back, feints toward PIGMEAT
with cocked fists. PIGMEAT leaps from his seat and escapes around
the table. As he is about to pursue PIGMEAT, SUSIE is arrested by
the rat-tat-tat of BABY SISTER's high heels on the lower stairs. His
enraged face momentarily reveals the conflict of his emotions.
Then, throwing a threatening look at PIGMEAT, he takes off after
her.

EXTERIOR.   116TH STREET   NIGHT

BABY SISTER comes out onto the sidewalk and looks up and
down the crowded, storefronted street. The nearest beauty parlor
where she can hide is too far away; she knows the barman next
door won't hide her, nor will any of the storekeepers take sides.
She can't hope to outrun SUSIE in the crowded street.

Panic-stricken, she notices UNCLE PIE's hearse parked at the
curb. The back doors are open. She climbs inside and gets the
doors closed just as SUSIE comes from the house so fast he skids
on the pavement, throwing out his arms like an ice skater trying
to keep balance.

Frightened senseless, BABY SISTER opens the lid of the wicker
basket inside of the hearse, intending to hide inside it. But the
wicker basket contains a black male body with its throat cut.
She lets out a scream that freezes passers-by in their tracks and
turns SUSIE into a motionless statue.

The next instant BABY SISTER comes tumbling from the back end of the hearse as though she has looked on the face of the devil. Abruptly SUSIE becomes mobilized, like a statue come to life, and grabs at her. She ducks beneath his arm and runs down the street.

A car pulls to a stop ahead of her and five big rough-looking workmen suddenly erupt. In a flash she realizes they have heard her scream and have seen her escaping from the hearse, and knows they are coming to her rescue.

BABY SISTER

(*screaming*) Rape fiend!

With outraged faces, the five big men converge on SUSIE. One hits him in the stomach, the second in the face; the third grabs his arms from behind and pins them to his body; the two others are trying to get a piece of him.

SUSIE

(*with frustrated fury*) Leave me loose, you crazy motherfuckers, she's my sister.

BABY SISTER

(*vindictively*) You dirty, lying rape fiend, I hope they beat you up.

The men throw SUSIE to the ground and kick and stomp him.

People converge from all directions.

LOUD JUBILANT VOICE

Hey, man, they is beating up on SUSIE.

ANOTHER JUBILANT VOICE

Tell 'em leave some for me.

BUDDY, UNCLE PIE and PIGMEAT suddenly join the melee.

BABY SISTER turns away and begins running down 116th Street toward Lenox Avenue.

BUDDY

(*shouting*) Leave him alone, it's our sister.

1ST MAN

It's his sister.

2ND MAN

Come on then, boy, and kick him in the things.

BUDDY

She's his sister too.

3RD MAN

His own sister.

2ND MAN

That makes it all the worse.

UNCLE PIE

(*pleadingly*) You done beat him enough, men.

PIGMEAT looks around for BABY SISTER, sees her far down the street, hurrying toward Lenox Avenue. He starts to run after her. She looks over her shoulder, sees him coming and begins running faster. She disappears around the corner but he follows her.

Finally the men quit beating SUSIE, go back and get into their car, which is holding up a long line of traffic, and drive off.

UNCLE PIE and BUDDY help SUSIE get to his feet. SUSIE walks with slow painful motions of an old man suffering from arthritis. He doesn't say a word.

INTERIOR.   LOUISES' FLAT   NIGHT

In the apartment they find MAMA praying on her knees at the table.

MAMA

Lord, what's going to happen to this fatherless girl? Lord, show me the light, show me the way, Lord. Lord, protect her from sin and trouble—didn't even go to her own father's funeral.

BUDDY

(*angrily*) What do you expect, Ma, the way she got to live. Sleeping on a cot in the dining room, ain't got no place to dress; can't do nothing without everybody seeing, can't even go to the crapper without having to climb over everybody in the family. (*giving* SUSIE *a defiant look*) And SUSIE beating on her all the time like she were a whore.

SUSIE has gone into the front room adjoining the living room which he shares with BUDDY and has lain across the bed, gentle as a lamb. He doesn't reply to the accusation.

UNCLE PIE

(*kneeling beside* MAMA) She ain't no whore, God, You knows that; I don't have to tell You. She's a good girl, I'll bet she's still a virgin; she just looks like a whore is all.

BUDDY lights a cigarette, sits on the bed in the corner where his mother and father had slept and leafs through a Negro picture magazine.

BUDDY

I hope she don't never come back.

INTERIOR.   CHURCH OF THE REDEEMED SINNER   NIGHT

When BABY SISTER comes abreast the church, she throws a look over her shoulder. PIGMEAT is nowhere in sight. She ducks inside. It is semi-dark inside the church.

BABY SISTER

(*standing in the aisle, calling*) REVEREND CONVERTED SINNER! Oh, REVEREND SINNER, it's me, BABY SISTER LOUIS.

There is no reply. She continues toward the back, goes behind the pulpit where the back end of the store is partitioned off and calls again. Then she knocks on a door in the partition. Receiving no answer, she tries the knob, finds the door unlocked and enters a room behind the church which is REVEREND CONVERTED SINNER's living quarters. It is a dirty, unkempt room with a single unmade bed on one side, a table beside a coal-burning stove in the center and a makeshift kitchen on the other side. Two black-painted windows, screened on the outside and barred on the inside, look out onto a courtyard behind.

She looks about the room curiously, turning on the single naked bulb hanging from the ceiling. She hears PIGMEAT calling to her from inside the church. She switches off the light.

VOICE OF PIGMEAT

I know somebody's there. I saw the light go off.

BABY SISTER

(*switching on the light again*) What you want?
Steps are heard, the door opens, PIGMEAT enters the room.

PIGMEAT

What you doing here?

BABY SISTER

I come to get some spiritual 'sistance, what you think?

PIGMEAT

From old Talking Zombie?

BABY SISTER

He our reverend, ain't he?

PIGMEAT

I guess so. When you coming home?

BABY SISTER

I ain't never coming home. I'm tired of SUSIE beating on me
all the time.

PIGMEAT

We ain't going to let him no more. You come on back with me.

BABY SISTER

I'm going away.

PIGMEAT

You can't go away. Where can you go?

BABY SISTER

Somewhere.

PIGMEAT

You got to come back sometime. The longer you wait, the
worser it gets.

BABY SISTER

I'm going to wait for our reverend, and if he say for me to go
back, I'll get him to take me.

PIGMEAT

(*turning to leave*) All right. I wish you'd hurry up. You ain't making it no better, staying away like this without nobody knowing where you are.

BABY SISTER

(*with sudden alarm*) Don't tell nobody where I am.

PIGMEAT promises and leaves. She watches him go up the aisle and out through the front door. From the front door she watches his receding figure until it turns the corner of 116th Street. She shrugs and looks about undecidedly.

EXTERIOR.   HARLEM STREETS   NIGHT

Then suddenly, as though she has made up her mind, she goes outside and begins walking rapidly north on Lenox Avenue, threading through the crowds of people returning from work. At the next intersection she crosses Lenox and continues uptown on the other side, glancing over her shoulder from time to time to see if she is followed. Her pace is rapid, but seems aimless.

A car draws to the curb in front of her, waits until she comes abreast. The horn says: Hello. She looks through the corners of her eyes. Emotions pass over her face. At first she tosses her head disdainfully and seems about to ignore it. Then she looks again and her face brightens. She turns quickly, as though making up her mind, and approaches it with a dazzling smile.

It is a new compact sedan with two-tone color. A good-looking brown-skinned man, flashily dressed in a beige sports jacket and blue sports shirt, flashes a smile at her, inviting and complacent.

YOUNG MAN

Come on, baby, hop in. Let's go places.

Coolly, she looks the car over, then looks him over. He leans over and opens the door. She gets in beside him and shuts the door, not looking at him directly but taking him in through the corners of her eyes.

BABY SISTER

(*finally*) Didn't you used to tend bar at Small's?

YOUNG MAN

No, baby, that's another boy friend. I'm JOE COOK.

BABY SISTER

I'm BABY SISTER.

JOE

(*looking her over with open appreciation*) What shall it be, BABY SISTER?

BABY SISTER

Let's eat some barbecue.

The car pulls out into the traffic and later draws up before a glittering new barbecue restaurant on Broadway, north of 145th Street. One side of the front is faced with white tile, the other contains a huge electric rotisserie, six feet high, placed back from the open window and protected by a counter. Two white-clad barbecue experts with high chef's hats are tending the sizzling pork ribs on the rack of slowly turning spits and serving short orders across the counter. Bright neon light spills over the dark-faced customers, standing at the counter, gnawing ribs; and the unforgettable smell of barbecue floats in the summer air.

JOE parks the car and he and BABY SISTER go inside and take a small table at the rear.

INTERIOR.   RESTAURANT   NIGHT

Dim, red-shaded wall lamps above the checkered tablecloths give a cozy atmosphere; and a fairyland jukebox gives out with muted jazz.

They sit opposite, looking at one another with admiration and open sex appraisal, drinking beer and eating red-hot barbecue with coleslaw and hot biscuits.

JOE

You like Count Basie?

BABY SISTER

Sure, but some of that old-time beat has got to go. I like Art Blakey's combo.

JOE

If I had my rathers I'd make up my own band. Art Blakey on
the skins, Charlie Mingus on the bass, John Coltrane on the sax,
Harry Edison on the horn—

BABY SISTER

(*interrupting*) Give me Roy Eldridge—

JOE

Aw, he's a show-off; he ain't no band man. You like Trummy
Young?

BABY SISTER

Natch.

JOE

Then on the keys, that's where I take the Count. (*suddenly
his eye catches a poster on the wall advertising a dance at the Renaissance Ballroom from ten o'clock until two*) Let's go to the
dance, baby.

BABY SISTER

I got to get home before then. I just slipped off.

JOE

Well, you is off now. And Choo-Choo's band is there.

BABY SISTER

(*following his gaze*) It don't start until ten. (*looking toward
the clock on the wall*) And it's just a quarter to nine now.

JOE

(*checking his wristwatch with the electric clock*) It's two minutes slow. (*suddenly inspired*) I know what we can do. I know
where some cats are having a reefer party.

INTERIOR.   HARLEM FLAT   NIGHT

JOE and BABY SISTER are inside an apartment filled with sporty
young men and teen-age girls dancing slowly, lasciviously, as

though trying to squirm inside one another's bodies, to the muted blues. Billie Holiday is singing, her low whining voice sounding like the climax of a sex act.

Through a double doorway is the dining room, lit by a blue-shaded lamp on a round-top table, where a couple sits eating fried chicken and potato salad, putting the food in each other's mouths and licking the grease from each other's lips.

The air is redolent with the fumes of marijuana; couples are sucking the marijuana sticks, faces distorted, passing them back and forth.

BABY SISTER is sitting at the end of a divan in the living room, almost unseen in the dark. JOE is sitting on the arm; a marijuana cigarette glows between his lips; he hands the stick to her.

JOE

Here, take some pot, baby.

BABY SISTER

I don't want any.

JOE

What's the matter with you?

BABY SISTER

I don't smoke it.

JOE

Hell, baby, if you're scared, go home.

BABY SISTER takes a puff from the cigarette, sucks in the smoke, gives it back. She stands up, moves into JOE's arms. They stand planted, twisting slowly in tight embrace, the cigarette dangling from his lips. He moves the cigarette and their mouths become glued.

A couple passes through the dining room into the dark corridor beyond, arms about each other. Another teen-age girl is trying to go with them; two young men are restraining her; she is struggling and writhing in their grasp.

GIRL

(screaming) Take me! Take me too!

Another girl embraces her, seemingly trying to calm her.

JOE

(*pulling* BABY SISTER *by the arm*) Come on, let's take a room.

BABY SISTER

(*pulling back*) No. No.

JOE

(*releasing her with disgust*) This is Sugar Hill, if one won't another will.

He turns away. Another girl drifts into his arms. They dance, belly-rubbing, mouth to mouth. BABY SISTER dances with a tall, light-complected man with yellow hair. She presses close to him, caressing his neck and ears, cheek against his shoulder. He caresses her buttocks.

Suddenly JOE wrenches her from the man's arms and slaps her.

The man clutches JOE by the coat collar, jerks him away from her.

MAN

If she don't want you, I'll take her.

JOE

You ain't that cute.

They back off in the dim light and draw knives. Dancing stops. The couples move away. Other men clutch them, hold them apart. Suddenly the proprietor, a stout yellow woman with a scar on one cheek, comes from the back of the hall.

PROPRIETOR

I won't have none of that. Put them knives away.

The fighters are cowed. They close their knives, pocket them, move apart, looking sullen.

PROPRIETOR

(*peering among the girls*) Who they fighting about?

GIRL

(*pointing at* BABY SISTER) Her.

PROPRIETOR looks at BABY SISTER, then takes the two fighters
by the arm, makes them sit at the table in the dining room.

PROPRIETOR

I'm going to give you boys some pot and you make up. Ain't
no piece worth fighting about.

The recording is changed. The dancing begins again. No one
dances with BABY SISTER. She starts doing a strip tease. The others
stop to watch her. She has got her sweater and skirt off and is taking off her stockings when the proprietor returns from her room
with marijuana sticks for the two men.

PROPRIETOR

(*angrily*) Put them clothes back on, girl. And you better get
out of here. I see you're a troublemaker.

BABY SISTER dresses, silent and blank-faced. JOE comes up to her.

JOE

I'll take you.

BABY SISTER

(*brightening*) Let's go to the dance.

JOE

We're on the way, baby.

INTERIOR.   BALLROOM   NIGHT

JOE and BABY SISTER are doing a wild, frenzied Funky Broadway
in front of the bandstand on the big dance floor of the Renaissance Ballroom. Their feet are planted; their bodies are twisting
like two snakes over a hot fire. Black couples all over the big,
brightly lit room are standing with their feet planted as though
nailed to the floor, twisting their bodies in all manner of sensual
volutions, as though procreating in full dress.

Behind them the big band is going wild; two sax players stand
and swap fours and eights; the trumpet lead jumps up and takes
eight beats; the drummer takes a solo, sticks flying in the air, then
the bass takes a solo.

Sweat pours from the musicians' faces, from the faces of the men and women dancing; the underarms of women's dresses are sweat-soaked as are the collars of men's shirts.

Then suddenly the music stops. The couples fall into one another's arms, leaning against each other, catching their breath.

The lights are dimmed; vari-colored beams play over the dance floor, slowly rotating, as the band goes into the moderate, restful rhythm of the "Jitterbug Waltz."

There follows an intermission.

JOE and BABY SISTER are standing at the soft drink bar to one side of the dance floor, drinking soft drinks. They are laughing at one another, exhilarated, talking nonsense.

The drum sounds. The couples crowd back onto the floor. The band gives out with the cha-cha-cha; the dancers go wild.

An hour later there is another intermission.

> BABY SISTER

What time is it?

> JOE

It's early yet. Just twelve-thirty.

> BABY SISTER

(*looking suddenly scared*) I got to go home now sure enough.

> JOE

(*wiping sweat from his face*) Hell, we're just getting warmed up.

> BABY SISTER

I got to get home; I'm gonna get killed as it is.

> JOE

Let's eat something first.

INTERIOR.   RESTAURANT   NIGHT

JOE and BABY SISTER are sitting at a table in the back corner of The Chicken Shack on St. Nicholas Avenue, north of 145th Street, eating crisp fried chicken-in-the-basket and french-fried potatoes, and drinking whiskey highballs.

BABY SISTER is on her second highball and has reached the giggly stage.

Farther front, a bald-headed pianist is sitting beneath a tiny spotlight, rippling the keys of an upright piano with his interpretations. Black couples are sitting at the tables along the walls; mixed couples and a party of white people are at the front. The white people are obviously tourists from downtown; the black people are of the Harlem upper class or else are racketeers with their special girl friends.

BABY SISTER steals the show by going up kissing the pianist on his bald head and leaving the print of her lips.

A single man at the bar gives her the eye and JOE becomes jealous and takes her out.

INTERIOR.   PARKED CAR   NIGHT

They have words in the parked car.

BABY SISTER

You don't own me.

JOE

Ain't you satisfied with one man at the time?

BABY SISTER

If he's nice.

JOE drives away from in front of The Chicken Shack and parks the car in the almost black dark stretch of 122nd Street between Seventh and Lenox Avenues, just around the corner from the Church of the Redeemed Sinner. The lights are off. The faces of JOE and BABY SISTER are barely discernible in the dark.

She is sitting with her head against the seat, face up; he is leaning over her, kissing her face and neck.

JOE

(softly) Ain't I been nice to you, baby?

BABY SISTER

Joe, I can't, don't ask me, Joe.

JOE

(*persisting; his hands moving over her*) Why not?

BABY SISTER

You'll get me into trouble.

JOE

I'll be careful.
She kisses him and draws away. He struggles with her. They move about in the semi-darkness, half struggling, half caressing. It is as though she feels she should not give in without a struggle. Her head goes back, her mouth open, her profile is that of surrender.

BABY SISTER

(*panting*) No-no . . . Oh. Oh, JOE.
Their bodies mold together.
BABY SISTER sits with her arm about JOE's neck, her face in the curve of his shoulder. His arm encircles her back; his hand cups her breast.

JOE

Stay with me tonight.
BABY SISTER snaps out of her reverie, suddenly straightens up, begins adjusting her clothes, combing her hair, repairing her makeup.

BABY SISTER

(*desperately*) Oh God, if I don't get an alibi I'm going to get killed.

JOE

Can't you slip in?

BABY SISTER

You don't know my brother. He's sitting by the door, waiting.

JOE

What you're going to do?

BABY SISTER

I'm going by Ma's preacher, and get him to say I've been there.

JOE

Will he do that?

BABY SISTER

He'll do anything for me—if don't nobody else know it.

INTERIOR. CHURCH NIGHT

BABY SISTER enters the storefront church, goes through to the back room, turns on the light. It is just as she left it. REVEREND CONVERTED SINNER has not yet returned. She lies across the bed to rest for a moment and is suddenly asleep.

The room is black dark. Suddenly there is the sound of a violent scuffle taking place on the bed; the bed scrapes across the floor; the muffled voice of BABY SISTER is heard cursing furiously; there are loud panting gasps of another. Then there is the sound of a body crashing against the table, followed by high-heeled footsteps running across the floor. The door is flung open. In the vague light filtering through the clear window glass from a distant street light is seen the figure of BABY SISTER running down the church aisle and out of the front door.

EXTERIOR. HARLEM STREETS NIGHT

When BABY SISTER emerges into the sketchy light of Lenox Avenue she looks flustered and disheveled but more flabbergasted than terrified. She runs a few steps to the nearest street light, then slows to a walk and straightens her skirt and runs a comb through her curly hair. Struck by a sudden premonition, she looks over her shoulder and distinctly sees SLICK coming down the street toward her, weaving slightly. Afraid of what he might do to her for the beating SUSIE gave him, she turns about and begins to run again. Once she looks back and sees SLICK still following. She runs full speed down Lenox Avenue, trying to get home before SLICK catches up with her, and does not see him take a woman by the arm and turn into a darkened doorway, so that when she looks back just before turning onto 116th Street he is nowhere in sight.

She is more terrified by not seeing him than she had been by the sight of him. When she passes the poolroom in front of which her father was killed, she moves over to the curb as though it is infested with ghosts. A man emerges from the dark alley beside the poolroom and moves to intercept her.

MAN

(*in a whiskey-thick voice*) You is for me, baby.

BABY SISTER screams. The man turns tail and flees back into the dark alley.

BABY SISTER runs posthaste to her tenement.

INTERIOR.   TENEMENT ON 116TH STREET   NIGHT

BABY SISTER pauses for breath in the entrance hallway. Light filters down through the stair railing from the single dim bulb on each side of the upper halls. Relieved, she starts running up the stairs, but when she turns on the first landing all the hall lights suddenly go out. The hall windows are blackened with grime and there are no outside street lights near enough to light up the stairway.

It is suddenly black dark on the stairway below and above, but it is the black-dark entrance hallway which frightens her most. If the outside door had been open as she had left it, there would be a vague rectangular outline. But the blackness is opaque and she knows the door has been closed, either from without or within. The stairways are unseen in the stygian dark. She stands stock still and holds her breath, draws her knife from her stocking and opens it.

In the almost complete silence she hears light footsteps bounding up the stairs as though taking three at a time on tiptoe. Panic-stricken, she turns to flee upward, but stumbles over the first steps and someone clutches her from behind. Her scream is cut off by a hard, rough hand over her mouth. She knows it is a man by his clothes and his smell.

There are muted sounds of a violent struggle, then the open-mouthed grunts of a man being jabbed in the ribs by sharp elbows. Then BABY SISTER bites the hand covering her mouth. When the hand is snatched away, she slashes out in the dark. The next instant BABY SISTER's scream explodes, shattering the night.

BABY SISTER

(*screaming*) SUSIE!!! SUSIE!!!

Footsteps are heard going down the stairs in frenzied flight, the front door is flung open, the vague silhouette of a man is seen disappearing in the night.

Cracks of light appear at the bottom of doors flanking the hallways. From up above there is the sound of a door being opened onto a chain.

MAN'S AGITATED VOICE FROM ABOVE

BABY SISTER!!! BABY SISTER!!!

BABY SISTER

(*still screaming*) SUSIE!!! SUSIE!!!

Footsteps thunder down the stairs from the total darkness.

VOICE FROM ABOVE

(*merging with the footsteps*) BABY SISTER!!! BABY SISTER!!!

The first footsteps are followed by other footsteps, then by still others, emanating from unseen shapes in the total darkness. The first footsteps reach the landing where BABY SISTER is crouching.

Suddenly the hall lights come on.

BABY SISTER

(*gasping convulsively*) BUDDY!!! Oh, BUDDY!!!

BABY SISTER crouches in a corner with an open knife in her hand. Her brown eyes, ringed with mascara, are stretched wide open with the limpid, inhuman senselessness of extreme terror. There is a slight scratch on one of her cheeks. Her sweater is torn from the neck down one shoulder. Drops of fresh blood gleam from the floor.

BUDDY is clad only in a pair of pants. His face is distorted with shock and fright. He has a meat cleaver in his hand.

Then PIGMEAT arrives, wearing only a pair of ragged underpants, a butcher knife in one hand, a rusty screw driver in the other.

MAMA comes last, clad in her old-fashioned cotton flannel nightgown and barefooted, carrying a red-handled fireman's ax.

Other black people come half undressed from all the lighted doorways.

BUDDY

(*finally*) You all right, BABY SISTER?

The shock and terror slowly leave her eyes. She looks at her three relatives, at their weapons. She sighs.

BABY SISTER

Where is SUSIE?

PIGMEAT

He went out 'bout midnight, and ain't come back.

BABY SISTER

What time is it now?

MAMA

(*bitterly, not looking at her*) Time you ought to be in bed, 'fore you gets the whole family killed. (*turning furiously to* PIG-MEAT) And you get upstairs and hide your nakedness. You're worse than a savage.

BUDDY

We ought to call the police.

NEIGHBOR

What for? What they gonna do but arrest y'all?

BABY SISTER

I ain't hurt.

BUDDY

What we need is a gun.

INTERIOR.   LOUISES' FLAT   DAY

An alarm clock rings for 6:30 A.M. Without moving her body, BABY SISTER gropes blindly along the floor beside the bed and shuts it off. She is sleeping face down beneath a sheet on a cot at one end of the dining room, the main part of which is taken up by a cheap dining room suite. In the corner at the head of her bed is an improvised clothes closet. At the foot of her bed the one window looks out onto the courtyard. The green shade is drawn but its cracks are lit by the early summer sunrise.

She tries to go back to sleep.

MAMA

(*from the front sitting room*) If you'd go to bed at night 'stead of gallivanting about getting us all into God only knows what kind of trouble you could get up on time.

BABY SISTER gets up, rubbing the sleep from her eyes. She is wearing sleeveless summer pajamas. Barefooted and still half asleep, she skirts the table, goes through the sitting room, skirting the big round table, and passes through the front bedroom shared by BUDDY and SUSIE into the bathroom. MAMA is lying awake on the double bed in the sitting room, BUDDY is asleep on one of the single beds in the bedroom. She notices that SUSIE's bed has not been slept in.

After having washed she returns to the dining room, takes a sweater and skirt from the curtained-off corner and dresses. After which she goes into the kitchen and draws a glass of water from the tap. PIGMEAT is asleep on a cot to one side of the kitchen stove. He doesn't awaken.

Again she passes through the sitting room, kisses her mother's cheek and goes out, down the stairs and joins the long line of workers hurrying toward the subway kiosk at the corner of Lenox Avenue. Most of the black people are going downtown to their service jobs, but she takes an uptown bus, transfers at 125th Street to an eastbound bus and gets off opposite the ugly 125th Street station of the New York Central railroad line. A commuters' train thunders to a stop on the overhead tracks as another takes off, shaking the ground.

INTERIOR.   CAFETERIA   DAY

She enters the front door of a cafeteria, ignores the whistles of the bums sitting at front tables behind the plate glass windows nursing cold cups of coffee and reading salvaged scraps of the morning newspapers, keeps on through to the pantry and hurries downstairs to the women's locker room.

She takes a key from her purse, opens the huge padlock on her locker and quickly changes into a starched white uniform. The locker room is crowded with other women workers changing, mostly blacks with a few whites.

It is a little past seven o'clock when she takes her station behind the fruit juice and coffee counter. The case has been iced for the juices and the big coffee urns have been filled by the night crew. She begins filling glasses with fruit juice, stacking the coffee cups and saucers and checking the milk, moving with quick efficiency.

White-uniformed men, mostly black, work behind the adjoining short-order counter, preparing the batter for pancakes and heating the hot plates.

COUNTERMAN

Hey, baby-o, how 'bout you?
BABY SISTER throws him a quick smile.

BABY SISTER

Lo, daddy-o, go slow.

COUNTERMAN

Every morning I wake up cold in hand, baby-o.

BABY SISTER

You been outside where it's cold at, daddy-o.

EVIL-LOOKING BLACK CUSTOMER

Is you going to serve me, miss, or is you ain't?

EXTERIOR.   HARLEM STREETS   DAY

BUDDY leaves the LOUISES' flat and gets a cup of white coffee and a sugar doughnut at the lunch counter across the street, which at that hour is crowded with other silent black men. The electric clock behind the counter reads: 7:37. When he finishes his breakfast, BUDDY walks toward Seventh Avenue and turns down to 115th Street, entering the first tenement between Seventh and Lenox.

INTERIOR.   TENEMENT ON 115TH STREET   DAY

He rings the bell of a first-floor flat. The door is opened by a man in his undershirt, razor in hand, face half lathered. BUDDY enters, takes out a pencil and notebook, follows the man back to the bathroom.

MAN

(*continuing to shave*) Give me two bits on 9-5-4; a dime on the 9 leading.

BUDDY

Ain't you going to play your usual?

MAN

That number don't know me; that number ain't fell out in so long it done forgot how to fall.

BUDDY

(*pencil hovering over pad*) Today might be the day.

MAN

(*giving* BUDDY *a jaundiced look*) You numbers writers is all the same, you git it in a man and he can't get it out.

WOMAN'S VOICE

(*from adjoining room*) Tell him to give me four bits on 1-2-3; I dreamt last night I was getting married.
MAN nicks himself, curses under his breath.
BUDDY writes out another slip.

MAN

Give me four bits on my usual then; if it comes out and I ain't on it, after all these months, I'm gonna feel like cutting my throat.

WOMAN'S VOICE

Give him the four bits for me, daddy.

MAN

(*grumbling as he counts out $1.25*) Must think I is made of money.
BUDDY gives him the original slip for his and the woman's play,

pockets the note pad with the carbon duplicate, goes to the front door and lets himself out.

He goes to the door of another flat and rings the bell.

EXTERIOR.   LENOX AVENUE   DAY

PIGMEAT is looking in the window of a small credit jewelry store on Lenox Avenue when BUDDY passes. The clock in the window reads: 9:15.

PIGMEAT

(*falling in beside* BUDDY) I been waiting for you.

BUDDY

(*coldly*) So I see.

PIGMEAT

Who you think jumped BABY SISTER last night?

BUDDY

(*irritably*) How I know; why don't you ask her, you and her so palsy-walsy.

PIGMEAT

She told me what she told you, she don't know.

BUDDY

Then what you ask me for?

PIGMEAT

She hid in REV'END SINNER's store church when she run away.

BUDDY

(*crossly*) Why didn't you tell Ma?

PIGMEAT

She made me promise not to tell.

BUDDY

Then what you telling me for?

PIGMEAT

I been wondering 'bout that.

BUDDY

Wondering 'bout what?

PIGMEAT

I been wondering where SUSIE was all night.
BUDDY stops dead still to look at him.

BUDDY

What you mean?

PIGMEAT

(*looking off*) He always beating her up, more like she's his girl
than his sister.

BUDDY

(*starting to walk on*) What would he jump her for, if she were
giving it to him?

PIGMEAT

(*walking fast to catch up*) Maybe 'cause she stayed out so late
. . . (BUDDY *doesn't answer*) Maybe 'cause she ain't, maybe that's
why . . . (*still* BUDDY *doesn't answer*) You think she is?

BUDDY

(*turning the corner into 112th Street*) He always slipping back
to her bed at night. Why don't you watch 'em, you want to know
so bad.

PIGMEAT

(*shamefacedly*) Aw, I don't care, so long as it ain't SLICK.

BUDDY

(*stopping before entrance to first tenement*) What you going
to do if it is?

PIGMEAT

(*vehemently*) I'll kill that motherfucker.

BUDDY

BUDDY

You go on and 'tend to your own business and let BABY SISTER 'tend to hers. And leave me alone. I got to get back to work. I ain't got my book made up.

INTERIOR. PRECINCT STATION DAY

MAMA LOUIS is sitting in a hard wooden chair in the booking room of the 123rd Street precinct police station. A uniformed white lieutenant sits behind the desk, looking bored. A uniformed black sergeant sits to one side at the radio dispatcher's desk.

DETECTIVE CORPORAL JOHNNY BROWN comes from a door to the rear and beckons.

CORPORAL BROWN

LIEUTENANT FISCHER will see you now, MISSUS LOUIS. Step this way, please.

MAMA gets up and follows him into a rear corridor and is ushered into a small office. The walls are covered with sectional maps of New York City, various typed notices and memoranda and photostat circulars of wanted criminals. LIEUTENANT FISCHER sits behind a cluttered desk with a green blotter. Behind him light floods in from an open window.

LIEUTENANT FISCHER

(*without arising*) Sit down, MISSUS (*looking at the memo pad on the desk*) LOUIS.

MAMA sits in a hard wooden chair, facing the light.

LIEUTENANT FISCHER

What can I do for you?

MAMA sits tearing at a black handkerchief in her hands.

MAMA

My husband was the man who was killed in front of that poolroom on 116th Street. Just yesterday we buried him.

Her face looks ravaged with grief.

LIEUTENANT FISCHER's face is framed in the bright light from the window behind him and his expression is barely discernible, but his voice is dry, noncommittal and uninviting.

LIEUTENANT FISCHER

We have all the known facts up to the present, MISSUS LOUIS. We are working on it; I am working on it personally.

MAMA

(*choking back sobs*) And late last night my baby daughter was attacked—

LIEUTENANT FISCHER

(*interrupting sharply*) With intent to rape, or assault and battery? I mean was he trying to rape her or rob her?

MAMA

Oh, he were going to rape her, what else?

LIEUTENANT FISCHER

(*taking pencil and pad*) You know the identity of the man?

MAMA

No, and she don't neither. She never got to see him.

LIEUTENANT FISCHER

(*fiddling with his pencil*) You reported this last night—to the police?

MAMA

(*guiltily*) No sir.

LIEUTENANT FISCHER

You called a policeman?

MAMA

No sir, it weren't no use. He had got away and she weren't hurt bad, and it wasn't any use of making all the fuss and bother and keeping folks up all night.

LIEUTENANT FISCHER

(*ducking his head to hide his face*) You should have called the police. But anyway, you can tell me now what happened.

MAMA

(*tearing her handkerchief to shreds*) She were coming home late, coming up the stairs—we live on the fourth floor—and suddenly the hall lights went out, and a man grabbed her.

LIEUTENANT FISCHER

(*voice slightly thickened*) What is your daughter's name?

MAMA

BABY SISTER.

LIEUTENANT FISCHER

(*voice thicker*) You say she was coming home late. At what time exactly?

MAMA

I don't know but it was well after midnight.

LIEUTENANT FISCHER

(*staring at empty pad without writing*) Where had she been?

MAMA

I don't know; she wouldn't tell.

LIEUTENANT FISCHER

How do you know she had been attacked?

MAMA

We heard her scream and started running downstairs. She were on the first landing—and when we got there the hall lights come on and—

LIEUTENANT FISCHER

(*beginning to write*) Who do you mean by "we"?

MAMA

Me and two of my sons, PIGMEAT and BUDDY.

LIEUTENANT FISCHER

(*poking in the typed script on his desk*) It says here you have another son, SUSIE. Where was he?

MAMA

He was out. He had gone out earlier and hadn't come back.

LIEUTENANT FISCHER

What time was it when he came back?

MAMA

He didn't come back.

LIEUTENANT FISCHER

Where is the switch for the hall lights?

MAMA

In the basement furnace room.

LIEUTENANT FISCHER

The janitor's suite is in the basement?

MAMA

We don't have no regular janitor; there's just a man who tends the furnace in the winter and comes by in the summer to turn on the lights and clean the halls sometimes.

LIEUTENANT FISCHER

How do you enter the basement?

MAMA

From the back yard.

LIEUTENANT FISCHER

You found your daughter?

MAMA

She were backed against the wall on the first landing with her sweater all torn and her knife out: and there was a little blood on the floor.

LIEUTENANT FISCHER

Then she must have cut her assailant?

MAMA

Must have.

LIEUTENANT FISCHER places his pencil on the desk and ceases to write. When he next speaks his voice sounds relieved.

LIEUTENANT FISCHER

We will look for him, MISSUS LOUIS. I will assign a detective to the case immediately.

MAMA

It ain't just that I come to see you about.

LIEUTENANT FISCHER remains silent without prompting, but MAMA stumbles on, forcing herself to speak.

MAMA

What I came most for was to ask the police to help me control that girl. She was always a wild girl, getting into all kind of trouble—

LIEUTENANT FISCHER

(*voice incontrollably harsh, angry*) What kind of trouble?

MAMA

Trouble with men. Men are always after her and she ain't got sense enough to take care of herself; and now that her pa is dead—

LIEUTENANT FISCHER

What exactly has she done?

MAMA

It ain't what she's done so far—not far as I know, anyway; but I'm afraid of what she might do, now her pa ain't here no more to control her.

LIEUTENANT FISCHER

(*in a blurred, harsh voice*) What do you think she might do?

MAMA

I'm scared of some man getting hold of her, making a whore out of her or making her pregnant.

LIEUTENANT FISCHER

How do you expect the police to protect a girl's virginity, lock her in a chastity belt?

MAMA

It was just that I thought—

LIEUTENANT FISCHER

(*in a tight, guilt-ridden voice*) You should go to the city welfare department or the juvenile court. All the police can do is try to give her physical protection—that is, against violent attack, assault, rape and such—and that only if she cooperates, informs us what to expect, who's after her. Otherwise we can't help her. If she gets herself pregnant we will arrest the man who did it— if she swears out a warrant. And if we find her engaged in prostitution, we'll have to arrest her.

MAMA

I thought maybe the police might sort of keep an eye on her.
LIEUTENANT FISCHER abruptly stands up, ending the interview.

LIEUTENANT FISCHER

We'll do the best we can.
MAMA also stands to leave.

MAMA

At least I'll feel better knowing the police are looking out for her.

LIEUTENANT FISCHER

(*softly*) Don't mention it.
As MAMA goes out the door, the LIEUTENANT's face twists in a grimace of guilt.

INTERIOR. DELUXE BARBERSHOP DAY

SUSIE is sitting in a barber chair in the big deluxe barbershop next door to Sugar Ray Robinson's "Enterprises." The clock over the glass-enclosed cashier's cage reads: 11:10.

SLICK enters the barbershop and sits in the chair beside him.
His face shows the marks of his beating.

SLICK

(*to the barber*) Give me the works.
He glances furtively at SUSIE through the corners of his eyes.
SUSIE deliberately ignores him.

SLICK's barber signals. A manicurist comes and attaches a tray
to the arm of SLICK's chair, gives him a professional smile, sits on
her stool and takes his left hand. She is an attractive, light-
skinned woman with a fresh coiffure, heavily made up, and wearing a spotless white form-fitting nylon uniform.

A shoeshine boy brings his shine box, a high footrest for the
client with a low seat for himself attached, sits in front of
the chair and takes SLICK's right foot, begins working on the narrow tan shoe.

SUSIE

(*speaking straight ahead*) What you follow me in here for?
A sudden tension envelops everyone within hearing, but no
one acts as though they've heard.

SLICK

(*looking toward* SUSIE) What you mean, followed? I had an
appointment. You can ask my barber.
SUSIE does not ask the barber. The barber ventures no remark.

SLICK

But since you is here, I want to talk to you.

SUSIE

(*deadpan*) Talk ahead.
The shoeshine boy looks up; looks down quickly.

SLICK

I seen her come from that whiskey head's storefront church
late last night.
SUSIE does not reply.

SLICK

Oh, you know 'bout that?

SUSIE

State your piece. What you want?

SLICK

(*lowering his voice*) See here, man, I can't get no five G's together all at once. I give you a grand and the rest on terms.

SUSIE

(*in his tight-throated, dangerous-sounding voice*) You give me five G's or keep away from her; or I'll cut your motherfucking throat.

Involuntarily the manicurist shudders but gives no other sign that she has heard. Both barbers continue to work with intense concentration on their client's hair. The shoeshine boy misses a beat with his shine cloth but makes up for it by a series of pops. SLICK stares straight ahead.

When SUSIE's barber removes the nylon wrapper about SUSIE's shoulders to replace it with a rubber one for "conking," SUSIE's left hand, resting on the arm of the chair, is momentarily exposed, revealing a fresh bandage across its palm; but no one seems to notice it.

Except for the sound of clippers, there is a period of complete silence. Finally SLICK speaks toward the wall.

SLICK

Five G's ain't a throwaway in Harlem, man. Besides which, she's been running wild; she might be latched on to all kind of studs and be more trouble than she's worth.

SUSIE

No she ain't. I done seen to that. She ain't hooked up to nobody. She's just right.

SLICK

It ain't a big deal anyway, with all the young stuff that's going free.

SUSIE

That's why I ain't hot on dealing with you Harlem pimps. All you think of is street girls. You is scared of big money.

SLICK

Who's scared of big money?

SUSIE

You is. I'll sell her downtown and get more than that for her. She a natural-born call girl.

SLICK

Where anybody going to find hundred-dollar Johns in Harlem?

SUSIE

That just goes to show how ignorant you is. Harlem is full of rich Johns who'd get off a C-note for her.

SLICK

Yeah, and they'd think they'd bought her.

SUSIE

Is Harlem all you can think of? What about the big hotels downtown? What about all them fat rich suckers in the garment industry? What about all them oil millionaires from Texas and Oklahoma who come here just for that? She's just what they're looking for; and a C-note ain't no more to them than a tip. You could get your money back in a month and buy a Cadillac besides.

SLICK

You is out of your head thinking white men is going to pay that kind of money for a colored girl.

SUSIE

Man, you're a solid square. Lots of these high-society women up here has been on that kick for years. How you think they're keeping up their sweet men? You think they're getting money from their stingy black husbands?

SLICK

If you're all that smart, why don't you work her yourself?

SUSIE

Don't think I wouldn't if she weren't my sister.

The two barbers exchange looks behind their clients' heads, then, smiling cynically, continue their work as though they'd heard this kind of talk all their lives.

SLICK

Supposing you is right—

SUSIE

I knows I'm right.

SLICK

I ain't got five G's right now; and I ain't got no way to get it unless I put her to work.

SUSIE

Then just pat your foot, daddy-o; I'll find me another buyer.

A sudden, wary silence, beginning at the front where clients are waiting their turns, sweeps over the big barbershop to the extreme rear. Faces turn toward the entrance as though drawn by a magnet, and become suddenly blank. Eyes become expressionless. It is as though life has become suddenly suspended.

LIEUTENANT FISCHER comes inside, a frozen look on his thin white face. CORPORAL BROWN follows, with the defiant, shamefaced look of a black man playing the role of an Uncle Tom before his black brothers.

They continue back into the shop and stand a little apart in front of SUSIE's chair. LIEUTENANT FISCHER and SUSIE stare at one another with instinctive hatred. CORPORAL BROWN takes his .38-caliber police positive from its shoulder sling and holds it loosely in his hand, so it is visible.

LIEUTENANT FISCHER

(*finally*) Where were you after midnight?

SUSIE

(*unblinking*) What's it to you?

LIEUTENANT FISCHER

How'd you like to come down to the station and say that? SUSIE's barber stops working and steps back out of range.

SLICK's barber moves suddenly away as though on forgotten business.

Brown and black faces look on with studied blankness.

SUSIE

(*tight-throated; defiant*) I was 'tending to my business, like you ought to be doing now.

LIEUTENANT FISCHER reaches out suddenly and lifts the rubber sheet. At sight of SUSIE's bandaged left hand he deliberately draws his pistol, and then with a motion lightning-fast hits SUSIE along the meat part of the jaw, knocking him out of the barber chair and onto the floor at the feet of SLICK.

SLICK jumps from his chair, over the top of SUSIE's sprawled figure, to get out of range.

SUSIE turns on his hands and feet like a big cat, comes up from the floor with his leg muscles, head bowed on the right side, left forearm forward in a knife fighter's crouch. A click is heard. The knife blade springs naked in his right hand.

The LIEUTENANT levels his pistol at the exact center of SUSIE's forehead.

LIEUTENANT FISCHER

(*softly*) I'm going to kill you.

SUSIE blinks and sanity returns as his body wilts.

CORPORAL BROWN

(*in his customary cynical voice*) Drop the chiv, daddy-o.

A fraction of a second goes by. The chiv hits the floor. SUSIE stands up, his body loose, flaccid, in the complete immobility of defeat.

CORPORAL BROWN reaches down, picks up the knife, inserts it between the metal arm of the barber chair and the fixture for the manicurist's tray, breaks two thirds of the blade off, extends it toward SUSIE. SUSIE ignores it. The CORPORAL tosses it onto the seat of the barber chair.

LIEUTENANT FISCHER

(*holstering his pistol; blue eyes pinned on SUSIE's face*) If she names you, say goodbye.

SUSIE pushes the knife to the floor, sits again in the barber chair, arranges the rubber sheet, looks at the LIEUTENANT defiantly.

SUSIE

She ain't going to name me.
Without another word or look in SUSIE's direction, the LIEU-TENANT turns and walks from the barbershop, followed by his shamefaced CORPORAL.
SLICK returns to his chair.
No one speaks.
The barbers take their posts.

SLICK

(*finally*) That's what I mean.

SUSIE

Chances go around.

EXTERIOR.   LENOX AVENUE   DAY

The whistles are blowing for noon. The sun is high in the sky. The air hammers of workmen digging up the water main on Lenox Avenue suddenly cease their nerve-racking clatter.
A big black muscular old workman wearing a soiled sweat shirt sings out jubilantly:

WORKMAN

Oh, how the ham do smell, when ah hears the dinner bell!

YOUNG WORKMAN

(*of the new generation*) Man, hush that slavery-time shit; you is free now.

OLD WORKMAN

(*looking about at the ditch, the picks and shovels, the air hammers*) Free? Does us look like us is free?
A black uniformed patrolman chatting with the white foreman of the gang laughs.

FOREMAN

Free for one hour.

In the background is the half-black-painted plate glass front of the Church of the Redeemed Sinner.

The head of REVEREND CONVERTED SINNER emerges through a crack in the doorway. He looks up and down the street. The head jerks back, like the head of a turtle seeing danger. The door seems to close itself. There is the faint sound of a lock clicking shut.

From the direction of 116th Street come the black-clad figures of MAMA LOUIS and UNCLE PIE. Her ravaged yellow face is grief-stricken and his pop-eyed, moon-shaped black face contains such an unbelievable expression of obvious sorrow they appear to be professional mourners going for an audition. The passers-by hurrying home for lunch pay them no attention.

MAMA

I hope he's still there.

UNCLE PIE

Where else he going to be? He lives there and ain't no funeral today.

They halt in front of the entrance and try the door. When they find it locked, MAMA knocks.

Inside, REVEREND CONVERTED SINNER is standing halfway down the aisle, arrested in a posture of listening. At the sound of the knocking he scampers back to the door of his room and pauses again like a small night rodent in front of its hole.

MAMA

He must not be in.

UNCLE PIE

Maybe he's asleep. (*taking a key ring from his pocket*) Anyway, I got a key, I'm a deacon.

INTERIOR.   CHURCH OF THE REDEEMED SINNER   DAY

At the sound of the key being inserted in the lock, REVEREND CONVERTED SINNER soundlessly flings open the door to his room, leaps inside and pulls the door shut behind him. The sound of his lock clicking shut is synchronized with the sound of the outer door lock opening. Moving rapidly on tiptoes, REVEREND CON-

VERTED SINNER spreads his bed, clears the table in the center of the room, opens a Bible and places it atop the table, places a tablet to one side of it on which several pages have been written, lays a pencil beside the tablet, seats himself at the table, lays his head atop his folded arms and feigns sleep.

MAMA and UNCLE PIE enter the church and stop halfway down the aisle.

UNCLE PIE

(*calling in a loud voice*) REVEREND CONSECRATED SINNER!
There is no reply.

MAMA

(*in a whisper*) It's REVEREND CONVERTED SINNER.

UNCLE PIE

(*replying in a whisper*) Ain't it the same? (*loudly*) Oh, REVEREND!
No reply.
They continue to the back and knock on the door to the REVEREND's living quarters.
No answer.

MAMA

He ain't here.

UNCLE PIE

(*bending over to look through the keyhole of the old-fashioned lock*) He must be asleep. His key's in the door.
Suddenly the sound of snoring comes from the room.

UNCLE PIE

Yeah, he's in there; I can hear him snoring. (*he bangs on the door and shouts*) Wake up REVEREND, it's SISTER LOUIS.

REVEREND CONVERTED SINNER

(*in muffled voice as though just coming awake*) Eh, who dat?

UNCLE PIE

(*shouting*) SISTER LOUIS!

REVEREND CONVERTED SINNER

(*shouting*) SISTER LOUIS! What you want, sister?

UNCLE PIE

(*shouting*) She wants some spiritual guidance.

REVEREND CONVERTED SINNER

(*continuing to shout through the locked door*) Spiritual guidance? At this hour of the day?

MAMA

Please, REVEREND SINNER. We can't pick our time.

REVEREND CONVERTED SINNER

Just a minute, sister.

Arranging his features into a solemn, sanctimonious expression, REVEREND CONVERTED SINNER arises from the table and crosses the room to open the door. His features are so set in his arrangement he is unable to show surprise.

REVEREND CONVERTED SINNER

Come right in, sister, and you too, BROTHER PIE. I must have fell asleep reading the good book. Ahem, in the arms of our Good Savior.

MAMA and UNCLE PIE look about for seats; MAMA takes the chair, UNCLE PIE sits on the edge of the bed. The REVEREND stands by the table, rubbing his hands together and trying to look inspiring.

REVEREND CONVERTED SINNER

Spiritual guidance. That's what your reverend is for.

MAMA

It's about BABY SISTER.

REVEREND CONVERTED SINNER

(*giving a start*) Her? What's she said—done rather. I ain't seen her since she flew in here and desecrated her pa's funeral. Is she done run away?

MAMA

(*tearing at the shredded black handkerchief in her hands*) It ain't exactly what she's done. She ain't done nothing really bad yet, as far as I know; less she done something when she was out so late last night.

REVEREND CONVERTED SINNER

Was she out late? Where was she at?

MAMA

(*worriedly*) She won't say. We been trying to make her tell, but she just shuts up.

REVEREND CONVERTED SINNER

(*sweating*) Don't force her. (*piously*) Show her that you trust her.

MAMA

It ain't that I don't trust her. But things just happen to her. She act like a slut and men is always after her. Just last night somebody tried to rape her.

The REVEREND gives such a violent start he becomes strangled and bends over, gasping for breath.

UNCLE PIE leaps to his feet and beats him on the back. Finally the REVEREND gets his breath.

REVEREND CONVERTED SINNER

(*gasping*) Rape! Lawd above, sister. Who done that?

MAMA

She never got to see him.

REVEREND CONVERTED SINNER

(*sighing*) Oh!

MAMA

He grabbed her on the landing as she was coming up the stairs.

REVEREND CONVERTED SINNER

(*suspiciously relieved*) Oh! Oh! And she never got to see him? Lawd lawd!

MAMA

It just ain't only that. It's just I'm so scared she's going to get into trouble I can't see. Lawd, I'm scared. If she don't get herself into trouble, she going to get the rest of us into trouble. Lawd, I can see it coming, as plain as Christ on the cross, and I don't see no way to stop it.

UNCLE PIE

It ain't like as if she were a bad girl. I'll bet my arm she's still a virgin. It's just what happens to her all the time. Mens won't leave her alone. You can understand that, REVEREND.

REVEREND CONVERTED SINNER

(*drawing back*) Me?

UNCLE PIE

(*clearing his throat*) Why, sure, you is a reverend and must understand all the sinful nature of mens.

REVEREND CONVERTED SINNER

(*clearing his throat*) 'Course she ought to get married. Then her husband could keep her at home.

UNCLE PIE

(*indignantly*) She can't just go out and get married like that; she got to find a husband first.

MAMA

And that's just the trouble; she hardly know one man from another. She's so cooped up in the house she can't entertain nobody and we can't afford no bigger place. Most of Pa's insurance money went to pay for the funeral; and SUSIE just can't seem to find no suitable job. BUDDY's got a little numbers book and helps out some, and LIL helps out some when she's working, and BABY SISTER brings home her pay—what's left of it, which ain't much. But it just don't seem enough to do. Lawd, I don't know.

REVEREND CONVERTED SINNER

(*solemnly*) There's only one thing left to do, sister. It never fails. Let us kneel in prayer.

The three of them kneel about the table before the open Bible.

EXTERIOR.   HARLEM STREETS   DAY

When the taxicab turns the corner of 125th Street into Seventh Avenue and draws to a stop in front of the Theresa Hotel, the big two-faced clock mounted on the pole in front of the credit jewelry store reads: 2:57.

A sound truck passes shattering the cab with jazz, advertising a dance at the Renaissance Ballroom.

LIL gets out of the taxi, assisted by the huge doorman in his well-worn livery, waves at the crowd of sporty characters assembled in front of the hotel windows and enters the hotel bar.

INTERIOR.   THERESA BAR   DAY

Slanted venetian blinds across the plate glass front window cast the inside in gloom.

DICKIE is sitting at the circular bar, chatting with friends, waiting for her. A bartender nods; DICKIE looks about, gets up, taking his drink, and leads her to a booth. The bartender pours her a Scotch on the rocks without being asked and pushes it toward the waitress.

She nods gratefully and takes a sip. She looks cool and voluptuous in a green linen suit and red coral beads.

DICKIE

(*smiling reassuringly*) Well, baby, what's the trouble?

LIL

(*looking suddenly worried*) Honey, I'm just plain scared. I'm so scared I can't sleep.

DICKIE

(*frowning in alarm*) Scared of what, baby?

LIL

Scared of trouble, honey, just plain trouble.

DICKIE

What kind of trouble, baby?

LIL

Killing trouble. It's BABY SISTER and that white detective. I feel it in my bones.

DICKIE

TIMME?
LIL nods.

DICKIE

What's he done?

LIL

I think he's made her pregnant.

DICKIE

What makes you think that, baby?

LIL

Something she said yesterday; rather it was more how she acted, the expression on her face. I asked her outright, but of course she denied it; and I didn't think any more of it at the time, but this morning I woke up thinking about her and it suddenly came back. It's just intuition, but I feel almost certain.

DICKIE

(looking as though he didn't put much stock in women's intuition) Just what was it, baby, just what did she do, or didn't do, or didn't say, or whatever it was.

LIL

Well, she had a new yellow dress and she said he gave it to her. She came to get me to say I gave it to her so she could take it home.

DICKIE

(suddenly serious) Well, that's something else. If he gave her a dress—but hell, I've given a lot of girls dresses I haven't made pregnant.

LIL

(*giving him a cold look*) Well, I'm sure you have, but you ain't a white man giving dresses to a little colored girl.

DICKIE

(*half smiling*) Well, that's for sure. But what you want to do about BABY SISTER, take her to a doctor and have her examined?

LIL

(*thoughtfully*) I don't know whether she'd let me for one thing. And it depends on TIMME, what kind of a man is he? If she is and she's told him, will he get her an abortion?

DICKIE

I'm sure TIMME would do that; but if you want me to I'll ask him. He ain't so bad.

LIL

Oh no! But if he fixes it he can do it easy, being a detective lieutenant.

DICKIE

Well, what are you scared of then?

LIL

(*face sagging, eyes widening*) It's SUSIE who scares me. I don't know what it is he's got against BABY SISTER: he acts like he's crazy. If he sees her so much as looking at a man, he'll knock her down. And if he finds out she's got herself pregnant by a white man and has had an abortion, he'll kill them both—or get killed. And that's for sure.

DICKIE

(*looking grave and thoughtful*) I guess you're right. But the only solution I see to that is to get her away from home.

LIL

I've thought of that. If I could get her with some little band. With a little training she could make it; and she holds herself good.

DICKIE

(*brightening with a sudden idea*) I can get her on the Apollo "Amateur Hour" and if she makes good on that she's in. Some band is bound to take her. And I can slip her in this Saturday night.

LIL

(*trying hard to look enthusiastic*) I sure do hope that she'll make it. 'Cause if she don't get away from home soon, SUSIE's going to kill her as sure as water is wet.

EXTERIOR.   HARLEM STREET   DAY

The clock on the dingy brick front of the 125th Street railroad station reads: 3:55. A train roars past on the trestle overhead. It is a mixed neighborhood of blacks and whites, catering to the needs of transients. Near the railroad station, on the same side of 125th Street, is the flashy cafeteria where BABY SISTER works.

PIGMEAT stands in a doorway across the street from the cafeteria, watching the entrance.

SLICK is sitting in his shiny convertible parked a few doors distant from the cafeteria entrance. The rock dents in the bodywork made by PIGMEAT are clearly visible.

PIGMEAT has seen SLICK but hasn't been seen himself.

CORPORAL BROWN and LIEUTENANT FISCHER drive up in front of the cafeteria and park in the "no parking" zone. The LIEUTENANT gets out and walks up to SLICK's car and puts his hand on the door.

LIEUTENANT FISCHER

What do you want here?

SLICK

(*defiantly*) I ain't breaking no laws; I'm just minding my business.

LIEUTENANT FISCHER

Have you got girls working this district?

SLICK

(*looking away indifferently*) I ain't got no girls working no district.

LIEUTENANT FISCHER

(*leaning forward*) Listen, I want your attention.

The words have magical effect on SLICK. He turns quickly about and looks up at the LIEUTENANT, fawningly.

SLICK

Yes sir, boss, you has got my attention. I am listening to you with my whole attention.

LIEUTENANT FISCHER

Good, because if I catch you speaking to this girl again, I'm going to arrest you, and then I'm going to take you up there under the trestle. (*pausing dramatically*) And then I'm going to let you escape. And then I'm going to kill you for attempting to escape. Understand?

SLICK

Yes sir, boss, I got the message. You ain't never going to find me over this way no more.

LIEUTENANT FISCHER

Good.

BABY SISTER comes from the cafeteria in time to see SLICK driving rapidly away. She looks after the car, puzzled, then looks around and sees the LIEUTENANT coming toward her. When the LIEUTENANT motions for her to get into the car, CORPORAL BROWN gets out, crosses the street and enters the bar beside which PIG-MEAT is standing. The LIEUTENANT takes the seat beneath the wheel vacated by CORPORAL BROWN and when BABY SISTER slips into the seat beside him, drives off.

INTERIOR.   POLICE CRUISER   DAY

BABY SISTER

(*sitting far over on her side of the seat*) What you looking so mean about?

LIEUTENANT FISCHER

I want to ask you some questions.

BABY SISTER

(*looking bored*) Ask 'em.

The LIEUTENANT keeps driving west on 125th Street, past Madison, Fifth, Lenox, Seventh Avenue.

LIEUTENANT FISCHER

Who attacked you last night?

BABY SISTER

(*giving a start*) Ma's been to see you.

LIEUTENANT FISCHER

Yes.

BABY SISTER

(*sullenly*) I've already said I didn't see him.

The LIEUTENANT says nothing else as he turns north on St. Nicholas Avenue. BABY SISTER looks out of the window.

The car stops in front of a fourteen-story apartment house on Edgecombe Avenue. It is a swank, well-kept street of private residences and fine apartment houses which face a clifflike park bordering the Harlem River. Affluent black citizens live here.

LIEUTENANT FISCHER

I've made an appointment with a doctor for you.

BABY SISTER

What's his name?

LIEUTENANT FISCHER

Dr. Archer. Just ask the elevator boy.

BABY SISTER

(*hesitating*) Is it going to hurt?

LIEUTENANT FISCHER

No, you won't feel a thing and it's not dangerous. You just have to be quiet for a time afterward.

BABY SISTER turns impetuously, throws her arms about the LIEUTENANT and kisses him passionately.

BABY SISTER

(*vehemently*) Oh, TIMME, I love you.

LIEUTENANT FISCHER

(*deliberately disengaging her arms*) Let's don't draw any attention. I'll wait for you.

BABY SISTER jumps from the car and runs rapidly up the stairs. A liveried doorman holds open the door for her and tips his hat. Two colored women, coming from the elevator, look her over with disdain. She hurries through the luxurious foyer, enters the waiting elevator.

BABY SISTER

(*to the operator*) Dr. Archer's office.

The elevator operator gives her a knowing grin.

BABY SISTER

(*furiously*) It's for my pa.

INTERIOR.   LOUISES' FLAT   DAY

MAMA LOUIS, BUDDY, LIL, PIGMEAT and SUSIE are sitting about the round-top table in the sitting room speculating on the whereabouts of BABY SISTER.

MAMA

Lawd, that chile, where is she now?

PIGMEAT

I done told you, Ma, I b'lieve the police done got her. They asking her 'bout last night is all. Ain't no need—

PIGMEAT breaks off to look suspiciously at SUSIE shifting nervously in his chair.

PIGMEAT

What the matter with you?

The discussion is interrupted by a knock on the door. PIGMEAT rushes to open it.

PIGMEAT

I knowed it!

BABY SISTER stands in the doorway, accompanied by CORPORAL BROWN. She seems poised to duck until she sees SUSIE sitting on the opposite side of the table, then calmly steps inside as though nothing has happened.

Wearing his customary cynical grin, CORPORAL BROWN follows her into the room, flashing his badge.

CORPORAL BROWN

(*addressing them all*) We had her down at the station. (*then staring directly at* SUSIE) Asking her some pertinent questions.

Everyone has been staring at him, now all of them stare at her, except PIGMEAT, who looks slyly at SUSIE.

CORPORAL BROWN

(*deadpan*) We got an idea who attacked her.

With the exception of PIGMEAT, who continues to peep at SUSIE, everyone stares back at CORPORAL BROWN expectantly, eyes questioning, but no one speaks.

BABY SISTER inches around the table to get behind LIL.

CORPORAL BROWN

Well, no one wants to know whom we suspect . . . (*pausing invitingly*) . . . then I'll mosey on along. I've done my good deed for the day. She was afraid to come home alone.

A sense of shamefaced guilt envelops them.

CORPORAL BROWN leaves.

SUSIE puts both hands on the table, pushes to his feet and gives BABY SISTER a threatening look.

SUSIE

(*harshly*) I don't b'lieve a word of that copper's shit. He— (*breaking off as he notices* BABY SISTER *staring at his bandaged left hand with a horrified expression*)

MAMA

(*not taking notice*) Now, SUSIE . . . (*silenced by the expressions of the others*)

PIGMEAT is swallowing audibly. BUDDY bows his head in an attitude of intolerable embarrassment. LIL's face ages from terror.

All, except MAMA, who looks bewildered, seem gripped in horror and repulsion.

BABY SISTER looks directly at SUSIE with a challenging defiance. SUSIE stares back mutely. After a moment BABY SISTER's lips twitch. SUSIE grinds his teeth.

BABY SISTER

(*defiantly*) SUSIE, I want you to give me back my yellow dress, you hear. I'm going to the club to hear LIL sing tonight. I'm tired of being cooped up all the time like a prisoner.

MAMA

(*gasping*) Well, I never!

PIGMEAT tries to catch BUDDY's eyes, but BUDDY looks away. LIL stares at SUSIE as though to discover his intentions. But SUSIE merely jams his fists into his pants pockets and shuffles toward his bedroom.

SUSIE

(*thick-voiced*) Okay! Okay! (*adding with feigned disgust*) You women! (*maliciously before passing from sight*) All of you!

MAMA

(*unable to get over her astonishment*) What's come over him?

EXTERIOR.   125TH STREET   NIGHT

SLICK's convertible is parked around the corner on Eighth Avenue, diagonally across 125th Street from the 88 KEYS NIGHT CLUB. The top is closed and he is barely discernible in the dark interior as he sits watching the entrance to the night club through his rearview mirror. He sees PIGMEAT alight from a crosstown bus in front of the club and hurry across the street, then loses sight of him.

PIGMEAT stands unseen in a darkened tenement entrance from which he can watch the entrance of the 88 KEYS. He sees SUSIE walking from the direction of Seventh Avenue and enter the club alone.

INTERIOR.   88 KEYS NIGHT CLUB   NIGHT

A long bar, curving at the front end, extends down to a heavily curtained doorway at the rear. The bar is crowded with noisy black men and women. From beyond the curtained doorway comes the sound of hot, licking jazz.

SUSIE passes through the bar without speaking and enters a curtained foyer before the night club where a big, hard-faced man charges him two dollars for a one-night membership; then he is admitted to the dimly lit clubroom.

Inside is a large, square, darkened room with most of its floor space taken up by small square tables filled with guests. Black men and women out for a night of dancing and drinking, listening and loving, sit shoulder to shoulder and back to back at the small square tables as though packaged for sale.

A dance floor, about the size of an eight-place dining table, is at the side known as the front; in an almost black-dark recess behind it sits the five-piece band.

LIL stands in the center of the dance floor, wearing a plunging-neck evening gown; her bare arms and upper torso with their smooth creamy skin are bathed in the soft blue beam of a baby spotlight. Her red, hennaed hair looks dark brown, and her dark brown eyes black; her purple-painted lips bright blue. She is singing the blues with far more sex than feeling.

SUSIE edges in among the standees along the back wall and his searching gaze immediately spots the yellow dress of BABY SISTER at a ringside table, limned against the blue beam of light. Beside her sits BUDDY, looking self-conscious in the new dark green suit he bought for the funeral.

LIL ends her song, stands smiling, waiting for the applause to die out.

The lights come on dimly, but not bright enough for the black guests to be entirely visible to one another.

LIL goes to sit at the table with BABY SISTER and BUDDY. A waiter comes with a bottle of iced champagne in a silver-plated ice bucket, and three champagne glasses.

The band begins playing for dancing and the dance floor becomes jammed with acrobatic dancers. BABY SISTER dances with BUDDY. DICKIE comes into the club, carrying his saxophone case, and sits beside LIL.

SUSIE watches unseen from the dimly lit background, then, after a time, goes outside to the bar.

BABY SISTER and BUDDY return to their table. DICKIE greets them, then continues his intimate conversation with LIL. BABY SISTER becomes bored and looks about at the other celebrants in the dim light. Her gaze rests on a good-looking brown-skinned young man sitting at a table with a heavy-set black woman much older than himself. He feels her gaze on him and looks up; their gazes lock, then she becomes coy and turns a scintillating smile on DICKIE and LIL, who are oblivious.

BABY SISTER asks DICKIE to dance the next dance with her. LIL is obviously annoyed. DICKIE shrugs and escorts BABY SISTER to the dance floor. LIL moves to another table to chat with a girl friend. Left alone at the table, BUDDY drinks more champagne.

The good-looking man has disappeared, leaving his black lady friend alone. She catches BUDDY's eyes and smiles invitingly. BUDDY looks away. The black woman frowns. Looking acutely embarrassed, BUDDY gets up and leaves.

BABY SISTER does not see the good-looking man who interests her, but she knows he is watching her, wanting her. She begins dancing suggestively with DICKIE to show off herself.

DICKIE

(*protestingly*) Girl, this ain't the place, nor the time, nor the man.

BABY SISTER

If you scared, go home.

DICKIE

If I thought you meant that, I'd tell LIL.

BABY SISTER

You got rust in your blood.

DICKIE takes her back to her table, then goes to the other table to join LIL and her girl friend.

While BABY SISTER is sulking at her table, the good-looking man suddenly materializes and asks her for a dance. She jumps to her feet and falls into his arms, looking sexy and victorious. Their dancing is so suggestive it draws instant attention.

The black woman, sitting alone, watches them with an expression of pure murder.

As though activated by intuition, SUSIE returns to the clubroom and watches them unseen from his post in the dimly lit background.

BABY SISTER and her partner are bumped by another acrobatic couple and BABY SISTER's gaze is drawn to SUSIE's stare. She appears suddenly alarmed.

BABY SISTER

Oh, I got to go.

GOOD-LOOKING MAN

(*astonished*) Go where?

Without replying, BABY SISTER breaks from his embrace and hurries toward the women's lounge, leaving her erstwhile partner standing alone on the crowded dance floor, looking silly. The good-looking man shrugs helplessly and starts wending his way back to his black lady friend. But she jumps up quickly and passes him on her way to the women's lounge.

The women's lounge consists of a small dressing room with dressing table and chair and one closed toilet at the far end. It backs against the recess for the bandstand and the sound of music is thunderous when BABY SISTER enters. She sits at the dressing table trying to compose herself after the fright given her by the sight of SUSIE, and she is repairing her makeup when the black woman enters and does not hear her. The first inkling she has of another person present is the sound of a key in the lock. Startled, she wheels about and sees the naked knife blade in the hand of the black lady friend of her good-looking man. She knows immediately and instinctively that the black woman has been made berserk by a jealous rage and intends to kill her.

She leaps to her feet, weak with terror, knocking over the dressing chair.

BLACK WOMAN

(*murderously*) You li'l slut, I'm gonna teach you to mess with my man; I'm gonna waste you for good.

BABY SISTER backs against the door to the toilet, hoists her yellow skirt and draws her own knife from the top of her stocking. But she is too weak with terror to attack. The black woman, seeing her hesitate, lunges and slashes at her. BABY SISTER ducks beneath the blade and dashes past the black woman, but stumbles over the overturned chair and falls to her hands and knees. Her knife is knocked from her hand. Seeing her defenseless, the black woman turns and bends over her deliberately to slash her across the back.

BLACK WOMAN

(*gloating*) I got you now, you slut.

BABY SISTER

(*screaming at the top of her voice*) SUSIE! SUSIE! HELP! Her loud, terrified scream is heard all over the club.

The locked door crashes inward and SUSIE looms in the doorway, the long blade of his knife gleaming in his right hand, a terrifying look on his face.

SUSIE

(*his harsh, grating voice sounding incalculably dangerous*) I'll cut your motherfucking head off! The black woman is now stricken with terror herself.

GOOD-LOOKING MAN

(*fearfully*) Don't cut her, man, please don't cut her.

SUSIE

(*tight-voiced, shoulders hunched, knife blade quivering*) If she cut my BABY SISTER she gone.

LIL pushes through the crowd and gets between SUSIE and the black woman. Other men, coming to the support of the good-looking man, draw their knives. SUSIE's look challenges them all.

BABY SISTER scrambles to her feet and gets behind LIL. Now her terror is inspired by SUSIE.

BABY SISTER

Leave her be. I ain't cut.

LIL puts an arm about her shoulder and takes her away. Gallantly the men stand aside to let the two women pass. With his knife still open and ready, SUSIE follows his sisters. The men look disapproving, but none attempt to stop him. Silently, the good-looking man goes to the aid of his black lady friend.

The band silences and dancing stops as LIL leads BABY SISTER toward the exit. SUSIE follows with his knife still open, eyes hot and challenging. The black celebrants move away from him as from death. The heavyweight ticket taker appears momentarily on the scene as though to see them out. Quietly and unnoticed, BUDDY follows in SUSIE's footsteps.

In single file, led by LIL, they pass through the silent barroom out into the street.

EXTERIOR.   125th STREET   NIGHT

From the dark tenement entrance across the street, PIGMEAT sees them emerge from the 88 KEYS and stand grouped on the sidewalk. He sees BABY SISTER throw herself into LIL's arms, her body shaking convulsively. He breaks from his hiding place and runs across the street to join them. At the same time SLICK's car pulls suddenly from the curb on Eighth Avenue and drives quickly out of sight.

BABY SISTER

(*crying in* LIL'*s arms*) I didn't go to cause no trouble, I just wanted to dance.

LIL

(*consoling*) Don't cry, baby, we all make mistakes. (*turning to* SUSIE) Call a taxi, just don't stand there.

EXTERIOR.   125th STREET   DAY

PIGMEAT is standing in a doorway across the street from the cafeteria where BABY SISTER works, watching the entrance. He sees LIEUTENANT FISCHER's car stop in front of the entrance. The LIEUTENANT is alone. He sees BABY SISTER come from the cafeteria, dressed in her street clothes, and get into the cruiser beside the LIEUTENANT. He sees them drive away. He steps out onto the sidewalk, hesitates, looking down the street in the direction the car has taken.

INTERIOR.   POLICE CRUISER   DAY

LIEUTENANT FISCHER

(*in a voice of concern*) You look ill. Did it hurt you?

BABY SISTER

(*sullenly*) No.

LIEUTENANT FISCHER

Didn't you want to be with me today?

BABY SISTER

(*voice muffled*) It ain't that.

LIEUTENANT FISCHER

Were you ill last night? Did something happen? Did you bleed?

BABY SISTER

(*with muffled sobs*) Nothing happened. It was just like you said it would be. I didn't feel nothing. I went dancing with my sister, LIL.

LIEUTENANT FISCHER

Then what's the trouble, darling? What is it now?

BABY SISTER

(*bawling unrestrainedly*) I wanted to keep our baby. I can't never have nothing I want.

LIEUTENANT FISCHER

(*bleak and distressed*) It's the wrong world for it.

He drives to the corner of Lenox Avenue and 116th Street and parks.

LIEUTENANT FISCHER

You go home now and rest for tonight. If they ask you where you've been, tell them I questioned you again.

BABY SISTER

(*suddenly brightening*) What will you give me if I win first prize tonight?

LIEUTENANT FISCHER

(*looking relieved*) I'll give you, er, er, a hundred dollars.

BABY SISTER

You will? Will you come up on the stage and give it to me? Won't nobody think nothing, they're always doing things like that.

LIEUTENANT FISCHER

No, but I'll wait outside.

BABY SISTER

We're going to have a party at our house afterwards.

LIEUTENANT FISCHER

Then I'll wait outside your house. You'll just have to come downstairs and get the . . . er . . . your . . . it.

BABY SISTER

All right, you do that.
She kisses him passionately before getting out of the car.

BABY SISTER

(*calling over her shoulder*) You've promised.

EXTERIOR.   125th STREET   DAY

SLICK comes quickly from the bar behind PIGMEAT and clutches him by the arms. When he recognizes SLICK, PIGMEAT fights desperately to get free, kicking backward at SLICK's shins. Passers-by look on, but no one interferes. One of the kicks lands on SLICK's shin and in a fury he hits PIGMEAT on the back of the head and knocks him down. He is about to kick him when two passing black men protest.

1ST BLACK MAN

Don't kick that boy; he's just a tadpole.

2ND BLACK MAN

What's he done, anyway?

PIGMEAT

(*scrambling to his feet*) Ain't done nothing.

SLICK

I ain't trying to hurt him; I just want to tell him something 'bout his sister.

PIGMEAT

(*standing apart but not moving off*) What about my sister?

1ST BLACK MAN

All right, beat it if you want to.

2ND BLACK MAN

Come on, man, he don't want to go.

SLICK

(*waiting for them to move away*) You saw her get into that white detective's car?

PIGMEAT

She being investigated. He took her in last night too.

SLICK

Boy, you believe that? She's his girl, didn't you know?

PIGMEAT

That's a lie. She wouldn't go with no white man.

SLICK

How dumb is you? She been his girl for a long time. He's going to take her away and put her in a whorehouse.

PIGMEAT

(*suddenly looking sick*) That's a dirty yellow lie.

SLICK

(*shrugging*) You don't have to believe it. I'm just telling you. I don't want to see a white man make a whore out of a colored girl.

PIGMEAT

He don't have no girls; he ain't like you. He's a lieutenant detective of the police.

SLICK

Hell, punk, who you think got all these black whores on the
line? These white detectives, that's who.

PIGMEAT

(*beginning to cry*) I'll kill him.

SLICK

Better kill him soon, 'cause he's taking her 'way tonight—if he
ain't already took her.

PIGMEAT

I know that's a lie. She's on the Apollo "Amateur Hour" tonight.

SLICK

(*laughing sneeringly*) That's their getaway. He's gonna take
her right after it's over.

PIGMEAT

I'm going to tell SUSIE what you said; I'm going to have him
beat you up again.

SLICK

(*giving another laugh*) SUSIE ain't going to mess with me no
more. You know why? 'Cause I got me a pistol, that's why. I keep
it right beside me in my car. If SUSIE comes toward me I'll shoot
him.

PIGMEAT

Liar!
SLICK starts toward him. PIGMEAT runs off, calling over his
shoulder.

PIGMEAT

Liar . . . liar . . .

SLICK

(*calling after him*) My sister ain't a whore.

PIGMEAT

(*running down the street; crying*) Liar . . . liar . . . liar . . .
liar . . . (*until he's out of sight*)

SLICK re-enters the bar and stands beside another pimp with
whom he's evidently been talking.

2ND PIMP

What you doing with that little boy?

SLICK

(*looking evil and vindictive*) I'm loading me a gun, man.

INTERIOR.   123RD STREET PRECINCT POLICE STATION   DAY

Inside the booking room, white and black uniformed patrolmen
stand about in groups. A white lieutenant in uniform sits behind the booking desk; beside him sits a uniformed black radio
dispatcher.

They all stop talking and stare at PIGMEAT as he walks up to
the desk.

PIGMEAT

Can I speak to the lieutenant?

LIEUTENANT

You're speaking to the lieutenant.

PIGMEAT

I mean the plainclothes lieutenant.

LIEUTENANT

There are two of them; what one?

PIGMEAT

The tall one with the light hair and blue eyes.

LIEUTENANT

You mean LIEUTENANT FISCHER. What do you want with him?

PIGMEAT

He's cross-questioning my sister. I want to tell him something.
The lieutenant switches on the intercom.

RADIO DISPATCHER

(*shaking his head*) FISCHER's not here. He's been gone since
ten o'clock and hasn't been back.

PIGMEAT

He must be here somewhere. He brought my sister in long time
ago and she ain't come back.

LIEUTENANT

(*switching off the intercom*) What's your sister's name?

PIGMEAT

BABY SISTER LOUIS.

LIEUTENANT

Oh, that good-looking girl who claims she was raped the other
night.

PIGMEAT

(*defendingly*) She weren't raped; just jumped.

RADIO DISPATCHER

Depend on FISCHER to get the good-looking ones.

LIEUTENANT

He didn't bring her here.

PIGMEAT

But where'd he take her if he didn't bring her here?

LIEUTENANT

(*with a straight face*) Oh, they're probably off investigating
somewhere. She's probably showing him how it was done.
There is an outburst of laughter in the background. The radio
dispatcher has a big grin on his face.
PIGMEAT looks puzzled. Then, as he gets the meaning of what

the lieutenant has hinted, a look of terrible consternation comes over his face. He turns and runs from the room, tears streaming down his face.

INTERIOR.   CAFETERIA   DAY

PIGMEAT enters through the back door of the cafeteria and finds the manager sitting in his office.

PIGMEAT

I want to see my sister, BABY SISTER LOUIS.

MANAGER

BABY SISTER? Why, she went home sick at ten o'clock.

EXTERIOR.   HARLEM STREETS   DAY

PIGMEAT walks north on Seventh Avenue, examining all cars. Finally he enters a bar and speaks to the bartender.

INTERIOR.   BAR ON SEVENTH AVENUE   DAY

PIGMEAT

You seen SLICK around?

BARTENDER

He was here, but he's been gone for a long time.

EXTERIOR.   HARLEM STREETS   DAY

Upon leaving the bar, PIGMEAT begins making the rounds of the popular bars of Harlem, asking for SLICK. SLICK has been seen at several of them, but no one knows where he has gone.

Finally PIGMEAT finds SLICK's car parked near a bar on Seventh Avenue. He opens the front door of the bar a crack to peep inside and sees SLICK standing at the bar talking to a man. SLICK has been watching the door in the mirror behind the bar and he sees PIGMEAT peep through the crack but gives no sign of recognition. It is only when PIGMEAT withdraws he begins to grin with evil satisfaction.

PIGMEAT returns to SLICK's car, tentatively tries the door, finds it unlocked. He looks up and down the street, opens the door quickly and gets inside.

SLICK has moved to the front window of the bar and is watching him over the top of the curtain.

PIGMEAT feels in the door pockets, then opens the glove compartment. He finds a pistol; takes it out and looks at it. The pistol is a .38 revolver and it is loaded. PIGMEAT sticks it down inside his pants, tightens his belt, pulls his shirt down over it. He waits his opportunity and gets quickly from the car and goes up the street in the opposite direction of the bar.

INTERIOR.   LOUISES' FLAT   DAY

BABY SISTER is lying on MAMA's double bed in the sitting room with the old-fashioned radio turned up loud, reading a *True Romance* magazine, when PIGMEAT enters.

PIGMEAT gives her one hateful, censorious look and hurries past to the kitchen without speaking, walking bent over as though he has stomach cramps. Quickly he hides the pistol beneath the mattress of his cot.

BABY SISTER follows him and scans the kitchen suspiciously.

> BABY SISTER

What have you been stealing?

> PIGMEAT

(*standing guard in front of his cot*) Ain't stole nothing. (*with hostility*) Where you been all morning?

> BABY SISTER

I been at work, where do you think?

> PIGMEAT

You're not going away, are you, BABY SISTER?

> BABY SISTER

Naturally I'm going away—if I win tonight and get to sing with a band.

> PIGMEAT

(*insistingly*) You're not going away tonight, are you?

BABY SISTER

(*looking at him searchingly*) What's got into you? I'll go away tonight if I want to. What you got to do with it?

PIGMEAT

BABY SISTER, don't go away tonight.

BABY SISTER

You're crazy.
She flounces back to the sitting room.
The radio is turned up loud again.
PIGMEAT sits on the edge of the cot, crying.

EXTERIOR.   HARLEM STREETS   NIGHT

LIL, BABY SISTER and BUDDY are sitting in a northbound taxi on Seventh Avenue. It stops for the red light at 125th Street. They look out of the window, fascinated.

The Harlem scene in all its legendary fantasy of light and laughter meets their eyes. Black, brown and yellow soul people are out in droves, milling up and down the sidewalks, jostling, gesticulating, putting out their voices, filling the summer night with an exciting pageantry. Lights are turned on in all the stores, shops, restaurants, bars and in the windows of hotels and tenements. The dense crowd in front of the Theresa Hotel seems to be rotating in a whirlpool. Diamonds glitter in the windows of the credit jewelers, reflected in the shining, wistful eyes of black couples peering at them.

LIL

(*lovingly*) Saturday night in Harlem.

BABY SISTER

I'm nervous, I need a drink.
Heavily made up and clad in a décolleté gown of LIL's, with her arms, shoulders and the seams between her ripe breasts exposed, BABY SISTER looks different, older, more seductive; but her face is tense and unsmiling.

LIL

We're meeting DICKIE at the Yucca Cafe.

When the light turns green, the taxi makes a left turn into 125th Street and pulls up before a brightly lit bar-restaurant resplendent with painted yuccas.

INTERIOR.   YUCCA CAFE   NIGHT

DICKIE meets them at the door and escorts them to the crowded bar where he has kept two high barstools for the two women.

Behind them, beyond a glass partition, seated at the small decorative tables, the elite of Harlem's underworld and the middle world of jazz musicians and show people are dining on "shack-fried" chicken and "minute" steaks.

At the far end, standing on a raised, glass-enclosed, soundproof platform, a black disc jockey with a shining smile is conducting a jazz program for a local radio station.

The atmosphere is gay, loose, whorish and fascinating.

DICKIE notices BABY SISTER's tense face and smiles reassuringly.

> DICKIE

Relax, baby, what you drinking?

> BABY SISTER

Champagne.

> DICKIE

(*to the bartender*) Champagne for the little lady.

The disc jockey is speaking into the microphone but he can only be heard at the bar from the radio tuned to his station.

> DISC JOCKEY

Tonight is a big night in Harlem. The famous Apollo Theatre Amateur Hour which gave the world such stars as Ella Mae Fitzgerald, Sarah Vaughan and Billy Eckstine is taking place tonight. Let's see if there are any amateurs in the house.

> MAN AT THE BAR

Hell, man, can't you see all these is professionals?

Sound of laughter. The prostitutes give him evil looks.

BABY SISTER suddenly giggles and feels relaxed.

INTERIOR.   DICE GAME SOMEWHERE IN HARLEM   NIGHT

In the center of a windowless room sits a billiard table beneath a bright, green-shaded drop light, cut in half by a small iron chain.

Various types of men are standing around it two and three deep, their black faces looking intent in the green upper glow, eyes moving back and forth as they track the white bird's-eye dice galloping on the green felt.

The dice jump the chain, come to a stop.

STICK MAN

(*in a monotonous, crooning voice*) Two treys . . . six . . . four's the point . . . little Joe from Kokomo.

He scoops up the dice and gives them back to SUSIE.

Low voices rise like smoke as bets are paid and laid.

SUSIE shakes the dice carelessly, throws them lazily. The dice jump the chain, come to a stop.

STICK MAN

Seven! . . . four-trey, the country way . . . Seven! . . . the loser.

He picks up the dice and holds them. The winner rakes in the pot. Side bets are paid; low words exchanged.

STICK MAN

Next shooter for the game.

Dirty money is piled on the table. The stick man counts it.

STICK MAN

Nine leaves in the circle. You got him, back man?

SUSIE

Pass me.

STICK MAN

Saddest words on land or sea. Who got him?

A ten-dollar bill floats down. The stick man throws back a dollar. The rack man picks up a dollar from the pot, throws back fifty cents.

Side bets are made.

STICK MAN

(*passing the dice to the new shooter*) You're covered, lover
. . . Turn 'em loose in the big cor-ral.

The dice spin out from the shooter's hand; one goes over the
chain, one stops short.

STICK MAN

(*picking up the dice*) No roll, nothing! . . . Jump the chain,
daddy-o. This is the big steeplechase . . .

The shooter takes the dice, rolls again. The dice jump the
chain, come to a stop.

STICK MAN

Boxcars! Craps! Twelve! The loser!
The winner picks up his money; side bets are paid.

STICK MAN

(*to shooter*) You going, or gonna get left?
The shooter throws down a five-dollar bill.

STICK MAN

Five in the circle! A fever! Winner's got him. Covered, lover.
He passes the dice to the shooter. Side bets are made. The
shooter rolls the dice. The dice jump the chain, come to a stop.

STICK MAN

EEE-leven from heaven. Six-five, eleven. The winner.

SHOOTER

Let it roll . . .
SUSIE turns away from the table and walks out.

EXTERIOR.   125TH STREET   NIGHT

CORPORAL BROWN parks the police cruiser in a "no parking" zone
three doors east of the Apollo Bar, gets out onto the street, walks
around the front of the car to enter the bar. LIEUTENANT FISCHER
remains seated in the cruiser; his thin white face is set in a brood-
ing melancholy as he stares up the street at the Apollo Theatre.

In the other direction, PIGMEAT stands motionless in the dark entrance to professional offices on the floor above, closed for the night. His hands are stuck into the deep side pockets of a cotton windbreaker; his right hand caresses the cold steel of the .38-caliber revolver he stole from SLICK. He is staring at the back of LIEU-TENANT FISCHER's head with a steady, unblinking malevolence.

Should the LIEUTENANT turn his head he will see PIGMEAT, but the LIEUTENANT does not turn his head.

EXTERIOR.   125TH STREET   NIGHT

The lights on the marquee of the Apollo Theatre read: TO-NIGHT—NINE O'CLOCK—AMATEUR HOUR.

A crowd has collected about the entrance, waiting for the motion picture to finish.

Four uniformed black policemen stand in the four corners of the crowded lobby, smiling and pleasant, looking out for friends, single women and pretty girls.

Two horse policemen sit astride their jittery horses at the curb.

Four police cruisers are parked at vantage points along 125th Street.

The crowd is boisterous, pushing, violent-looking, but good-natured. Violence seems to hang in the very atmosphere, ready to erupt. But nothing happens. The loud, sudden curses, the dangerous-sounding threats float away, ignored. The pocket play and swagger, the bad-man pantomime are reminiscent of a B Western motion picture.

Suddenly there is a ripple in the crowd. The horse policemen pull aside to let a big shiny black hearse pull to the curb.

VOICE IN THE CROWD

Here's FAT SAM. Who he want?

ANOTHER VOICE

Watch out he don't get you.

MAMA LOUIS alights from the hearse, clad in her black widow's weeds, and stands in the waiting crowd.

UNCLE PIE steers the hearse from the curb and cruises down the street, looking for a place to park.

No one comes out of the theater, but suddenly there is a concerted rush toward the entrance.

WOMAN'S VOICE

Let's go, daddy, the picture's over.

INTERIOR.   APOLLO THEATRE   NIGHT

Flanking the curtained stage are three tiers of old-fashioned boxes. Beyond, the low mezzanine continues unbrokenly into the balcony, which rises steadily to the rear wall and the protruding projection room.

The theater is brightly lit. The few people who saw the motion picture remain seated. Now come those to see the amateur show, pouring in like stampeding cattle, racing for the best seats, noisy, boisterous, bringing an electric excitement, a happy attitude of expectancy. Black people of all ages and descriptions, all touched by emotions deeper than those inspired by anticipated entertainment.

It is an occasion, an exhibition of unknown black talent, an opportunity for young black people to show the world what they can do, what they have that others haven't; inspiring in the audience strong racial pride, racial loyalties, deep partisan emotions.

Here and there are a few parties of white people, smiling, genial, slightly uncomfortable amid this throng of emotional black people, struggling to look and act their democratic best.

BUDDY is arguing with another young man about the seat beside him in the front row which he is trying to hold for PIGMEAT, who arrives just in time to head off a fight.

MAMA LOUIS and UNCLE PIE find seats toward center.

SUSIE is sitting beside an empty seat in the last row of the balcony beside the projection room in the section known as the "Reefer Roost." He is smoking a reefer. Other young hoodlums come and look at the empty seat, but after looking at SUSIE, move on.

Suddenly SLICK appears. SUSIE beckons with his head. SLICK squeezes through and takes the empty seat. SUSIE passes him the marijuana stick. SLICK takes a puff, sucks the smoke down into his lungs, takes another, passes it back to SUSIE, who takes another puff, squeezes out the fire and sticks the "soldier" behind his ear.

The bright lights go out; the curtain rises, revealing a surprisingly big, deep, wide stage.

A smooth brown-skinned MASTER OF CEREMONIES in a sharp tuxedo steps out onto the stage in the glare from the bright footlights, conked hair shining, white teeth gleaming, and announces the program.

MASTER OF CEREMONIES

Tonight, ladies and gentlemen, is the umpteenth thousandth presentation of the world-famous Apollo Theatre Amateur Hour.

Applause.

MASTER OF CEREMONIES

You are all familiar with the applause meter, which accurately registers the volume of applause for each contestant—

VOICE FROM THE AUDIENCE

Can the corn and get to the meat.

MASTER OF CEREMONIES

A comedian. Come up, sir, and take your turn.

Laughter.

An attendant steps from the wings to exhibit the applause meter, a box-shaped electronics instrument.

VOICE FROM THE AUDIENCE

Do it cook?

MASTER OF CEREMONIES

Another one. Who left open the jackass stall?

Laughter.

MASTER OF CEREMONIES

Now, ladies and gentlemen, these are the prizes: First prize for ensemble or solo act: one week's engagement at the famous Green Meadow Roadhouse in New Jersey; first prize for instrumental solo: a tryout and a week's engagement with a popular band; first prize for vocalist: waxing a disk for Universal Records with a name band and one week's engagement with the same band. And now the grand prize: the winner of this renowned, rare and coveted prize, the fabulous Apollo Gold Medal, will have a week's engagement at that equally fabulous jazz haunt, Birdland.

Big volume of applause.

MASTER OF CEREMONIES

And here is our first contestant, Miss BEULAH LAND, gospel singer.

Fanfare by the band.

A young, fat, pleasant-faced, brown-skinned girl wearing a red evening gown showing huge areas of broad shoulders and tremendous arms comes onto the stage smiling.

MASTER OF CEREMONIES

(*leading the applause*) Let's give the little lady a big hand.

The deafening applause is more for the beginning of the contest than for the individual singer.

MASTER OF CEREMONIES

(*toothily*) Applause preceding performances don't count.

He retires from the stage.

The band gives a lead and BEULAH LAND launches into a rendition of Negro spirituals.

INTERIOR.   YUCCA CAFE   NIGHT

Sitting at the bar of the Yucca Cafe between LIL and DICKIE, BABY SISTER finishes the glass of champagne before her. She's not quite tight, but she's frisky, her body is alive, her face is animated, half smiling; her eyes sparkle.

DICKIE

How do you feel now?

BABY SISTER

(*wriggling her shoulder*) Great.

LIL

(*dryly*) Well, you ought to after four glasses of champagne.

BABY SISTER

Just three. And I feel like I could dance all night.

DICKIE

You got to sing, not dance. (*glances at his watch*) And it's time for us to go.

LIL

I got her on last.

DICKIE

Time anyway.
He calls the bartender, pays the bill.

INTERIOR.   APOLLO THEATRE   NIGHT

LIL

(*whispering*) We're just in time. You're on next.

BABY SISTER

I'm ready.

MASTER OF CEREMONIES

(*waiting a moment as though for the applause to end*) And now, ladies and gentlemen, last but not least, we have that charming little songbird, whose elder sister you all know—BABY SISTER LOUIS. (*leading the applause*) Come out, BABY SISTER, and let us look at you.

BABY SISTER comes out in a mincing, sexy walk, doing things with her body to get attention before she opens her mouth, turns to the audience and winks, shaking a leg like a girl waiting for a man.

The audience goes wild. A man throws his hat up on the stage, another jumps up and starts trucking down the aisle.

MALE VOICE FROM AUDIENCE

Hey, baby, if I could only cook.

WOMAN'S VOICE

(*faintly heard*) Don't you go after that hat.

In the front row BUDDY and PIGMEAT are beating wooden blocks together.

But high up in the "Reefer Roost," eyes stretched, pupils distended, tight-faced, SUSIE is sitting muscle-taut, unsmiling, unmoving, his gaze riveted on BABY SISTER. SLICK looks at him from the corners of his eyes and smiles evilly to himself.

The MASTER OF CEREMONIES holds up his hands for the applause to cease. Finally the band gives a lead and BABY SISTER gives out with the naughty, suggestive song "In the Night," in the whining, breathless voice that goes with sexual intercourse, taking her body through all the motions.

Again the audience goes wild. Male voices shouting, women screaming, young hoodlums in the aisles doing suggestive twists.

Again the MASTER OF CEREMONIES has to come on stage and plead for quiet so she can do her encore. She encores with another suggestive song, and minces off stage.

Again the wild applause. The MASTER OF CEREMONIES calls her back to take a bow. The applause goes on and on. She stands there smiling, using her body teasingly, waiting for the applause to die down; and then finishes with a blues song.

It seems as though the applause will never stop; and it comes on in volume again when she is announced winner of the vocalist prize.

PIGMEAT gets from his seat, crosses in front of the stage, goes up the wall aisle and out the front exit.

EXTERIOR.   125TH STREET   NIGHT

PIGMEAT runs from end to end of the block, looking for the LIEUTENANT's car; then he turns into the areaway beside the theater to the stage entrance, looks about in the alley back of the theater and comes in through the stage entrance into the wings. He sees LIL and DICKIE peering onto the stage and joins them.

INTERIOR.   APOLLO THEATRE   NIGHT

The MASTER OF CEREMONIES is going through the final formality of presenting the grand prize. All of the contestants are lined up on the stage in front of the footlights. The MASTER OF CEREMONIES holds a baton over the head of each one, and the meter registers the applause. It is a foregone conclusion that BABY SISTER will win it.

The other contestants leave the stage while the MASTER OF CEREMONIES presents her with the Apollo Theatre Gold Medal and a signed contract for a week's engagement at Birdland.

Famous black jazz musicians and singers in the audience come on stage and hug and kiss her. The audience applauds wildly each time she is bussed.

When the curtain is lowered for the late movie, LIL joins BABY SISTER on the stage and invites everyone present to the party at MAMA's flat. Then, escorted by DICKIE, she and BABY SISTER leave by the stage door. Although uninvited and ignored, PIGMEAT follows closely with the pistol in the pocket of his windbreaker, determined not to let BABY SISTER out of sight.

EXTERIOR.   125TH STREET   NIGHT

Out in front of the theater a crowd collects about BABY SISTER. MAMA squeezes through and embraces her. The big hearse pulls to the curb and UNCLE PIE climbs out and pushes through the crowd to embrace BABY SISTER also.

WHITE HORSE COP

Hey, Reverend, get this hearse away from here.
UNCLE PIE hurries back; MAMA starts to follow.

LIL

MAMA, don't ride in that thing, come with us.

MAMA

His feelings will be hurt.
MAMA gets in and the hearse drives off. People grin.
DICKIE hails a taxi; LIL is giving the address to people she has invited to the party. The taxi stops; BABY SISTER, LIL and DICKIE get in; LIL gives BUDDY some money before they drive off.

BUDDY

(to PIGMEAT) Come on, let's get a taxi too.

PIGMEAT

You go ahead. I'm coming later.

EXTERIOR.   EIGHTH AVENUE   NIGHT

SUSIE and SLICK are sitting in SLICK's parked car around the corner on Eighth Avenue in front of a popular bar.

SLICK

She ain't no good to me now at any price. The sweet men take
over.

SUSIE

You had your chance, daddy-o.

SLICK

Yeah, you had yours. What you gonna do now?

SUSIE

I'm gonna get mine, you kin bet on that.

SLICK

Watch out for that white detective.

SUSIE

What you mean? You think I scared of that motherfucker?

SLICK

Don't let him get her.

SUSIE

Ain't nobody gonna get her but me.

INTERIOR.   LOUISES' FLAT   NIGHT

The flat has been made ready for the party: the bed has been
moved from the sitting room and stacked atop the bunks in the
brothers' bedroom; BABY SISTER's cot has been moved from the
bedroom into the kitchen and stacked atop PIGMEAT's cot; and
the dining room furniture has been shoved back against the wall.
    In the dining room, couples are dancing to the late-night jazz
program pouring from the radio in the sitting room, rubbing bellies with exuberance, their black laughing faces shining with sweat.
SUSIE is dancing with BABY SISTER; her face is expressionless; his

reveals a masochistic self-torture; nevertheless their bodies are close in tight embrace.

The loud, husky voice of Satchmo is heard over the din: "*What did Ah do tuh be so black 'n' blue . . .*"

UNCLE PIE and MAMA are sitting at the round-top table in the sitting room in front of the radio.

MAMA

(*shouting*) Thank the Lord, PIE, she safe now. I thought she were gonna get us all kilt before she were done with.

UNCLE PIE

(*shouting*) BABY SISTER never meant no harm. BABY SISTER is a good girl. I bet she the only virgin in Harlem.

DICKIE and LIL are entertaining friends in the kitchen, mixing drinks.

DICKIE

(*bracing himself against the stacked cots*) Feel better, honey?

LIL

(*speaking to everyone*) Nobody knows the scare that girl has given me.

WOMAN FRIEND

Now it is just a question what sweet man gonna take her money. Everyone laughs.

The disc on the radio comes to an end and the sweating couples separate. SUSIE wheels out of the embrace of BABY SISTER and rushes through the sitting room into his bedroom and slams shut the door, his face like a thundercloud before a storm. BABY SISTER looks indifferent as she follows slowly into the sitting room.

MAMA

(*looking at* BABY SISTER *suspiciously*) What's got into him?

BABY SISTER

(*indifferently*) How would I know.

MAMA continues to regard her with suspicion. UNCLE PIE'S indignation is directed toward the absent SUSIE.

Thinking no more about it, BABY SISTER strolls casually to the open front window and looks down at the street.

VOICE OF THE DISC JOCKEY

The time is exactly thirty seconds past 1 A.M.

BABY SISTER

(*casually*) I'll be back in a minute, Ma.
She moves in the direction of the front door.

MAMA

(*sharply*) Where you going, girl?

UNCLE PIE

(*indulgently*) She can't come to no harm, she famous now.
BABY SISTER leaves without replying, and runs quickly down the stairs.

SUSIE is standing before a shard of mirror stuck to the wall of the bedroom, staring at his reflection as he plays with his open knife. Once he lays the naked blade against his throat, another time against his left wrist.

SUSIE

(*softly but with intense feeling*) Motherfucker!

EXTERIOR.   116TH STREET   NIGHT

When BABY SISTER comes to the bottom of the stairs PIGMEAT steps from the darkness beside the doorway and blocks her path, shocking her into immobility.

BABY SISTER

(*hand flying to mouth*) Oh! (*adding furiously when she recognizes him*) You're not funny!

PIGMEAT

(*tensely*) You ain't going. I ain't gonna let you.

BABY SISTER

(*bewildered*) Going where? What you talking 'bout?

PIGMEAT

(*deadly serious*) I ain't gonna let you run away with that white man.

BABY SISTER

Oh! You been spying on me, you li'l snotnose tattletale.

PIGMEAT

I know all about it.

BABY SISTER

(*trying to pass*) About what? You don't know what you talking about.

PIGMEAT clutches her by the right arm and blocks her path with his body.

PIGMEAT

I know I ain't gonna let you run away with no white man and be a whore.

BABY SISTER

(*blindly furious*) Turn me loose or I'll knock your block off. It's none of your business what I do.

With a quick movement, PIGMEAT switches hands and pulls the pistol from his jacket pocket.

PIGMEAT

If you go out there I'll kill you.

Sight of the pistol so enrages BABY SISTER she slaps his face.

BABY SISTER

(*in a rage-constricted voice*) You worse than SUSIE. If you don't get outa my way I whip your ass.

With a violent wrench she breaks from his grip and runs out into the street.

PIGMEAT

(*leaping after her*) BABY SISTER!!! BABY SISTER!!!

She keeps on running toward the police car where LIEUTENANT FISCHER waits with her present.

PIGMEAT begins shooting at her retreating back, screaming hysterically.

PIGMEAT

BABY SISTER . . . BABY SISTER . . . COME BACK, BABY SISTER!!!

Flame lances through the night followed by the sound of pistol shots. Glass shatters as a bullet penetrates the windshield of the police cruiser and burns LIEUTENANT FISCHER across the cheek.

BABY SISTER loses a high-heeled slipper and stumbles, falling face downward on the pavement.

Thinking she has been shot, LIEUTENANT FISCHER puts three wired-together bullets through his shattered windshield, while with his other hand he snaps on the car's bright light. With the same flow of motion he snaps open the door and leaps to the street. Before him, caught in the car's bright lights, BABY SISTER lies face downward on the dirty sidewalk, bloodstains on the hem of her evening gown. Behind her, PIGMEAT is crumbling slowly to the ground, the gun slipping from his lifeless fingers. The LIEUTENANT jerks out his police whistle and begins blowing frantically.

INTERIOR.   LOUISES' FLAT   NIGHT

The sound of shooting echoes through the LOUISES' flat, panicking everyone. SUSIE, the first to move, wheels toward the open bedroom window and peers downward. The next instant his big, muscular body erupts into motion as though exploding. He emerges from the bedroom as though fired from a catapult, runs over MAMA as she jumps from her chair, knocking her flat, leaps over her body without looking down, snatches open the hall door and goes down the stairs in a power dive, open knife clutched in his right hand, stretched eyes blinking like motion picture shutters. Behind him, the others come running.

EXTERIOR.   116TH STREET   NIGHT

Up and down the street, lights come on. Heads and shoulders of black people pop into lighted windows. Other black people come running from the edges of darkness, as though spewed up from the dirty street.

LIEUTENANT FISCHER stands spread-legged in the beam of his car's bright lights.

LIEUTENANT FISCHER

(*sounding inhuman*) Stand back! Keep back! I'll shoot!

From the distance comes the answering shrill of a police whistle.

SUSIE leaps from the tenement doorway and heads into the beam of bright lights, knife held outward in a thrusting position. His left arm is raised as though to ward off attack.

LIEUTENANT FISCHER

Halt or I'll shoot!

SUSIE's pace doesn't slow, doesn't alter. He is coming toward the detective like a charging bull.

SUSIE

(*through clenched teeth*) Motherfucker!

LIEUTENANT FISCHER fires twice. SUSIE shows no sign that he's been hit. With his outstretched left arm he knocks aside the LIEUTENANT's pistol, and with his right hand plunges his knife blade in the LIEUTENANT's heart.

Time stands still. From above comes the anguished cry of MAMA LOUIS, blending with the swelling scream of police sirens.

EXTERIOR.   PANDEMONIUM ON 116TH STREET   NIGHT

Pandemonium reigns on 116th Street.

Police cruisers filled with black and white uniformed cops, official cars filled with precinct detectives, homicide detectives, District Attorney assistants, Medical Examiner assistants, police hearses, police ambulances, uniformed policemen on foot, hordes of half-clad black people erupting from the surrounding slum tenements, strange white men looking out of place on that black slum street, are all milling about, churning up confusion, choking the street.

MAMA being led away between BUDDY and LIL, wailing convulsively, tears streaming down her anguished face.

MAMA

My sons! BABY SISTER! My God! God, I beg you!

DICKIE

(*shouting senselessly*) Taxi!!! Taxi!!!

UNCLE PIE is beating on the side of his shining, immaculate hearse with one half of a brick as he curses it.

UNCLE PIE

Motherfuckin' buzzard!

A ragged black hoodlum trying to steal a white cop's pistol from its holster.

A white plainclothes detective shaking his foot like a cat after stepping into a puddle of blood.

BABY SISTER, dripping blood from the back of her gown, being eased onto a stretcher.

The bodies of PIGMEAT, SUSIE and LIEUTENANT FISCHER being tagged D.O.A. by the assistant medical examiner and lifted into wicker baskets.

INTERIOR.   CHURCH OF THE REDEEMED SINNER   DAY

A funeral is taking place in the storefront church on Lenox Avenue known as the Church of the Redeemed Sinner.

The scene is almost the same as at the recent funeral of JOHN LOUIS, the dead brothers' father, except there are two coffins in front of the homemade pulpit instead of one.

Now MAMA LOUIS sits between her daughters, BABY SISTER and LIL. BUDDY, wearing the same green suit which he wore to his father's funeral, sits on the inside. UNCLE PIE sits beside him.

The other two sons of BROTHER JOHN LOUIS who created so much confusion at his funeral, PIGMEAT and SUSIE, are now in their own coffins. It is reminiscent of an expression in Harlem, "Chances go 'round."

REVEREND CONVERTED SINNER, the resident minister of the Church of the Redeemed Sinner, is preaching almost the same funeral sermon for the sons as he preached for the father, except to change the references. It is as though the words of the sermon have got stuck in his brain from so much repetition.

REVEREND CONVERTED SINNER

(*in his customary funeral voice*) Lawd, people is dyin' ev'y day in ev'y way in Harlem fuh ev'y reason under the sun. From the rimbone of the world to the dark streets of Harlem is these sinful young womens, gettin' mens kilt, corruptin' they families, sowin' trouble ebrywhere. Young girls with hot tails who have not yet got religion . . .

BLACK CONGREGATION

(*rhythmic response*) Young girls, lawd, with trouble in they tails, lawd, an' nothin' in they heads, lawd, gib'm 'ligion, lawd, send'um salvation . . .

BABY SISTER

I can't stand it! I can't stand it!

MAMA

(*harshly*) Hush yo' mouth, you hussy. Gettin' us all kilt an' yo'self with chile—

LIL

(*interrupting*) Not here, Ma.

REVEREND CONVERTED SINNER

Young brothers cut down in de spring uv life, daid in de dangerous street, tryna 'fen de chasty uv they baby sister.

CONGREGATION

'Fen de chasty uv they baby sister, lawd . . .

MAMA

(*bitterly*) Won't even tell yo' ma who the father was.

BABY SISTER

I can't stand it!

LIL

It were that white detective SUSIE kilt, Ma.

BABY SISTER jumps to her feet, hikes up her skirt and runs frantically down the aisle toward the exit, her high, iron-capped heels drumming on the wooden floor.

BABY SISTER

(*screaming hysterically*) I can't stand it! I can't stand it!

REVEREND CONVERTED SINNER's jaw hangs open; he looks flabbergasted.

The CONGREGATION begins to buzz.

BUDDY jumps to his feet and squeezes past UNCLE PIE and runs down the aisle after BABY SISTER.

MAMA

God, wut now?

LIL

Don't worry, Ma, I'll get her.

LIL jumps to her feet and runs after BUDDY.

REVEREND CONVERTED SINNER begins jumping up and down in his homemade pulpit, screaming.

REVEREND CONVERTED SINNER

(*screaming*) 'Nfidels, blasphemers! Sinners! Stop 'em! Stop 'em!

Black church brothers and sisters jump up and start chasing the trio.

REVEREND CONVERTED SINNER

(*frothing from his mouth*) Catch 'em! Catch 'em! Bring'um back tuh de Lawd!

BABY SISTER pushes through the startled crowd of black people in front of the church. BUDDY dashes from the church and gives chase. LIL goes running after them, wobbling on her high-heeled shoes. Following LIL comes a stream of black church people erupting from the church. Black people from the crowd outside join in the chase. All of them are chasing BABY SISTER, like hounds chasing a fox.

BUDDY overtakes BABY SISTER and clutches her from behind. She fights to break free, screaming hysterically.

BABY SISTER

Let me go! Let me go, BUDDY! I can't stand it!

LIL catches up with them and puts her arms about BABY SISTER and kisses her consolingly.

LIL

Don't cry, baby, don't cry! Life ain't worth it.

Black church people catch up and encircle them and stare disapprovingly, shaking their heads and clucking their tongues.

LIL

You don't have to go back, baby. We'll bury them ourselves.

OLD BLACK MALE SPECTATOR

Whass d'mattah wid her?

BLACK CHURCH BROTHER

She don't want to go to her own brothers' funeral.

Black church people look horrified. Condemnatory looks are exchanged.

BLACK CHURCH SISTER

Jezebel!

OLD BLACK MALE SPECTATOR

Deez young gals t'day is no good! All dey wants is close 'n' men.

NINE SHORT STORIES

Harold Price who lived across the hall, the tall, fair, colored man who was Fay's common-law husband, was just leaving the house for his afternoon tonk session down at the smoke shop at 100th Street and Cedar when Joe Wolf called from the drugstore at 97th and Cedar at about three o'clock. Fay told him to come on up. He passed Harold between 93rd and 94th and nodded to him. They'd seen each other around Bunch Boy's smoke shop at various times, but Harold had no suspicion that Joe might be going with his old lady, although Joe knew where Harold fitted in, and everything there was to know about Fay. She had told him all herself, thinking he was wise and superior and would find out anyway.

She hadn't expected Mr. Shelton, the old white man she went with on the side, to call that afternoon. He had telephoned that morning as was customary but hadn't said anything about stopping by. She and Joe were lying on the bed getting ready when he knocked on the door.

It was a second-floor front bedroom of one of those old houses on 89th Street with the door opening into the hall. The landlady, Miss Lou, an evil old ex-whore with a grudge against the world, having seen Joe come in right after Harold had left, had sent Mr. Shelton on up to catch him there in the hopes of ranking Fay's play. Fay was too independent for her, kept by a rich white John out of Shaker Heights, and living with a fine-looking, hard-working, tall yellow boy on the side who dumped his paycheck to her as regular as it came, then cheating on them both with this broke, ragged lunger who claimed he was some kind of writer or poet or something.

So she had told Mr. Shelton that Fay was alone and that he could go on up. Then she slipped up behind him to eavesdrop in the hallway, waiting for the rumpus to break.

But at his knock Fay hit the deck like an oldtime fireman, made a frantic dash to the window and spotted his car, waved Joe into the clothes closet with frenzied gestures, smoothed the bedcovers, opened the book, *Anthony Adverse,* to the center pages and laid it face down on the bed, gave one last searching glance about the room for telltale bits of evidence, then said languidly, "Who is it?"

Joe had grabbed his shoes and scampered into the cluttered closet, had just closed the door behind him in time to hear the muffled answer, "It's me, dear."

He heard her open the door and gush, "Oh, darling, I'm so glad you came. I was just lying here trying to read but I couldn't keep my mind on it for thinking about you. Here, sit on the bed and let me kiss you. I love you, darling," and he thought laughingly, *what a bitch!*

Now he heard the slight kissing and then the man's voice, smug and condescendingly possessive. "It's nice to kiss you when you're not wearing so much gooey lipstick," and he thought, *why, you old bastard.*

"Mrs. Shelton and I are going to drive East—we'll stop in Philadelphia and New York and probably at a resort in Michigan. You won't be able to write to me this time so I stopped by to leave you enough money so you won't be strapped."

All Joe heard were the two words *Mrs. Shelton,* and it came to him suddenly that in the five weeks he'd been going with Fay he'd never heard her refer to him as anything but *Mr. Shelton,* always with a kind of respect as if to insist that he, too, think of the bastard as some kind of benefactor instead of the sucker that he was; and now hearing him refer to *Mrs. Shelton* with the same insistence for respect, he began getting angry. *What the hell was she, the guy's mistress or his slave?*

"I'll really need two hundred dollars, darling," he heard her say; then his startled reply, "So much? I gave you a hundred last week for clothes, you know."

"You'll be away, darling, and I won't have anything to do with all my time," he heard her sugared jive. "I'll just take my time and shop and buy all the little things I need; then I want to take Edna and Lil to a show—they've been so nice to me."

"Dear, you must try to understand," came his slightly impatient voice. "I've been trying to tell you, but you don't seem to realize what is happening. That damned Roosevelt has taxed me bone dry—why, during the past three years my income has shrunk to less than one fourth. What makes me so furious," his voice rose in a rage, "he's just throwing our money away on these damned shiftless lazy beggars. By God, if I had my way, I'd make them work for what they get like people used to do in America—"

"Darling, don't get so excited about old Roosevelt," he heard her try to soothe him. "Maybe he'll die or get sick or something. Think of me, your little brown sugar, darling—you've still got me. Roosevelt can't take me away from you."

Joe heard him chuckle suddenly, and then his voice, half amused and half exasperated, "If the rest of the colored people are as sensible as you, dear, we might get rid of him this time. By God, we'll put enough money behind Landon to get him there, then we'll see these damned lazy beggars work . . ."

Now Joe's anger left him and he was amused. *These old bastards sure die hard*, he thought, remembering suddenly the time the Belle Vernon Milk Company dumped hundreds of gallons of milk into the gutters of Cedar Street when the relief rolls in Cleveland were the highest they'd ever been and down in the slums babies were dying like flies for the lack of proper food. *What the hell do old sons of a bitches like this want—to see the people starve?* he wondered.

His thoughts had cut out the sound of their voices and when he listened again, he heard him say, "Stop it! I tell you stop it! I can't make love to you today, my dear."

"I want it."

"Why can't you be serious for once, dear? I enjoy it as much as you, but my God, dear, with the country going to the dogs and—

"Now, stop! Must I tell you I am not as young as I once was?"

"You're young enough for me, darling. You're all I—"

"No, I'm not. I'm an old man and I know it. But I'm not a fool; I'm not so vain that I don't know—"

"You're not old at all."

"You know, dear, sometimes I think of advising you to marry some young colored boy your own age. If I could be assured there was one good enough—"

"You know I couldn't live with a colored man, darling—"

Why, you goddamn whore, Joe thought.

"However, I realize my own capabilities—"

"Here, then!"

"You have beautiful legs, my dear. Brown and smooth. But I'm not in the mood today. I have a number of—"

"Here!"

"Stop it! Stop it this instant. You're getting beside yourself . . ."

What in the hell is she trying to do? But Joe was too proud to bend down to the keyhole to see for himself. He stood sweating in the center of the closet between the two racks of close-packed garments bought for her by *Mr. Shelton*—he thought of him as *Mr. Shelton* without being aware of it—his stockinged feet cramped and uncomfortable among the scatter of shoes, suddenly overcome with the sense of having sold his pride, his whole manhood, for a whore's handout, no better than the pimps down on Central Avenue, only cheaper—so damn much cheaper. One flicker of light came through the keyhole to which he was too proud, even, to bend down and look at the man who had controlled his eating for the past five weeks, and now at this moment was controlling his movement and emotions and even his soul. Too proud now to look even while accepting the position, as if not looking would lessen the actuality; would make it more possible to believe he hadn't accepted it. Sweat trickled down his face and neck and legs and body like crawling lice, and the mixture of the scent of the twelve bottles of perfume she kept on her dresser like a stack of thousand-dollar bills, along with the sharp musk scent of her body, stale shoe smell and underarm odor, in the dense sticky closeness, brought a sickish taste to his mouth. Then a flood of cold reality. *Just don't look at him . . .*

". . . one of your faults, dear, is that you can never learn the proper exercise of the power of your charms."

"I'm mad; you don't love me anymore."

Hell, I've known she was a slut; that's what attracted me. Do I have to puke, goddammit, because she demonstrates it?

"What is the matter with you today, my dear? You've appeared upset and nervous ever since I arrived. You don't want to make love to me, I'm sure. Have your neighbors—"

I'm what's the matter with her, you old senile bastard, Joe thought. *She's afraid I'll come out and kick you in your old white ass.*

But that didn't help it any. He was still hiding in the closet from a nigger bitch's white lover.

If I can only get it funny, he thought. *It is funny! Funny as hell! Goddamn, we're some simple people.*

He tried to get far enough away from it to see it like it was. The guy is just another square. Just like all the other white squares he'd seen being debased by Negro women after their sex had gone from their bodies into their minds, no longer even able to give or receive any vestige of satisfaction from younger women of their own race, their wives long past giving or requiring. Turning to Negro women because in them they saw only the black image of flesh, the organ itself, like beautiful bronze statues endowed with motion, flesh and blood, instinct and passion, but possessing no mind to condemn, no soul to be outraged, most of all no power to judge or accuse, before whom the spirit of exhausted sex could creep and crawl and expose its ugly nakedness without embarrassment or restraint.

He was in this joint down on 40th when he was seventeen years old, back in 1928, when every other door opened into a cathouse or a lightning joint, and this little white lain pulled up out front in a big Lincoln touring a block long. He was a little fat cherubic-looking bald-headed bastard with pink cheeks and watery blue eyes. Big Mama May, the landprop, a six-foot muscular mannish blue-gummed whore, damn near bald, with more razor scars than Cuts Callie, sporting an ankle-length black satin dress and size 11, straight-last Stacy-Adams shoes, lamped the lain when he drew up, and made the three of them who had been sitting around the table drinking burnt-sugar colored lightning, himself and Howard and the yellow whore, Little Bit, take their drinks into the next room, then closed the French doors leaving a crack large enough for them to peep. Before the John could even ring she swung the front door in, and without so much as a how-de-do, grabbed him by both shoulders, jerked him through the doorway, and flung him savagely into the heavy round-top oaken table. He ricocheted off, fell over a chair, sprawled face down on the rough pine floor. She kicked shut the door with her heel, started after him, gritting her teeth and cursing. He scrambled to his feet and fled around the table, trying to escape her, face blood-red, eyes terror-stricken. She lit right in behind him, looking vicious and murderous, mouthing obscenities, around and around the table, first one way and then the other, until he stumbled and she had him, planting her number 11's in his rump, beating him about the face and head with her

*open hand, befouling him, debasing him, until he shuddered and
went limp. He got up a few minutes later and began straightening
his collar and tie without looking at her. She got a whisk broom
and began brushing him off. He extracted his wallet from his pocket
and handed her two yellow-back bills, extremely careful to keep
his hand from touching hers, still not looking at her, then departed
without having from beginning to end said one word, his fat face
sagging at the edges in utter exhaustion. With them laughing like
hell in the back room.*

But it wasn't funny now. He couldn't get it funny. The fact was,
he, Joe Wolf, had been maneuvered by a whore into a spot too low
for a dog.

Slowly, without sound, he slid a dress from a wire hanger, took
down the hanger from the rack and in the dark untwisted the
ends and straightened the wire, looped the now separate ends to
form handfolds for a garrote, took a deep breath and tried to set
it in his mind. He'd go out fast with the garrote in his left hand,
throw a hard right at the bastard's face—that'd hold him for a
moment—then put the wire quickly around her neck and twist it
in the back. His breath oozed out and with it his determination—
God knows, I don't want to kill them. But he knew that he would;
he always did every crazy thing he knew he shouldn't do.

How long he had missed the sound of voices, he didn't know,
when suddenly he heard Fay's stricken cry,

"NOT THAT DOOR! THAT'S THE CLOSET!"

The door opened quickly and Joe blinked into the light, and
for one breathless instant he stared straight into the small blue
sardonic eyes of a stout bald-headed white man with a fringe of
gray hair and a puffy vein-laced face. Then the door closed quickly,
shutting out the light, and words walked evenly through the exploding chaos of his thoughts, "I can never tell which door is
which," in a controlled, urbane, slightly amused voice. He stood
there, unable to breathe, feeling as foolish and idiotic as a hungry
man leaving a cathouse where he'd spent his last two bucks. Then
rage scalded him from tip to toe. He flung open the door to spring
into the room, slipped on a shoe and went sprawling, the wire
garrote cutting a blister across the back of the fingers of his left
hand. The noise of the falling shook the house, but Fay and *Mr.
Shelton*—he still thought of him as *Mr. Shelton*—were at the bot-

tom of the stairs, and *Mr. Shelton's* voice, making his farewells, was chatty and unalarmed.

Joe got up painfully and stood in the middle of the room waiting for her, and finally when she returned, he accused, "The goddamn bastard saw me!"

She shut the door with a long nervous sigh of relief and fell across the bed laughing hysterically. Finally she rolled over and looked up at him and said, "He didn't see you," in a voice shaken with hysterical laughter. "God!" she breathed. "I thought for a moment he had seen you for sure. Phew! I didn't know his eyesight was that bad."

"Goddammit, **he did see me!**" Joe snarled. "He looked right into my eyes!"

All of a sudden it hit him that *Mr. Shelton* had opened the door deliberately, knowing he was there, and after having satisfied himself that he was right, had refused to acknowledge Joe's existence.

"He couldn't have seen you, darling," Fay was saying. "He gave me the two hundred dollars—see!" She waved a wad of bills at him. "He even kissed me goodbye," she added.

Joe stood there looking at her without hearing, hardly seeing her. *Why, he had not only refused to recognize him as a rival, not even as an intruder; why, the son of a bitch looked at him as if he was another garment he had bought for her.* It was the first time he had ever felt the absolute refusal of recognition.

Then he felt her arms around him. "Come on, snap out of it," he heard her say. "Suppose he did see you—so what? He didn't let it make any difference."

He hit at her with his right fist, caught her on the shoulder and spun her away. She jerked her head around to scream at him just in time to catch a corner of the wire loop about his left hand straight across the bridge of her nose. A lump jumped up where the wire had struck while he was still looking, then her mouth came open in a scream. He tried to shift the wire to his right hand so he could flay her with it, but she rushed him, clawing and biting and screaming; and he began hitting her across the head and neck and shoulders with the length of the wire.

Trying to make him accept it! The man refused to even acknowledge his existence. And she wanted him to accept it! Why, goddammit, he'd kill her!

Miss Lou burst into the room pointing a long-barreled .38 and said, "You dirty nigger bastard! If you hit her again I'll kill you!"

Joe jackknifed his right leg and kicked Fay in the stomach, sent her somersaulting over the bed, made a half-shoulder turn and slashed a vicious backhand stroke at Miss Lou with the length of heavy wire, catching her across the right arm and breast just before she pulled the trigger. The sound of the shot shattered his rage, filled his mind with flight. He leaped through the door, bumped Miss Lou back across the hallway into the wall, slipped on the polished floor when he wheeled toward the stairs, and went down half falling, half stumbling, clinging to the rail, with Miss Lou blasting at him from above. Panicky but unhurt, he made the street, didn't stop running until he was back in his hot tiny room on 97th Street.

He locked the door and sat down on the bed, gasping for breath. The wire was still looped about his left hand, and he looked at it blankly for a moment before taking it off and dropping it to the floor. Sweat ran down his face and dripped from the point of his chin to make a dark wet stain on the dry board floor, but he didn't notice. The frown tightened in his face until his eyeballs hurt. He wanted to just crawl away somewhere and die.

For deeper than his resentment was his shame. The fact was he had kept standing there, taking it, even after he could no longer tell himself that it was a joke, a trim on a sucker, just so he could keep on eating off the bitch and people wouldn't know just how hard up he really was. Just to keep on putting up a cheap front among the riffraff on Cedar Street, just to keep from having to go back to his aunt's and eat crow, had become more important to him than his innate pride, his manhood, his honor. Uncle Tomism, acceptance, toadying—all there in its most rugged form. One way to be a nigger. Other Negroes did it other ways—he did it the hard way. The same result—*a nigger*.

TANG

[1967]

A man called T-bone Smith sat in a cold-water slum flat on 113th Street east of Eighth Avenue in Harlem, looking at television with his old lady, Tang. They had a television set but they didn't have anything to eat. It was after ten o'clock at night and the stores were closed, but that didn't make any difference because they didn't have any money. It was a two-room flat so the television was in the kitchen with the table and the stove. Because it was summertime, the stove was cold and the windows were open.

T-bone was clad only in a pair of greasy black pants and his bare black torso was ropy with lean hard muscles and decorated with an elaborate variety of scars. His long narrow face was hinged on a mouth with lips the size of automobile tires and the corners of his sloe-shaped eyes were sticky with matter. The short hard burrs on his watermelon head were the color of half-burnt ashes. He had his bare black feet propped up on the kitchen table with the white soles toward the television screen. He was white-mouthed from hunger but was laughing like an idiot at two blackfaced white minstrels on the television screen who earned more money every week by blackening their faces and acting foolish than T-bone had earned in all his life.

In between laughing he was trying to get his old lady, Tang, to go down into Central Park and trick with some white man so they could eat.

"Go on, baby, you can be back in an hour with 'nuff bread so we can scoff."

"I'se tired as you are," she said evilly. "Go sell yo' own ass to whitey, you luvs him so much."

She had once been a beautiful jet-black woman with a broad flat face and softly rounded features which looked as though they had been made by a child at play; her figure had been something to invoke instant visions of sex contortions and black ecstasy. But both face and figure had been corroded by vice and hunger and now she was a lean, angular crone with burnt red hair and flat black features which looked like they had been molded by a stamping machine. Only her eyes looked alive; they were red, mean, disillusioned and defiant. She was clad in a faded green mother hubbard which looked as though it had never been laundered and her big, buniony feet trod restlessly about the dirty, rotting kitchen linoleum. The soles were unseen but the tops had wrinkled black skin streaked with dirt.

[Suddenly, above the sound of the gibbering of the blackface white minstrels, they heard an impatient hammering on the door.] Both knew instantly someone had first tried the doorbell, which had never worked. They looked suspiciously at one another. Neither could imagine anyone it could be except the police, so they quickly scanned the room to see if there were any incriminating evidence in sight; although, aside from her hustling about the lagoon in Central Park, neither had committed any crime recently enough to interest the police. Finally she stuck her bare feet into some old felt slippers and rubbed red lipstick over her rusty lips while he got up and shambled across the floor in his bare feet to open the door.

A young black uniformed messenger with smooth skin and bright intelligent eyes asked, "Mister Smith?"

"Dass me," T-bone admitted.

The messenger extended a long cardboard box wrapped in white paper and tied with red ribbon. Conspicuous on the white wrapping paper was the green and white label of a florist, decorated with pink and yellow flowers, and on the lines for the name and address were the typed words: *Mr. T. Smith, West 113th Street, 4th floor.* The messenger placed the box directly into T-bone's outstretched hands and waited until T-bone had a firm grip before releasing it.

"Flowers for you, sir," he trilled.

T-bone was so startled he almost let go of the box, but the messenger was already hurtling down the stairs, and T-bone was too slow-witted to react in any fashion. He simply stood there holding the box in his outstretched hands, his mouth hanging open, not a thought in his head; he just looked stupid and stunned.

But Tang's thoughts were working like a black IBM. "Who sending you flowers, black and ugly as you is?" she demanded suspiciously from across the room. And the fact of it was, she really meant it. Still he was her man, simple-minded or not, and it made her jealous for him to get flowers, other than for his funeral, which hadn't happened yet.

"Dese ain't flowers," he said, sounding just as suspicious as she had. "Lessen they be flowers of lead."

"Maybe it's some scoff from the government's thing for the poor folks," she perked hopefully.

"Not unless it's pig-iron knuckles," he said.

She bent over beside him and gingerly fingered the white wrapped box. "It's got your name on it," she said. "And your address. What would anybody be sending to your name and your address?"

"We gonna soon see," he said and stepped across the room to lay the box atop the table. It made a clunking sound. The two blackfaced comedians danced merrily on the television screen until interrupted by a beautiful blonde reading a commercial for Nu-cream, which made dirty skin so fresh and white.

She stood back and watched him break the ribbon and tear off the white wrapping paper. She was practically holding her breath when he opened the gray cardboard carton, but he was too unimaginative to have any thoughts one way or another. If God had sent him down a trunk full of gold bricks from heaven he would have wondered if he was expected to brick up a wall which wasn't his.

Inside the cardboard box they saw a long object wrapped in brown oiled paper and packed in paper excelsior in the way they had seen machine tools packed when they had worked in a shipyard in Newark before she had listened to his sweet talk and had come to Harlem to be his whore. She couldn't imagine anybody sending him a machine tool unless he had been engaged in activities which she didn't know anything about. Which wasn't likely, she thought, as long as she made enough to feed him. He just stared at it stupidly, wondering why anybody would send him something which looked like something he couldn't use even if he wanted to use it.

"Pick it up," she said sharply. "It ain't gonna bite you."

"I ain't scaird of nuttin bitin' me," he said, fearlessly lifting the object from its bed of excelsior. "It ain' heavy as I thought," he said stupidly, although he had given no indication of what he had thought.

She noticed a typewritten sheet which had been lying underneath the object which she instantly suspected was a letter. Quickly she snatched it up.

"Wuss dat?" he asked with the automatic suspicion of one who can't read.

She knew he couldn't read and instinctive jealousy provoked her to needle him. "Writing! That's what."

"What's it say?" he demanded, panic-stricken.

First she read the typed words to herself: *WARNING!!! DO NOT INFORM POLICE!!! LEARN YOUR WEAPON AND WAIT FOR INSTRUCTIONS!!! REPEAT!!! LEARN YOUR WEAPON AND WAIT FOR INSTRUCTIONS!!! WARNING!!! DO NOT INFORM POLICE!!! FREEDOM IS NEAR!!!*

Then she read them aloud. They alarmed him so much that sweat broke out over his face and his eyes stretched until they were completely round. Frantically he began tearing off the oiled wrapping paper. The dull gleam of an automatic rifle came into sight. She gasped. She had never seen a rifle that looked as dangerous as that. But he had seen and handled the M-14 used by the United States Army when he had served in the Korean war.

"Iss a M-14," he said. "Iss uh army gun."

He was terrified. His skin dried and appeared dusty.

"I done served my time," he continued, adding, "Efen iss stolen I don't want it. Wuss anybody wanna send me a stolen gun for?"

Her eyes blazed in a face contorted with excitement. "It's the uprising, nigger!" she cried. "We gonna be free!"

"Uprising?" He shied away from the thought as though it were a rattlesnake. "*Free?*" He jumped as though the snake had bit him. "Ise already free. All someun wants to do is get my ass in jail." He held the rifle as though it were a bomb which might go off in his hand.

But she looked at the gun with awe and love. "That'll chop a white policeman two ways sides and flat. That'll blow the shit out of whitey's asshole."

"Wut?" He put the gun down onto the table and pushed it away from him. "Shoot the white police? Someun 'spects me tuh shoot de white police?"

"Why not? You wanna uprise, don't you?"

"Uprise? Whore, is you crazy? Uprise where?"

"Uprise here, nigger. Is you that stupid? Here we is and here we is gonna uprise."

"Not me! I ain't gonna get my ass blown off waving that thing around. We had them things in Korea and them cats kilt us niggers like flies."

"You got shit in your blood," she said contemptuously. "Let me feel that thing."

She picked the rifle up from the table and held it as though she were shooting rabbits about the room. "Baby," she said directly to the gun. "You and me can make it, baby."

"Wuss de matter wid you? You crazy?" he shouted. "Put that thing down. I'm gonna go tell de man 'fo we gets both our ass in jail."

"You going to tell whitey?" she asked in surprise. "You going run tell the man 'bout this secret that'll make us free?"

"Shut yo' mouth, whore, Ise doin it much for you as I is for me."

At first she didn't take him seriously. "For me, nigger? You think I wanna sell my pussy to whitey all my life?" But, with the gun in her hand, the question was rhetorical. She kept shooting at imaginary rabbits about the room, thinking she could go hunting and kill her a whitey or two. Hell, give her enough time and bullets she could kill them all.

Her words caused him to frown in bewilderment. "You wanna stop being a whore, whore?" he asked in amazement. "Hell, whore, we gotta live."

"You call this living?" She drew the gun tight to her breast as though it were a lover. "This the only thing what made me feel alive since I met you."

He looked outraged. "You been lissenin to that black power shit, them Black Panthers 'n that shit," he accused. "Ain't I always done what's best?"

"Yeah, put me on the block to sell my black pussy to poor white trash."

"I ain' gonna argy wid you," he said in exasperation. "Ise goan 'n get de cops 'fore we both winds up daid."

Slowly and deliberately, she aimed the gun at him. "You call whitey and I'll waste you," she threatened.

He was moving toward the door but the sound of her voice

stopped him. He turned about and looked at her. It was more the sight of her than the meaning of her words which made him hesitate. He wasn't a man to dare anyone and she had sounded as though she would blow him away. But he knew she was tenderhearted and wouldn't hurt him as long as he didn't cross her. So he decided to kid her along until he could grab the gun, then he'd whip her ass. With this in mind he began shuffling around the table in her direction, grinning obsequiously, playing the part of the forgiving lover. "Baby, I were jes playin—"

"Maybe you are but I ain't," she warned him.

"I weren't gonna call the cops, I were jes gonna see if the door is locked."

"You see and you won't know it."

She talking too much, he thought, shuffling closer to her. Suddenly he grabbed for the gun. She pulled the trigger. Nothing happened. Both froze in shock. It had never occurred to either that the gun was not loaded.

He was the first to react. He burst out laughing. "Haw-haw-haw."

"Wouldn't have been so funny if this thing had been loaded," she said sourly.

Suddenly his face contorted with rage. It was as though the relief felt by the dissipation of his fear had been replaced by fury. He whipped out a springblade knife. "I teach you, whore," he raved. "You try to kill me."

She looked from the knife to his face and said stoically, "I shoulda known, you are whitey's slave; you'll never be free."

"Free of you," he shouted and began slashing at her.

She tried to protect herself with the rifle but shortly he had cut it out of her grasp. She backed around the table trying to keep away from the slashing blade. But soon the blade began reaching her flesh and the floor became covered with blood; she crumpled and fell and died, as she had known she would after the first look at his enraged face.

THE NIGHT'S FOR CRYIN'

[1937]

Black Boy slammed his Tom Collins down on the bar with an irritated bang, turned a slack scowl toward Gigilo.

Gigilo, yellow and fat like a well-fed hog, was saying in a fat, whiskey-thickened voice: "Then she pulled out a knife and cut me 'cross the back. I just looked at 'er. Then she threw 'way the knife and hit me in the mouth with her pocketbook. I still looked at her. Then she raised her foot and stomped my corns. I pushed her down then."

Black Boy said: "Niggah, ef'n yo is talkin' tuh me, Ah ain' liss'nin'." Black Boy didn't like yellow niggers, he didn't want no yellow nigger talking to him now, for he was waiting for Marie, his high yellow heart, to take her to her good-doing job.

Gigilo took another sip of rye, but he didn't say anymore.

Sound bubbled about them, a bubble bursting here in a strident laugh, there in accented profanity. A woman's coarse, heavy voice said: "Cal, Ah wish you'd stop Fo'-Fo' frum drinkin' so much" . . . A man's flat, unmusical drone said: "Ah had uh ruff on 632 and 642 come out." He had repeated the same words a hundred solid times . . . "Aw, she ain' gibin' dat chump nuttin," a young, loud voice clamored for attention . . . A nickel victrola in the rear blared a husky, negroid bellow: "*Anybody heah wanna buy . . .*"

The mirror behind the bar reflected the lingering scowl on Black Boy's face, the blackest blot in the ragged jam of black and yellow faces lining the bar.

Wall lights behind him spilled soft stain on the elite at the tables. Cigarette smoke cut thin blue streamers ceilingward through the muted light, mingled with whiskey fumes and perfume scents and Negro smell. Bodies squirmed, inching riotous-colored dresses up from yellow, shapely legs. Red-lacquered nails gleamed like bright blood drops on the stems of whiskey glasses, and the women's yellow faces looked like powdered masks beneath sleek hair, bruised with red mouths.

Four white people pushed through the front door, split a hurried, half apologetic path through the turn of displeased faces toward the cabaret entrance at the rear. Black Boy's muddy, negroid eyes followed them, slightly resentful.

A stoop-shouldered, consumptive-looking Negro leaned over Black Boy's shoulder and whispered something in his ear.

Black Boy's sudden strangle blew a spray of Tom Collins over the bar. He put the tall glass quickly down, sloshing the remaining liquid over his hand. His red tongue slid twice across his thick, red lips, and his slack, plate-shaped face took on a popeyed expression, as startlingly unreal beneath the white of his precariously perched Panama as an eight ball with suddenly sprouted features. The puffed, bluish scar on his left cheek, memento of a pick-axe duel on a chain gang, seemed to swell into an embossed reproduction of a shell explosion, ridges pronging off from it in spokes.

He slid back from his stool, his elbow digging into a powdered, brownskin back to his right, caught on his feet with a flat-footed clump. Standing, his body was big, his six foot height losing impressiveness in slanting shoulders and long arms like an ape's.

He paused for a moment, undecided, a unique specimen of sartorial splendor—white Panama stuck on the back of his shiny shaved skull, yellow silk polo shirt dirtied slightly by the black of his bulging muscles, draped trousers of a brilliant pea green, tight waisted and slack hanging above size eleven shoes of freshly shined tan.

The woman with the back turned a ruffled countenance, spat a stream of lurid profanity at him through twisted red lips. But he wedged through the jam toward the door, away from her, smashed out of the Log Cabin bar into a crowd of idling avenue pimps.

The traffic lights at the corner turned from green to red. Four shiny, new automobiles full of laughing black folks, purred casually through the red. A passing brownskin answered to the call of "Babe," paused before her "nigger" in saddle-backed stance, arms akimbo, tight dress tightened on the curve of her hips.

Black Boy's popped eyes filled with yellow specks, slithered across the front of the weather-stained Majestic Hotel across the street, lingering a searching instant on every woman whose face was light. Around the corner, down on Central Avenue, he caught a fleeting glimpse of a yellow gal climbing into a green sedan, then a streetcar clanged across his vision.

He pulled in his red lips, wet them with his tongue. Then he broke into a shuffling, flat-footed run—through the squawk of a horn, across suddenly squealing brakes, never looked around. A taxi-driver's curse lashed him across the street. His teeth bared slightly, but the bloated unreality of his face never changed.

He turned right in front of the Majestic, roughed over a brown dandy with two painted crones, drew up at the corner, panting. The green sedan burnt rubber, pulled right through the red light in a whining, driving first.

But too late to keep Black Boy from catching a flash of the pretty, frightened face of Marie and the nervous profile of the driver bent low over the wheel. A yellow nigger. He turned and watched the red tail-light sink into the distant darkness, his body twisting on flatly planted feet. His lower lip went slack, hung down like a red smear on his black face. His bulging eyes turned a vein-laced red. Sweat popped out on his face, putting a sheen on its lumpy blackness, grew in beads on his shiny head, trickled in streams down his body.

He turned and ran for a cab, but his actions were dogged now instead of apprehensive. He'd already seen Marie with that yellow hotel nigger. He caught a cab pointing the right way, said: "Goose it, Speed," before he swung through the open door.

Speed goosed it. The cab took sudden life, jumped ahead from the shove of eight protesting cylinders. Black Boy leaned tensely forward, let the speedometer needle hit fifty before he spoke. "Dar's uh green sedan up front, uh fo' do' job. Latch on it 'n earn dis dime, big dime."

The lank, loose-bodied brown boy driving threw him a careless, toothy grin, coiled around the wheel. He headed into the red light at Cedar Avenue doing a crisp seventy, didn't slacken. He pulled inside the line of waiting cars, smashed into the green while the red still lingered in his eyes. The green turned to red at Carnegie, and the car in front stopped, but he burst the red wide open doing a sheer eighty-five, leaning on the horn.

"Ri' at Euclid," Black Boy directed through lips that hung so slack they seemed to be turned wrong side out. He was gambling on those yellow folk seeking the protection of their white folk where they worked, for they had lost the green sedan.

The driver braked for the turn, eyes roving for traffic cops. He didn't see any and he turned at a slow fifty, not knowing whether the light was red, white or blue. The needle walked right up the street numbers, fifty-seven at 57th Street, seventy-one at 71st. It was hovering on eighty again when Black Boy said: "Turn 'round."

Marie was just getting out of the green sedan in front of the Regis where she worked as a maid. When she heard that shrill cry of rubber on asphalt she broke into a craven run.

Black Boy hit the pavement in a flat-footed lope, caught her just as she was about to climb the lobby stairs. He never said a word, he just reached around from behind and smacked her in the face with the open palm of his right hand. She drew up short against the blow. Then he hit her under her right breast with a short left jab and chopped three rights into her face when she turned around with the edge of his fist like he was driving nails.

She wilted to her knees and he bumped her in the mouth with his knee, knocking her sprawling on her side. He kicked her in the body three rapid, vicious times, slobber drooling from his slack, red lips. His bloated face was a tar ball in the spill of sign light, his eyes too dull to notice. Somehow his Panama still clung on his eight ball head, whiter than ever, and his red lips were a split, bleeding incision in his black face.

Marie screamed for help. Then she whimpered. Then she begged. "Doan kill me, Black Boy, daddy deah, honey darlin', daddy-daddy deah. Marie luvs yuh, daddy darlin'. Doan kill me, please, daddy. Doan kill yo' lil' honeybunch, Marie . . ."

The yellow boy, slowly following from the car, paused a moment in indecision as if he would get back in and drive away. But he couldn't bear seeing Black Boy kick Marie. The growth of emotion was visible in his face before it pushed him forward.

After an instant he realized that that was where he worked as a bellhop, that those white folk would back him up against a strange nigger. He stepped quickly over to Black Boy, spoke in a cultural preëmptory voice: "Stop kicking that woman, you dirty black nigger."

Black Boy turned his bloated face toward him. His dull eyes explored him, dogged. His voice was flatly telling him: "You keep outta dis, yellow niggah. Dis heah is mah woman an' Ah doan lak you no way."

The yellow boy was emboldened by the appearance of two white men in the hotel doorway. He stepped over and slung a weighted blow to Black Boy's mouth. Black Boy shifted in quick rage, drew a spring-blade barlow chiv and slashed the yellow boy to death before the two white men could run down the stairs. He broke away from their restraining hands, made his way to the alley beside the theater in his shambling, flat-footed run before the police cruiser got there.

He heard Marie's loud, fear-shrill voice crying: "He pulled a gun on Black Boy, he pulled a gun on Black Boy. Ah saw 'im do it—"

He broke into a laugh, satisfied. She was still his . . .

Three rapid shots behind him stopped his laugh, shattered his face into black fragments. The cops had begun shooting without calling halt. He knew that they knew he was a "dinge," and he knew they wanted to kill him, so he stepped into the light behind a Clark's Restaurant, stopped dead still with upraised hands, not turning around.

The cops took him down to the station and beat his head into an open, bloody wound from his bulging eyes clear around to the base of his skull—"You'd bring your nigger cuttings down on Euclid Avenue, would you, you black—"

They gave him the electric chair for that.

But if it is worrying him, he doesn't show it during the slow drag of days in death row's grilled enclosure. He knows that that high yellow gal with the ball-bearing hips is still his, heart, soul and body. All day long, you can hear his loud, crowing voice, kidding the other condemned men, jibing the guards, telling lies. He can tell some tall lies, too—"You know, me 'n Marie wuz in Noo Yawk dat wintah. Ah won leben grands in uh dice game 'n bought her uh sealskin—"

All day long, you can hear his noisy laugh.

Marie comes to see him as often as they let her, brings him fried chicken and hot, red lips; brings him a wide smile and tiny yellow specks in her big, brown, ever-loving eyes. You can hear his assured love-making all over the range, his casual "honeybunch," his chuckling, contented laugh.

All day long . . .

It's at night, when she's gone and the cells are dark and death row is silent, that you'll find Black Boy huddled in the corner of his cell, thinking of her, perhaps in some other nigger's loving arms. Crying softly. Salty tears making glistening streaks down the blending blackness of his face.

When headwaiter Dick Small pushed through the service hall into the main dining room, he ran smack into an early dinner rush. The creased, careful smile adorning his brown face knotted slightly in self-reproach. He should have been there sooner.

For a brief instant he paused just inside the doorway, head cocked to one side as if deferentially listening. A hum of cultured voices engaged in leisurely conversation, the gentle clatter of silver on fine china, the slight scrape of a chair, the tinkle of ice in glasses, the aroma of hot coffee and savory, well-cooked food, the sight of unhurried dining and hurried service blended into an atmosphere ineffably dear to his heart; for directing the services of this dining room in a commendable manner was the ultimate aim of his life, and as much a part of him as the thin spot in his meticulously brushed hair or the habitual immaculateness of the tuxedos which draped his slight, spright frame.

But he could sense a hint of exasperation in the general mood with that surety of feeling which twenty years as headwaiter at the Park Manor Hotel had bestowed upon him, and his roving gaze searched quickly for flaws in the service inspiring it.

There was fat Mr. McLaughlin knuckling the table impatiently as he awaited—Dick was quite sure that it was broiled lobster that Mr. McLaughlin was so impatiently awaiting. And Mrs. Shipley was frowning with displeasure at the dirty dishes which claimed her elbow room as she endeavored to lean closer to her boon companion, Mrs. Hamilton, and impart in a theatrical whisper a choice morsel of spicy gossip—Dick had no doubt that it was both choice and spicy. When Mr. Lyons lifted his glass to take another sip of iced water, he found to his extreme annoyance that there was no more iced water to be sipped, and even from where he stood, Dick could see Mr. Lyons' forbearance abruptly desert him.

The white-jacketed, black-bowed waiters showed a passable alacrity, he observed without censure, but they were accomplishing very little. Direction was lacking. The captain, black and slow, plodded hither and yon in a stew of indecision.

Dick clapped his hands. "Fill those glasses for that deuce over there," he directed the busboy who had sprung to his side. "Take an ashstand to the party at that center table. Clear up those ladies." He left the busboy spinning in his tracks, turned to the captain who came rushing over. "I'll take it over now, son. You slip into a white jacket and bring in Mr. McLaughlin's lobster."

His presence was established and the wrinkles of exasperation ironed smoothly out.

The captain nodded and flashed white teeth, relieved. He turned away, turned back. "Mr. Erskine has a party of six for seven-thirty. I gave it to Pat. Here's the bill of fare." He gave Dick a scrawled slip of paper.

Dick pocketed the order, aware that this party was something in the way of an event, for Mr. Erskine had been the very first of the older residents who had sworn they would never set foot within the dining room again until the "obnoxious"—Mr. Erskine himself had employed the term—syncopatings of "Sonny" Jenkins and his body-rocking "Cotton Pickers" had been everlastingly removed. His glance strayed involuntarily to the band dais at the rear where until just the day before Sonny and his black, foot-stomping troubadours had held forth; but deprived of their colorful appearance and cannonading rhythms it had a skeletoned, abandoned look.

Well, after all it was the older residents like Mr. Erskine who comprised the firm foundation upon which the hotel so staunchly rested, he reflected, agreeing with them (although he would not have admitted it) that the noticeable absence of Sonny and his boys was more to be desired than their somewhat jarring presence.

But he quickly pigeonholed the thought, the press of duty making no allowances for idle reflection. He went straight to the setup and scanned it quickly, his head to one side. After a moment's careful study, he leaned across the table and aligned a fork, smoothed an infinitesimal wrinkle from the linen, shifted the near candlestick just a wee bit to the left; then he rocked back on his heels and allowed his eyes to smile. He was pleased.

Flawless service for discriminating guests evoked in him a complete satisfaction. And who among the many to whom he had catered during his twenty years at the Park Manor had ever showed a finer sense of discrimination than Mr. Erskine, he thought, or a broader sense of appreciation, he added with a glow.

He nodded commendation to Pat, tan and lanky, who was spooning ice cubes into the upturned glasses with slim, deft fingers; and Pat acknowledged it with his roguish smile.

"Here's the bill of fare, Pat," he said in his quick, crisp voice. "Put your cocktails on ice and have everything prepared by a quarter after seven." He glanced at the wall clock and noticed that it was forty-seven minutes after six.

He stepped away, circled an unoccupied table and came back, frowning slightly. "This is Mrs. Van Denter's table, Pat. Did the captain select it?"

"Cap called the desk, chief," Pat explained. "They said Mrs. Van Denter had gone into the country to spend a week with her sister."

His breath oozed slowly out. "You know how stubborn she is. Been that way for twenty years to my knowledge, ever since her husband died and left her—" he caught himself and stopped abruptly. Gossiping with a waiter. Chagrin bit him lightly, putting snap into his voice: "Put your reserved card on, Pat. Always put your reserved card on first, then—"

The sight of Mrs. Van Denter coming through the entrance archway choked him. She made straight for her table, plowing aside everyone who got in her way. Tonight she looked slightly forbidding; her grayish, stoutish, sixtyish appearance rockier than ever and the tight seam of her mouth carrying an overload of obstinancy. At first glance he thought that she had had a martini too many, but as she lumbered closer with her elephantine directness, he decided that it came from her heart, not her stomach.

Perhaps she and her sister had had a rift, he was thinking as he bowed with more than his customary deference and inquired as to her health: "And how are you this evening, Mrs. Van Denter?" After a pause in which she did not reply he began his apology: "I am very sorry, Mrs. Van Denter, but the captain was under the impression that you were in the country—"

She brushed him aside and aimed her solid body for her table, on which Pat was just placing the reserved card. Dick turned quickly behind her, his mouth hanging slack. There was the hint of a race. But she won.

And for all of the iced glasses and party silver and crimped nap-

kins and bowl of roses and engraved name cards at each plate; for
all of the big black-lettered card which read: *RESERVED,* staring
up into her face, she reached for the nearest chair, pulled it out,
planted her plump body into it with sickening finality and reached
for an iced glass.

Dick dropped a menu card before her and signaled Pat to take
her order, his actions registering no more than a natural concern.
He picked up the bowl of flowers and the reserved card and placed
them on another table, then moved casually away. It was an era of
change, he told himself. It made the old more stubborn and the
young more reckless—he didn't know which were the more difficult to please. But here were Mrs. Hughes and her guest right beside him who seemed to be pleased enough even if no one else
was, he noted with obvious enjoyment of the fact.

"How do you do, Mrs. Hughes," he addressed the stately, white-
haired lady. "And this is your sister, Mrs. Walpole, of Boston, I
am sure. We're delighted to have you with us again, Mrs. Walpole.
I remember quite well when you visited us before."

Mrs. Hughes smiled cordially and Mrs. Walpole said, "I've been
here several times before."

"But I was referring to your last visit; it was in August three
years ago."

"What a remarkable memory," Mrs. Hughes murmured.

Dick was gratified; he prided himself upon his memory and when
someone took notice of it he felt rewarded. Turning away he
caught his tuxedoed reflection in a paneled mirror and the slightly
disturbing thought came to him that the blue and gold decora-
tions of this dining room were too ornate for the casual informality
which now existed. A vague regret threaded his thoughts as he recalled the bygone age when dressing for dinner had been the rigid
rule. It took a slight effort to banish such recollections and when
he spoke again his voice was brusque.

"Clear that table," he ordered a busboy as if the busboy alone
was to blame for the change of things.

Then a party of seven at a center table demanded his personal
attention. "Good evening Mr. and Mrs. Seedle," he greeted the
elderly hosts, knowing that they considered the service lacking until
he made his appearance. "And how is this young gentleman?" he
inquired of their seven-year-old grandson.

"I'm all right, Dick," the boy replied, "but I ain't no gentleman
'cause Gramma just said so—"

"Arnold!" Mrs. Seedle rebuked.

"Why does Granpa eat onions, Dick?" the boy asked, not to be
repressed, but Dick bowed a smiling departure without replying.

"So Gramma can find him in the dark," he heard Mr. Seedle elu-
cidate, feeling that "Gramma" could very likely find him right then
in the dark without the aid of onions as lit as he was.

"Fill these glasses," he directed a busy waiter to hide his growing
smile, then filled them himself before the waiter had a chance to
protest.

"Pst, pst," he called a busboy, received no reply. He hurried
across the floor, light lumping slightly on the irritation in his face,
shook the boy's shoulder. "What's the matter with you, are you
deaf?" he demanded.

"No sir, I—I—er—"

"Go get the salad tray," he snapped and hurried away in his lop-
ing walk to greet Mrs. Collar, eighty and cross, who hesitated undecidedly under the entrance archway.

"It's a rather nasty night, Mrs. Collar," he remarked by way of
greeting, seating her in a corner nook. "It doesn't seem to be able
to make up its mind whether to rain or sleet, but I feel that it will
clear up by tomorrow."

Mrs. Collar looked up at him over the rim of her ancient spectacles. "That isn't any encouragement to me," she replied in her
harsh, unconciliatory voice.

Confusion took the smoothness out of Dick's speech. "I am not
really sure, er—rer, I wouldn't be surprised if it continued, er, being indefinite."

"You're indefinite enough yourself," she snapped, scanning the
menu card.

He laughed deprecatingly, signaled to a youth less than a year
out of prison to take her order. "I'd make a poor gambler," he confessed ruefully.

Her head jerked quickly up again. "You don't gamble, do you,
Dick?" she asked sharply.

"No, Mrs. Collar, I do not gamble," said headwaiter Dick Small,
gambling then his job at five hundred a month to give an ex-con
another chance. "Nor do I employ any man who does."

"You couldn't tell if they did," she pointed out matter-of-factly.

"Not unless you had every one of them shadowed night and day."

The indelibleness abandoned his smile. He turned away from her, annoyance tight in his throat, and greeted a sudden influx of diners. But before he had finished seating them the indulgence came back to him. Mrs. Collar was really a very nice old lady, he admitted to himself, and he liked her. She was like olives, you had to acquire a taste for her. And he sincerely hoped that she was pleased with the service.

But after all, Mrs. Collar was just one diner, and he had neither the time nor the inclination to analyze her disposition for the dining room was rapidly filling with younger and more demanding guests.

It was an unusual weekday crowd, and search his mind as he would, he could not think of one reason for it. There were no conventions in town as he knew of, and there were no more than the usual dinner "specials." And then he had it, and he wondered why he had not thought of it before. It was no more or less than the return of the dissenters, recalled by the serene and comfortable knowledge that "Sonny" Jenkins and his "Cotton Pickers" had no longer to be endured.

A repressed snort of laughter pushed air through his nose. But this was no laughing time, really, he censored himself. It was a time for smooth, fast service. His reputation as a headwaiter, and even the prestige of the hotel itself, were dependent upon the guests being served with the least possible delay.

He started kitchenward to recruit more waiters from the room service department, he just simply must have more waiters, when something about a busboy halted him. He glanced down, looked up again.

"What kind of shoe polish do you use, son?" he inquired disarmingly.

"Paste," the boy replied, unthinking.

He let his gaze drop meaningfully to the boy's unshined shoes. "Try liquid next time, son," he suggested.

The boy jumped with sudden guilt. Dick stepped quickly around him and passed from the dining room before the boy had a chance to reply.

In the service hall Dick bumped into a waiter gobbling a leftover steak, said pleasantly enough, "Food is like drink, son, it's a habit. There's no place in service for the glutton or the drunkard."

The waiter strangled, blew steak all over the floor, but Dick passed on without a backward glance.

Over by the elevator where the room service was stationed, a waiter lounged indolently by a serviced table and yelled at the closed elevator doors, "Knock knock!"

Dick drew up quietly behind him, heard the slightly muffled reply from within the elevator: "Who's there?"

"Mr. Small, the headwaiter," he said crisply.

The waiter who had been leaning so indolently by the serviced table jumped. His hand flew up and knocked over a glass of water on the clean linen. The elevator doors popped open, emitting two more waiters in an impressive hurry.

"If you fellows don't care to work—" Dick began, exceedingly unimpressed.

The first waiter hoisted the room service table on his shoulder and started into the elevator without a word. The other two stammered in unison: "Yes sir, no sir, er—rer—"

"Put down that table," Dick grated at the first waiter.

The waiter let it drop as if it was hot.

"All three of you go into the dining room and report to the captain," Dick ordered.

They scampered quickly off.

"Here, serve this dinner," Dick directed a busboy who had performed a magical appearance.

"But I don't, er, know, er—"

"Find out," Dick snapped, at the end of his patience.

When he returned to the dining room he noticed that patrons were still entering. He greeted an incoming couple, seated them and took their order on note paper, being unable to locate an idle waiter.

A bellboy passed through from the kitchen. Dick stopped him. "Give this order to Howard," he directed.

"But I'm a bellboy," the boy objected.

Dick stood stock still and looked at him. "All stages of existence have their drawbacks, son," he began in a lazy, philosophical vein.

But the boy was not to be fooled. Dick had such a smooth way of telling a servant that he was fired. He took the note and hurried away in search of Howard.

Dick's quick sight scanned the sidestand before he turned away, exploring for negligence; but the pitchers were filled and the butter was iced and the silver was neatly arranged in the drawers. He allowed a slight expression of commendation to come into his smile. The busboys whose duty it was to keep the sidestands in order had earned stars in their crowns, although they would never know it if they waited for Dick Small, headwaiter, to tell them.

Dick turned back to his guests, feeling a benign omnipotence in caring for their needs. He was as the captain of a ship, he reflected, the master of this dining room and solely responsible for its service. He seemed to derive a becoming dignity from this responsibility.

These people were his passengers; he must feed and serve and humor them with an impartial respect. They were his life; they took up his time, his thoughts, his energy. He was interested in them, interested in their private lives and their individual prosperity. He knew them; knew about them. His most vital emotions absorbed their coloring from the emotions of these dining room patrons; when they were pleased, he was pleased; when they were hurt, he was hurt; when they failed or prospered in their respective endeavors it had a personal bearing on the course of his life.

Each day when he stood looking over them, as now, he received some feeling which added to his life, although it seldom showed in the imperturbableness of his smile.

Now his gaze drifted slowly from face to face, reading the feelings and emotions of each with an uncanny perception.

There were Tommy and Jackie Rightmire, the polo-playing twins. And did they have healthy appetites? And several tables distant he noticed their sister dining with a Spanish nobleman whom he had never been quite able to admire.

And there were Mr. Andrews and Mrs. Winnings, engaged as was their custom of late in animated chatter as they dined in the dubious seclusion of a rear column. Crowding forty, both of them, he was quite sure, and as obviously in love with each other as a pair of doves. But if the slightest censure threaded his thoughts as his gaze moved slowly on, it did not show in the bland smoothness of his expression.

He wondered what would happen if Mrs. Andrews, forty-two and showing it, and reputedly very jealous of Mr. Andrews' affections, should choose this dining room in which to dine some evening and inadvertently bump into their tête-à-tête.

And coincidentally, as it happens even in masterpieces, Mrs. Andrews did. She came through the entrance archway at the front and beat a hard-heeled, determined path straight toward her spouse's table.

Dick's compelling thought was to deter catastrophe, for catastrophe indeed it would be, he sincerely felt, should Mrs. Andrews encounter Mr. Andrews in such an inexplicable predicament. He headed her off just in time.

"Right this way, Mrs. Andrews," he began, pulling a chair from a conspicuously placed center table.

"No, no, not that," she discarded with a gesture. "I want something—remote, quiet. I'm expecting a friend." Her eyes dared him to think no more than that which she had explicitly stated.

"Then this will be just the ticket for you," he purred smoothly, seating her across the dining room from her husband with her back toward him and the column between them.

"Thank you, this will be just fine," she smiled, pleased, and he had the feeling of a golfer who has just scored a hole in one.

The voice of a waiter halted his casual strolling as he moved away from her: "Chief, see that old man over there at the window? The one with the white goatee?"

Dick did not look at the old man "with the white goatee," he looked very pointedly at the waiter slouching with propped elbows on the sidestand and lacking in a proper respect for the hotel's patrons, not to mention the hotel's headwaiter.

"He says all a nigger needs is something to eat and someplace to sleep," the waiter continued, unaware of the pointedness of Dick's frown. "He says he knows 'cause he's got a plantation of them—"

"Do *you* see that table over there from which Mrs. Van Denter is now arising?" he cut in, a forced restraint blunting his voice.

"Yes sir," the waiter replied quickly, sensing his mistake.

"Well, service it for six," he directed, the displeasure breaking through his restraint.

"Yes *sir*." The waiter was glad to be off.

Dick followed him over to Mrs. Van Denter's table and bowed to her again with that slightly exaggerated deference. "Was your dinner enjoyable, madam?" he inquired.

But dinner, enjoyable or not, had not softened the stone of Mrs. Van Denter's face. "Dick," she snapped, "I find your obsequiousness a bit repugnant." Then she plodded smilelessly away.

Dick admitted to himself with a sense of reproach that it had been a *faux pas* but he couldn't take time to explore into it further for he noticed that the table of two women needed clearing and he went in search of a busboy to clear it.

The boy, a greenhorn, approached timidly from the rear of the thin, reedy lady with the lashing voice and reached around her for her plate, taking great care not to disturb her. The lady saw the stealthily reaching hand; "the clutching hand" she might have said had she said it. Her sharp mouth went slack like a fish's. "Oh!" she gasped.

The boy grew panicky. He grabbed the plate as if to dash away with it, as indeed he did. The thin lady clutched the other rim and held on for dear life. There was a moment's tug of war. A chicken bone fell to the table. Then anger jerked the thin lady around in her chair.

"Let loose!" she shrilled.

And "let loose" the now thoroughly frightened boy most certainly did. He not only let loose but he jumped a full yard backward, his nostrils flaring like a winded horse's and his eyes white-rimmed in his black face.

"Always taking my plate before I'm finished," the thin lady added caustically.

But she had no further need to fear that particular boy taking her plate ever again, finished or not finished, for he didn't stop running until he was downstairs in the locker room changing into his street clothes. Dick sent the captain down to bring him back, but the boy had definitely resigned.

"Well, he wouldn't have made a waiter, anyway," he remarked. "He has an innate fear of white people which he couldn't overcome. It makes him nervous and panicky around them." But he was annoyed just the same.

A stag party of four in the rear offered a brief respite from peevish old ladies and frightened busboys. He noticed that a raised window beside them slashed wind across their table and hastened quickly in their direction, concern prodding him.

"Is there too much draft for you, gentlemen?" he inquired solicitously, pausing in a half-bow. But on closer observation he saw that they were all strangers to him and slightly drunk and not gentlemen, after all.

They all stopped eating and ogled him. "That's a good-looking tux, boy," one remarked. "Where'd you get it? Steal it?"

"No sir, I purchased it—" he began restrainedly.

"What makes you black?" another cut in. A laugh spurted.

Anger broke loose in him then. It shook him like a squall. But his smile weathered it. When the breath had softened in his lungs he said politely, "God did, gentlemen," and moved away.

At a center table a high-pressure voice was saying, "Just talked to the governor at the capitol. He said—" It sounded unreal to Dick. He turned his glance obliquely, saw the latecomer sit opposite his comely, young wife. It was the wife who signed the checks, he recalled; and who was the woman he had seen him with the other day and had intended to remember?

But the sight of old Mr. Woodford standing in the entrance archway snapped his line of thought before Mnemosyne could come to his aid. He rushed to meet him. "And how are you this evening, Mr. Woodford, sir?" he asked, and then added without awaiting a reply, knowing there would be none, "Right this way, sir. I reserved your table for you." He had already noted that Mr. Woodford's table was unoccupied.

He received Mr. Woodford's grudging nod, led the way rearward, head cocked, arms swinging, recalling reluctantly the time when Mr. Woodford was genial and talkative and worth many millions— broke now since the stock market crash and glum, with slightly bloodshot eyes from drinking a little too much, he suspected.

When he turned away he caught the beckoning finger of old Mrs. Miller, a resident for many years at the Park Manor and a special friend of the Rumanian countess who resided there on her visits to America. He moved quickly toward her, his smile becoming more genuine, less careful.

"And when have you heard from our good friend, her highness, Mrs. Miller?" he inquired with assured familiarity.

"I was just going to tell you, Dick," she replied in a reedy, year-thinned voice. "I had a cablegram from her daughter just this afternoon."

"And when is she going to pay us another visit? Soon, I hope."

"Never, Dick," she quavered. "She died last week."

Dick went rigid. The brown of his face tinged ashily. Then he noticed that Mrs. Miller's eyes were red and swollen from crying and he upbraided himself for not having noticed immediately.

He could find no suitable words for the moment. He pitied her in a sincere, personal way, for he knew that the countess was the one person in all the world whom she considered as a friend. But he could not express his pity. He was only a headwaiter. He thought there was something sublime in her gallantry which would not let her grief prostrate her; and he knew the countess would have wished it so.

Oddly, for a fleeting instant he was a young black waiter in Atlantic City, thirty-six years ago. It was his afternoon off and he had seven dollars. The pretty brown girl beside him was saying, "I want the five-dollar one." It was a wedding ring, and she was to be his bride. Seven dollars—and now he was headwaiter at five hundred a month, had bought a seven-thousand-dollar home, had a few thousand in the bank. That afternoon seemed a long way behind. He said aloud, a sincere depth of feeling in his voice:

"We shall miss her so much, Mrs. Miller. The world can little spare the loss of one so fine."

And by that sincere tribute to one who was dead he earned for himself five thousand dollars in Mrs. Miller's will.

"Indeed we shall miss her, Dick," Mrs. Miller replied, barely able to stem the flow of tears.

When he moved away from her his actions were slowed, groggy, as if he had taken a severe beating. In a very short time he would pass the sixty mark. Sixty was old for a waiter in a busy hotel. He shook himself as if he were awaking from a bad dream, stepped forward with renewed pounce.

Perhaps he wasn't looking, perhaps he couldn't see. He bumped into a busboy with a loaded tray. China crashed on the tiled floor, silver rang. The sudden shatter shook the room. He patted the stooping boy on the shoulder, the unusual show of feeling leaving the boy slightly flustered, turned quickly away, head held high, refusing to notice the shattered crockery. And by his refusal to notice it he averted attention.

The ringing of the telephone in the corner brought relief to his thoughts. He hurried over, picked up the receiver. "Dining room, the headwaiter speaking," he said. Faint traces of emotion still lingered in his eyes.

Behind him a woman's husky voice was saying, "But Mildred is selfish. No matter what you give in material things, my dear, unless you give something of yourself—" He recognized the voice as Mrs. Porter's, of Porter Paints and Varnish . . . The telephone began speaking and drew his attention.

He hooked the receiver, stuck a reserved sign on the table, started kitchenward to get a glass of water when the question jerked him up short like the snap of a noose:

"Boy, didn't you get a pardon from the penitentiary about a year back?"

The voices of the other three men and four women at the table stopped and hung rigidly suspended in an all-enveloping gasp. Motion froze as solid as the ice cubes tinkling in the glasses. Silence came in a tight clamp, restricting the breath.

But the waiter to whom the question had been addressed remained placid. "Yes sir," he replied.

Dick turned toward the party, brushing the apprehension from before him with a widespread gesture.

"First degree?" the voice persisted.

A woman said, "Oh!"

"Yes sir," the waiter repeated.

Dick entered the conversation then. "I engaged him, sir," he addressed the genial-faced man who had put the questions. "Turned out to be one of my best boys, too."

"Why?" the man wanted to know, more from curiosity than reprobation. "I imagine that the residents of the hotel here would resent it if they knew. I might myself."

"I felt that he was a good boy and that all he needed was another chance," Dick explained.

The man's eyes lingered a moment appraisingly upon Dick's face, then switched to the waiter's. "Let's give it to him," he decided, closing the incident. Ease came back into the diners and the dinner moved serenely on.

But the genial-faced man had earned Dick's everlasting gratefulness, although he would perhaps never know it.

Dick had forgotten that he was thirsty, drawn again into the maelstrom of duties confronting a headwaiter.

The rush gradually subsided. Dick was made aware of it by the actions of his waiters. They had begun to move about with that Negroid languor which bespoke liberal tips. He was reminded of the Negro of Mark Twain legend who said he didn't want to make a dime 'cause he had a dime. His smile was indulgent. He knew his boys.

His rapid sight counted twenty-one remaining diners. So he released the first shift of waiters with the ironic suggestion: "Don't disappoint your money, boys. Give it a break and spend it."

He watched their happy departure for a moment, knowing full well that they would be hanging over their favorite bars before the hour was passed, then his attention was drawn to a drunken party at a center table, overflow from the bar no doubt. The coarseness of their speech and actions spread a personal humiliation within him. He wanted to feel that his guests deserved the respect which he bestowed upon them.

Someone of the party made a risqué remark and everyone laughed. Everyone except one woman. She was looking at the lobster in front of her with mouth-twitching nausea. Then horror came into her face. "It moved! It moved!" she cried, voice rising hysterically. "It moved!" She backed away from the table, crying over and over again, "It moved!"

Dick stepped quickly forward, his careful smile forced, and whisked the platter of lobster from the table. "Is there something else you desire, madam?" he asked politely, presenting her with a menu.

A man swung leisurely from his seat and winked at him. "She desires a bit of air, that's all," he said.

A waiter smothered a laugh in a napkin.

"Take that napkin from your face!" Dick chastened with severe voice. "Get some side towels and use them, and don't ever let me catch you using a napkin in such a manner." His harshness was an outlet.

He moved toward the side windows, trying to stifle the buildup of emotion in the smoothness of his mind. The guests were always right and a waiter was always impersonal, in action and in thought, no matter what occurred: that was the one rigid tenet in the waiter's code. But platitudes helped him very little. He decided that he must be tired.

George, tall and sepia, passed him. He noticed that George needed new tuxedo trousers. But he didn't say anything because he knew that George had a high-yellow woman who took most of his money. And George knew what a waiter needed, anyway. He'd give him enough rope—

He was surprised to see that it was Mr. Upshaw whom George was serving. Mr. Upshaw had once said he didn't like "yellah niggers," as if they could help being yellow. Maybe Mr. Upshaw didn't consider George as being yellow . . .

He thought no more about it for he had just noticed Mr.

Spivat, half owner of the hotel, dining alone at a window table. He went over and spoke to him. "Nasty weather we're having, Mr. Spivat."

"Yes, it is, Dick," Mr. Spivat replied absently, scanning the stocks final.

The window behind Mr. Spivat drew Dick's gaze. He raised his sight into the dark night. Park foliage across the street was a thick blackness, looking slightly gummy in the wet sleet and rain. On a distant summit the museum was a chiseled stone block in white light, hanging from the starless night by invisible strings. Street lights in the foreground showed a stone wall bordering the park, a strip of sidewalk, slushy pavement.

A car turned the corner, its headlights stabbing into the darkness. Motor purr sounded faintly as it passed, the red taillight bobbed lingeringly into the bog of distant darkness. Dick stared into the void after it, feeling very tired. He thought of a chicken farm in the country, where he could get off his feet. But he knew that he would never be satisfied away from a dining room.

When he turned back traces of weariness showed in the edges of his smile, making it ragged. But his eyes were as sharp as ever. They lingered a moment on the slightly hobbling figure of Bishop. A little stooped, Bishop was, a little paunched, a little gray, with a moonface and soiled eyes and rough skin of midnight blue. A good name, Bishop, a descriptive name, he thought with a half-smile.

He noticed Bishop lurch once, so he followed him into the kitchen, overtook him at the pastry room and spun him about, sniffing his breath. He caught the scent of mints and a very faint odor of alcohol.

"You haven't been drinking again, have you, Bishop?" he asked sharply. He liked Bishop, but Bishop would drink, and a drinking waiter could not be tolerated.

Bishop rolled his eyes and laughed to dispel such a horrid idea. "Nawsuh, chief. Been rubbin' my leg with rubbin' alcawl. Thass what you smell. My n'ritis is terrible bad, suh."

Dick nodded sympathetically. "You need to watch your diet, Bishop," he advised. "Go home when you serve that dessert."

Bishop bobbed, rubbing his hands together involuntarily. "Thank you, suh, Mistah Small."

Dick turned back into the dining room followed by Bishop with coffee and cream. He stopped just inside the doorway, his gaze lingering on Bishop's limp.

But his frown was inspired by thoughts of his own wife more than by Bishop's limp. She was using an exceeding amount of money lately. He didn't want to start thinking unfair thoughts of her, that was the way so many marriages were broken up.

He caught himself and brought his mind back to the dining room. He tried to recall whether he had assigned Bishop to wait on Mr. Spivat. He certainly wouldn't have, he knew, had he known that Bishop was limping so badly for Mr. Spivat was convinced, anyway, that all Negro waiters were drunkards; and Bishop did appear drunk.

It all happened so quickly that the picture was telescoped in his mind and his body started moving before thought directed its motions.

Bishop's right leg buckled as he placed the tiny pitcher of cream. He jackknifed forward on his knee. Cream flew in a thin sheet over the front of Mr. Spivat's dark blue suit.

Mr. Spivat blanched, then ripened like a russet apple. Insensate fury jerked him erect. His foot began motion as if to kick the kneeling figure, froze in knotted restraint.

Dick was there in three swift strides, applying a cold, damp towel to Mr. Spivat's suit. "Clean up, George," he directed the other waiter, trying to avert the drama which he felt engulfing them. "Sorry, Mr. Spivat, sir. The boy's got neuritis, it's very bad during this nasty weather. I'll lay him off until it gets better."

But neither could cold, damp towels help Mr. Spivat's suit, nor could expressions of sorrow allay the fury in his mind.

He mashed the words out between his clenched teeth: "Dick, see that this man gets his money, and if I ever see him in this hotel again I'll fire the whole bunch of you!" He wheeled and started walking jerkily from the room, his body moving as if it were being snatched along with slack strings. "Drunk!" he ground out.

Dick motioned Bishop from the dining room and followed behind. He had the checker make out a requisition for Bishop's pay, an even thirteen dollars. He couldn't meet the doglike plea of Bishop's eyes.

Bishop stood at a respectful distance, his shoulders drooping, his whole body sagging; very black, very wordless. Bishop had al-

ways like Mr. Spivat, had liked serving him. He and Mr. Spivat used
to discuss baseball during the summer months.

After a time he said irrelevantly, a slight protest in his voice, "I
got seven kids."

Dick looked down at his feet, big feet they were, with broken
arches from shouldering heavy trays on adamant concrete, big and
flat and knotty. He felt in his pockets, discovered a twenty-dollar
banknote. He pressed it into Bishop's hand.

Bishop said, "I wasn't drunk, chief," as if Dick might think he
was.

Dick wanted to believe that, but he couldn't. Bishop as a rule
did not eat mints; he didn't like sweets of any kind. But mints would
help kill the odor of whiskey on his breath. Dick sighed. He knew
that Bishop liked serving Mr. Spivat. There was very little of the
likes and dislikes of all his waiters, of their family affairs and personal lives, that Dick did not know. But of them all, he sympathized
most with Bishop.

But what could he do? Bishop would drink.

He said, "Accidents will happen, son. Yours just cost you your
job. If there's anything I can ever do for you, anything in reason,
let me know. And even if it isn't in reason, come and let me say so."
He stood quite still for a moment. His face showed extreme weariness.

Then he shook it all from his mind. It required a special effort.
He blinked his eyes clear of the picture of a dejected black face,
donned his creased, careful smile and pushed through the service
hall into the dining room. His head was cocked to one side as
though he were deferentially listening.

This is the story of an illiterate black man whom men and women, both black and white, called *God*.

When this man was serving ten years for rape in one of America's very tough prisons, his official name, the name printed on his wooden label above his prison number, was *Smith*. Unofficially, during his ten years of incarceration, he was designated *rat, fink, black bastard, prison preacher, degenerate, corn doctor,* and many other descriptive appellations which were less flattering. In truth, he was all of these; but he was more.

He was a short black man with a mouth full of cheap gold teeth which caused his breath to be intolerably offensive, even though he kept them scrupulously shined with Old Dutch cleanser, ashes, sand, metal polish, and toothpaste when he could get it. There was a rapidly growing bald spot in the middle of his short kinky head which wrinkled as completely as did his forehead when he suddenly frowned or stretched his white-rimmed eyes.

His body was thick and muscular, with the suggestion of a paunch to come in later years when his appetite could be sated, and his shoulders sloped like an ape's. He had huge, muscle-roped arms and weird, long-fingered hands of enormous size and grotesque shape, a strangler's hands. He could scratch the calf of either leg without stooping. Flat, splayed, fantastic feet, which could not be comfortably encased in any shoe smaller than a size 16, grew from abnormally small legs as straight as sticks.

His eyes squinted and his gold teeth gleamed in his black face when he grinned. While in prison he always grinned for white people, be they convicts or guards, no matter what they said or did to him. Usually they just goosed him because that made him jump and strike out at whatever was in front of him. Once a guard goosed him and he struck another guard in front of him and the two of them lit on him like ducks on a June bug and beat some of the black out of him.

He had the reputation of being the strongest man in prison. There were convicts who swore they had seen him stand flat-footed and, gripping both wheels, lift a Georgia buggy full of wet concrete. A Georgia buggy of wet concrete will weigh easily upward of five hundred pounds and to push it along is no easy task for a husky man.

But his prodigious strength did not prevent angry convicts from putting a blanket over his head from time to time and slugging him with iron pipes for ratting on them. Nor was he falsely accused. He was a rat. He informed the officials whenever he saw a fellow inmate break a rule.

Out of this grotesque black man who looked half frog and half ape there came a voice that transcended all human qualities. It was perhaps one of the greatest speaking voices ever to be heard upon this earth. It startled a person, coming from this black man's mouth, made one look around in bewilderment then back to the man to stare with foolish amazement. If one can imagine the voice of God speaking from the burning bush of biblical legend, one can imagine the voice of Smith.

At the end of eight years the deputy warden granted him privilege to open a small "office" over the courtroom, where he extracted aching corns from both guards' and convicts' feet. He could do more with a corn than a monkey can with a coconut. Big tough hacks, like "Forty Four," "Kill Crazy," and "Pick Handle Slim," would break down in his office and cry from sheer gratitude after he had peeled off their corns.

It was perhaps during that time that he learned how pliant people were when relieved of suffering, although that probably was not the way he thought of it. He could not charge for his services, but the deputy had not prohibited him from mentioning what things he needed, and he learned to tell from the expressions of his clients whether to need a new pair of shoes or a sack of Bull Durham smoking tobacco. He did not smoke and new shoes hurt his feet; it was the money he wanted.

He was an ardent Christian, although his particular sect was never clearly designated, being covered more or less by the blanketing term Protestant which the prison applied to any form of belief not Catholic, Jewish, or Christian Science. Nor was his idea of

Christianity gleaned wholly from the Bible, as he could neither read nor write. But he had an active imagination and a good memory, and between the two he concocted a doctrine which was tangible and near to the earth and in which he believed fervently. When his fellow convicts accused him of coming to prison to find God he was not abashed.

He had a penchant for personal adornment in the form of bracelets made from shiny copper wire and bronze stickpins and red, yellow, and green celluloid rings, and when he attended the Sunday exercises he bedecked himself with his most brilliant articles of jewelry, sometimes wearing as many as two rings on each finger and a half-dozen bracelets on each wrist. Never was he so consummately elated as when the chaplain, in a prankish mood, called upon him to pray.

His prayers were singular. Above the muted and not-so-muted booing of his fellow convicts, he beseeched God to bless the warden and the deputy warden and the chaplain and the guards and the parole board and the outside judges and the governor and the sovereign state itself, and to have mercy upon the convicts' souls. He entreated God to save them all a place in heaven, particularly the officials and himself, and to carefully preserve their wings which he hoped some of his fellow convicts might someday deserve (although he made it plain he doubted it). And he always asked God to send them pork chops and fried chicken and big fat biscuits and roast "possum" to sustain them until that final day arrived. Perhaps he was not such a fool at that.

His prayers were long and eloquent. His eloquence had been acquired as a means of defense against the prison protocol where the head-hunting guards had field day on black rapists and the guerrilla bands of convicts were death on rats. A conviction for rape seems always to imbue men with an intimacy with God.

The deputy warden had permitted Smith to hold church services on Sunday and Wednesday evenings in the dormitories where the colored convicts were quartered. Smith waxed even more eloquent on these occasions.

His voice contained an astounding resonance and volume. When wrath at the sinners (who customarily played Georgia skin down at the lower end of the dormitory during his services) shook his short, powerful body, he threw a thunderous, echoing sound at them which drowned out their voices seeking more bets and rocked the concrete building. It mattered little what he said for usually his sermons were no more than incoherent gibbering and prolonged bellowing, such as, "an' de Lawd said, 'Adam, oh Adam, ef'n you eat dat fruit you'll sholy die,' an' whut Adam do? Whut Adam do, Ah asts yuh?" His voice would lower to a confidential lull, as gentle as the babbling of a brook. "Ah asts yuh, whut Adam do?" Then it would thunder out like the roar of a cannon, "He et it, dass whut he done, he et it!" and the whole big dormitory would jump, the sinners in the gambling games would turn loose the dice as if they were hot and the guard would drop his fresh cigar in the cuspidor. Then Smith would continue, bellowing like a bull, "De sinnah guina be zoomed 'way in smoke, but de sheeps guina live in de land of plenty an' po'k chops fuever. Now ain't dat whut de Lawd say, bruthah, ain' dat whut de Lawd say?"

He rocked his congregations, he scared them, he startled them if by nothing else except his colossal ignorance, he browbeat them, he lulled them, he caressed them. He made hardened convicts want to shout, he made gambling addicts repent and give away their ill-gotten gains and stay away from the games for two or three whole days. He played upon people's emotions. His voice was like a throbbing tom-tom, creeping into a person's mind like an insidious drug, blasting the wits out of the witty and filling the hearts of the witless with visions of everlasting bounty.

It had an indescribable range, sliding through octaves with the ease of a master organ. It was like a journey on a scenic railway, dropping from notes as clear and high as Satchmo ever hit on his golden trumpet, like the sudden, startling dive of a pursuit plane, to the reverberating roar of heavy artillery. You could see hell, in all its lurid fury, following in its wake, and then with as abrupt a change the voice took you to green pastures lush with manna.

When Smith got in his ten years and was called before the parole board, this august body of gentlemen, having been informed of his chummy relationship with God, called upon him to pray. He fell upon his knees and lifted his voice in a prayer which lasted a full half hour. Sweat beaded on the bald spot atop his head and ran down his face, it wet the back of his hands and saturated his heavy prison shirt, while January snow stood knee deep on the outside ground. He was eloquent, he was loquacious, he employed every tone of his amazing voice; he begged God to bestow his blessings upon each member of the parole board, upon their offspring and forebears, to bring them wealth, happiness, fame, and everlasting salvation, and to fill their hearts with mercy. He quoted passage after passage of what he thought was scripture. Never before had he prayed so earnestly.

But it was his voice which gained him his freedom. It touched those gentlemen's emotions like a live wire on raw nerves. They summarily dismissed him, signed him up for an immediate parole, and went out to give vent to their emotional urges which his voice had inspired in them, one by getting disgustingly drunk, another by going to bed with a harlot, while the third raced his high-powered automobile over hundreds of miles of highway at a dizzy speed.

The world was prosperous when Smith was dumped into it. Jobs were plentiful and easy to get, but he continued to preach as he had done in prison. "Ah looked up in de sky an' Ah saw uh message up dare writ in burnin' flame—Go *preach the gospel*," he informed his congregations. But it is unlikely that God sent Smith a written message.

He carried his pulpit about in his hand and set it upon street corners and wrestled with the sin of the world as ardently as if he, himself, had been forever sinless. From somewhere he acquired a moldy Prince Albert coat which had faded to a puking green and which hung to the tops of his run-over shoes. Supplementing this with an incredibly filthy stiff-bosomed shirt and a wing collar minus a tie he formed a picturesque sight, standing on his soapbox somewhere in the heart of the red-light district, bedecked in all his jewelry which he had brought out of prison, exhorting the hideously painted street crones and consumptive gamblers to change their ways. "Laff," he would shout at them. "Go 'head an' laff, laff yo' fool haids off, but w'en de panic cum an' de Lawd tek yo' food an' yo' clothes an' de rooves off'n yo' haids, den laff, laff den, you grinnin' fools!"

Perhaps he suspected as little as they that this prophecy could come true. It sounded to him like everything else which he had heard from the Bible which seemed always to be foretelling some catastrophe to come, and so he said it.

When curious passers-by asked him his name he replied that it was "Fathah."

During the days he did odd jobs to eke out a living—flunkying around sporting houses, cleaning up gambling dives, doing day labor, anything which an "illiterate nigger" could get to do. At night he preached. Every night.

He took to the road after a time, gandy-dancing on a section gang. He preached every chance he got. The name of Fathah stuck to him. He never admitted of any other.

During this time, the only mentionable inclination which he showed in sex was a preference for light-complected teen-age girls at whom he would ogle and leer when the opportunity presented itself. But girls found him indescribably repulsive and never ventured near enough to him to arouse his savage lust, nor did he approach them, for his urges were violent and uncontrollable and he had a cripple's sensitiveness about being repulsed. When women involuntarily drew away from him it filled him with such a fury that the veins turned red in his eyes and the arteries swelled in his neck and his muscles roped and corded. It required all his superhuman strength to restrain from clutching them with his powerful hands and venting his lust against their will, but he always did restrain himself. His ten years in prison helped.

Vanity, oddly, was the strongest force in his character, and rather than admit, even to himself, that women found him repulsive he forswore all sexual relationship as a tenet of his religion and imagined himself something on the order of a priest.

Once when taking a short cut across country to where his section gang was camped he accidentally stumbled upon one of his fellow hands raping a country maiden. In the ardor of his recently attained self-abnegation an insensate rage shook him and he slew the man with his bare hands as punishment for such brutal sin.

He had to run away to preserve his liberty, but his conscience did not trouble him. He told himself that God had inspired his act and thereafter he became obsessed with the belief that he was the instrument of God. Inspired by this newly discovered righteousness, he convinced himself that all manner of sex life, even that in the state of matrimony, was sinful, and he crusaded violently and tirelessly against it.

Luckily in the southern state where he committed this murder a dead section-hand nigger wasn't worth the trouble of an investigation, for he would surely have been apprehended before he got out of the state.

A month later, hiking down dusty country roads and riding slow freights, he arrived in a northeastern city. The panic which he had prophesied was on hand and already soup lines had come into existence. He had saved about a thousand dollars from his wages as a gandy-dancer and for one hundred and fifty dollars he leased a storefront church in the heart of the slums and poverty and had a red-lettered sign painted across its boarded front: I GUARANTEE TO MAKE YOU SHOUT. Old planks supported by boxes served as pews.

He opened wide the doors one Sunday night and began preaching to the empty benches. His powerful voice could be heard outside and up and down the street for half a block in each direction. Soon the hungry prostitutes and the hungry bums and the hungry men and women who were neither prostitutes nor bums but just people without jobs, attracted by the sound of his voice, drifted inside and took seats.

He preached to them, he gave them "gravy," he gave them consolation, he threw pictures of a burning hell at them, then painted visions of a heaven with golden streets and platters of fried chicken for them. But they did not shout. He bellowed at them and sang to them and bounced up and down on his huge, splayed feet, shaking his arms above his head so that his swallow-tailed coat spread out behind him like a bird about to take wing, and sweat glistened in the corrugations of his bald head and ran down his black face in rivulets and saturated his dingy stiff-bosomed shirt and wilted his starched wing collar to a rag. But still they did not shout.

"Why doesn't yuh shout?" he asked them. "Why doesn't yuh git happy an' praise de Lawd? Doesn' yawl know who Ah is?" And then his voice thundered at them like the boom of surf: "Ah is God! Ah is de Lawd! Praise be! Glory! Hallelujah! Git happy! Git de sperit in yo' souls!" And when he ran out of words he just threw back his head and bellowed: OwwwWWWWWWWAAAAAA!" And when he got back his breath he repeated, "Git happy! Ah is God! Ah is cum tuh make you happy! Ah has uh message fo' yawl! Ah is cum straight frum heaven!" He had worked himself into a state where he did not know what he was saying, trying to make them shout.

A half-drunk harlot, her black face rouged to a brilliant purple and dusted with flour-white powder, sitting in the front row, looked up and said defiantly, "Ef'n yo' is God, den gimme somp'n tuh eat. Ah ain' et uh bite dis day an' mah belly feels lak mah throat wus cut."

Then everybody took it up, all those hungry, Depression-hit people. "Yes, ef'n yo' is God, den feed us."

He stood stock-still in his pulpit while sweat ran down his wet black face and his cheap gold teeth gleamed between slack lips. "Ah is God," he kept mumbling over and over to himself as if he was very surprised to find it out. "Ah is God an' mah chilluns is hongry." Minutes passed, one minute, two minutes. His congregation kept grumbling. Three minutes. Emotions dropped over his face like picture slides. Four minutes. Then he lifted his voice so that the very timbers of the church shivered: "Ah is God an' Ah gwina go out in de street an' turn de cobblestones tuh po'k chops."

He got down off the pulpit and walked with erect carriage toward the door, looking neither to the right nor to the left, and his long arms hung down his sides like an ape's and his swallow-tailed coat dragged on the floor. His wet black face, set like a sleepwalker's, turned obliquely up toward the dusty rafters and the holes in the roof where the stars shone through, contained a look not of this earth.

When his congregation wanted to follow him outside and witness this miracle of turning cobblestones into pork chops he pushed them back and locked the door.

Later, when he returned with a two-wheel cart, such as junk dealers sometimes employ, loaded with fried pork chops and loaves of bread, gravy and potatoes, a huge can of coffee, a tray of knives and forks, stacks of plates and cups, he was just in time to keep his impatient congregation from battering down the door.

"Has yawl no faith?" he lashed at them with a two-edged voice. "Has yawl no faith in God?"

They drew away from him in awe. He rolled his cart down to his pulpit through a thick silence, those black hungry people rolling white eyes in his wake. He made them come and kneel before his pulpit and receive his blessings. He gave each of them a heaping plate and a scalding cup of coffee and they took time out to eat.

Then he collected the dirty dishes and began preaching again with his inexhaustible energy. "OwwwWWWWAaaa! OwwwWW-

WWAaaa! W'en yawl had money, yawl had frien's fur miles 'round. Now ain' dat so, chillun, ain' dat so?"

"Dass so, dass so," they chanted, a slight bodily motion moving into them as they began to catch the spirit.

"But w'en yawl got broke an' hongry, yawl ain' had but one single frien' in all dis town. Now who dat frien', chillun, who dat frien'?"

"Dass God, dass God," they chanted, bouncing up and down in their seats.

Then Fathah turned on the heat, he let his voice roll out like peals of thunder: "Ah is God! Follow me, mah chilluns, an' Ah shall lead yawl outta de land uf starvation into uh evahlastin' paradise uf po'k chops." Here he stopped and pointed a grotesque finger at them. "Whut is yawl jes been eatin'?" he asked them.

"Po'k chops!" they shouted, jumping from bench to bench. "Po'k chops!"

"Is yo' bellies full?" he asked in tones as gentle as the fall of spring rain on budding heaven.

"Our bellies is full!" they cried, hugging each other and laughing.

"Is yawl happy?"

"We is happy!" they shouted, joyishly intoxicated, drunk from the sound of his voice. A feeling of well-being pervaded them, their hunger seemed far in the past. Sweat ran down their faces, glistening on the black shiny faces of working people out of work, ditch-diggers and cooks and maids and foundry hands who could no longer find employment, streaking the powdered faces of harlots who could not find "Johns" and bums who could not find suckers. Tears ran down their eyes and mixed with their sweat.

With the skill of a seasoned performer Fathah chose this opportune moment to thunder at them in tones which allowed of no denial, "Who is Ah?"

"Yuh is God! Yuh is God!"

Fathah reared back on his run-down heels and let his voice roll out in a sonorous, compelling bellow. "Dare gwina be plattahs uf chicken an' pans uf steamin' brown biscuits ri' outen de oven. Dare gwina be food fuh mah chillun an' sheltah. Dare gwina be clean beds wid white sheets on dem. Dare gwina be clothes fuh mah chillun an' sheltah. Dare gwina be clean beds wid white sheets on dem. Dare gwina be clothes fuh mah chilluns' backs.

Dare gwina be plenty fur ev'body. Now ain' dat so?" he asked them. "Ain' dat so? Ain' mah chillun got faith?"

"He is God!" they shouted. "He is God!"

Didn't he turn the cobblestones of the very street into pork chops, and didn't they touch them with their hands and see them with their eyes and eat them with their mouths? Didn't Badeye Cora, who walked the street down in the lower end where it was dark, swear upon the name of her dead mother that she saw a whole section of the pavement gone when she returned that night to the hovel she shared with four other prostitutes; pavement which hadn't been gone that morning? Nor had there been any street workmen about, not that day nor any day in a long time. How were they to know that Fathah bought the pork chops from neighborhood restaurants? They didn't have any money to patronize restaurants.

Fathah found that it wasn't hard to make these hungry people believe that he was God when he fed them. They had been suddenly cast aloose from every security which they had known: tenements confiscated for taxes; pawnshops gone bankrupt; work which couldn't be got; banks, even, where there had been stacks and bushels and bales of money, which were closing. And poor Christ, crying on his cross like they were on theirs, couldn't help them none. They were starving and scared. Sure, they wanted salvation. But they didn't want to die to get it. Salvation was all right in its place. It was a mighty good thing. Sure, they wanted to go to heaven where the streets were paved in gold. Sure, they wanted their snow-white wings and their golden harps. That was all right when that final day came. But what they wanted then and there was something solid and edible to sustain them until that day did come. They wanted to believe in something tangible. When they prayed for food, they meant food for the belly, not food for the soul. They wanted a God who would put platters of pork chops down on the table before them, pork chops which they could see with their eyes and feel with their hands and eat with their mouths.

Fathah did just that. He kept his church doors open. Every single morning he appeared with a stack of bills. Every single morning he went out and bought food which he fed to the hungry. He never took up a collection. He never asked his congregation for a single penny. He said he changed old newspaper into money during the night so he could buy pork chops because if he kept on turning the pavement into pork chops there wouldn't be no place for the automobiles to run.

They believed him. They brought him batches of old newspaper to turn into money. Why shouldn't they have believed him? How else was he going to get so much money? Even the white folks didn't have that much money. The panic had hit everybody. Even Wall Street was closed up, so they had heard, and they didn't make no more money at Uncle Sam's mint. The white folks had lost their houses and their automobiles and had to fire their cooks and do their own cooking. How else could this black man who didn't do nothing else in the world but come there every day with a big stack of money and give away food get so much money if he didn't make it from old newspaper like he said? Crumpled one-dollar bills, stacked one on top of the other, looked like a whole lot of money to folks who were broke and hungry. Thus these black, hungry folks who flocked to his church and ate his free dinners of fried chicken and hot biscuits and succulent, greasy pork chops, these black, scared folks who lost their fear in the lull of his voice and reached their emotional peaks in its thunder reasoned.

Every single day Fathah fed his faithful children. Every single night they gave themselves up to their emotional gratitude and shouted until the street and the houses all about were filled with the sound of their voices, shouting: *"He is God!"* Every single night there were new converts.

It would have taken a man stronger than Fathah to have remained unconvinced of it himself. And so he came to believe sincerely that he was God. Then he began to establish the rules of his new, strange religion.

He had learned as a corn doctor in the penitentiary how easily were people managed when they were dependent on one for relief. He had learned that the man wanting a favor would do almost anything. So he created tenets which made his followers as near like himself as possible. He banned sex. He outlawed marriage. He separated men from their wives and children from their homes. He made them ugly. He prohibited the use of all cosmetics. He made them nameless. In the place of names he gave them appellations, such as: "Faithful" and "Angel" and "White Wings" and "Heaven Bird" and "Golden Harp." *"He created man in His*

Own Image." The possession of worldly goods was declared a sin. God had spoken. His herd must obey.

Had not he hit upon this brilliant stratagem his cult might have come to a rapid and dismal end, for his small bank roll was rapidly diminishing under the strain of feeding so many people. For all who came after the first hungry few were not destitute.

Some were working folk who still had jobs, folk who made eighty and ninety dollars monthly and saved out of that. They had never run number houses and seen a daily accumulation of nickels and dimes and quarters grow into millions with underworld mobs fighting like mad dogs for control. Some were wise folk, wise in the ways of the world, smart folk who couldn't be conned, clever folk hipped to every wrinkle in the racket; folk who had accumulated money by their wits and their skill and business acumen—who lost their smartness and cleverness and wisdom and wit and skill and acumen in the rush and roar and lull and sweep of Fathah's astounding voice, entwining them like creeping tentacles, engulfing them like treacherous quicksand, entrancing them like a beautiful symphony to make them fall down on their knees before him and raise their hands and their voices and shout, "*He is God!*" Wealthy people and working people. White people and black people. Awed and impressed by these hungry people's utter faith. "*He is God!*" Falling under the insidious spell of his voice, falling to their knees to sing his praise: "*He is God!*"

It was natural to believe the man; it was in his voice. So they gave their possessions to him to do with as he would: their salaries; their savings; their real estate; their jewelry and trinkets and all items of value, extra suits and dresses and coats and furniture; their nickels and dimes and quarters; everything which they possessed. They did not want worldly goods, the possession of which was sinful. "God" would look out for them forever. They had no worries.

And he fed them that needed feeding and clothed them that needed clothing. As his fame spread, his church grew. The old storefront was disbanded and headquarters established in a huge temple. A speaker system was installed to throw his powerful voice even farther. A radio carried it to the four corners of the world.

He grew a mustache, bought a dozen swallow-tailed coats and silk hats and a Rolls-Royce automobile to ride to and from his temple every day, and a blood-red airplane to fly over the world and look down upon his children, and five hundred rings with large bright stones, and dozens of bracelets and anklets and earrings of gold, to all of which the bills of sale were made out to the name of "God."

And that voice rolled on, like an irresistible flood, like an incoming tide, like the parade of years, like Wellington's army marching on its belly . . . "Ah is God! Do yawl heah me, chillun? Do yawl heah me? Ah gwina feeds mah chillun. Ah gwina clothe mah chillun. Ah gwina sheltah mah chillun. Ah gwina lead mah chillun outta de land uf Canaan intuh uh po'k chop paradise." And so he did. Hungry, shelterless, ragged people could ask for no more of any God. So they shouted afar: *"He is God!"* "Sister Lily of the Valley," and "Brother Snow on the Mountaintop."

He became a power in the community and his support was dickered for by big politicians. Smart people, intellectual people, great white people, doctors and lawyers and judges became interested in this amazing phenomenon of a man establishing himself as God. They pried into his affairs, trying to solve the equation which he presented to them, but with no avail. They investigated, seeking to find the source of his income. But all they found out was what his "sheep" told them, that he made crisp new money out of old newspapers. Fathah owned nothing, but God owns everything, his flock informed them.

Newspapers took up the hue and cry. They tricked Fathah into court on "test cases," trying to unveil the mystery which enshrouded him. But Fathah was cunning. Or perhaps he avoided revelation by his utter conviction that he was God.

His life was exemplary. He was himself the most staunch conformer to his tenets. He lived a stern and rigid life. He avoided all manner of vice. He could be seen any time of day or night. His life was an open book to his flock. And he remained as sexless as a rock.

It was by this unbending example which he made of himself that he kept his flock in hand.

And then he met a high-yellah gal, a three-quarter keltz, from down Harlem way, and she sent him to the dogs. Sent him to the dogs.

She came into his temple one summer night while he was preaching to his flock, her face made up like a burlesque strip queen, lips rouged scarlet and eyebrows circling half her forehead and her powdered cheeks painted crimson. Her fingernails looked like blood drops and she had mascara-rimmed blue eyes and black artificial lashes a half-inch long and platinum blond hair puffed up atop her head in an Afro plume. She was wearing a light yellow silk and wool turtleneck sweater which made her breasts look over-size on her small round body and a brown plaid skirt fitting tight about her hips. She had three cheap rings on her fingers and long green pendants hanging from her ears. Her shapely yellow legs were bare and her scarlet-painted toenails gleamed out from white sandals. She was half drunk and she pushed her way through the crowded aisles to get a better view of what was going on.

She made a startling contrast with those decorously gowned women with their scrubbed white and black faces shining with righteous sweat.

When Fathah caught sight of her his powerful voice faltered and shortly afterward he brought his sermon to a close and retired to his sanctum behind the pulpit. He sent "Sister Faithful" out among the congregation with orders to bring that "painted hussy" straight to him. Sister Faithful quaked from the wrath in his voice.

A few minutes later she led the woman into Fathah's sanctum and quickly departed, closing the door behind her.

"What you want, man?" the girl asked Fathah.

"Whuss yo' name?" he asked in a disarming voice.

"Cleo."

Then he leveled his grotesque, thrice-ringed finger at her and thundered, "Wipe dat paint frum yo' face!"

"Whaffaw?" she asked, unabashed.

He looked startled. After a long moment he asked her, "Does yawl know who Ah is?" There was a note of bewilderment in his voice.

"Naw, who is you?" she asked, taking a stick of gum from her pocket and unwrapping it, dropping the wrappers on the floor and sticking the gum in her mouth.

"Ah is God!" he pronounced in imperious accents.

She looked at him and chewed her gum. "Is you?" she asked at last. "You looks like a big black nigger to me."

His face contorted in a sudden spasm of emotion. Her remark had sparked, not anger, but a sudden uncontrollable lust in him. He asked her to go with him to his rooms. She contemptuously re-fused. He begged. He cajoled. She laughed at him. He got down on his knees before her. She leaned forward and let the tips of her breasts rub across the bald spot on his head then swirled quickly away from him and started out the door.

Fathah lost his head. Lost his head over a half-drunk chippy. He sprang at her like a wild beast, gibbering undistinguishable sounds and drooling slobber from the mouth. He threw her to the floor and assaulted her.

When he was ready to let go she threatened to have him arrested. His face turned a sick gray as realization of his act came to him. He offered her money to keep silent, then more money. She saw she had him in her power and bled him.

During the weeks that followed she made him buy her an expensive violet-colored sport phaeton and hire her a liveried chauffeur. She made him buy her thousands of dollars' worth of clothes and jewels and furs and rent her the finest apartment which she could find in all of Harlem.

He fell in love with her. He followed her around like a dog. He deserted his flock. She made him escort her into night clubs and bars where she publicly mocked him. She made him smoke pot and when he got jagged and shot through with blinding lust she put him out on the street.

His "chillun" soon discovered his perfidy. Word of it spread like grass fire among them. They lost their faith. Men took back their wives and women their husbands. Children returned to their homes. Then the people who had given up their possessions wanted them back.

They formed a committee to call on Fathah and demand the return of their property. Fathah would not see the committee, so they had him arrested for accepting money under false pretenses and sent him back to the penitentiary.

That yellow gal, Cleo, is on the town again. She's sold her car and pawned her jewels and she's often hungry.

There is a shortage of chops in paradise now.

LUNCHING AT THE RITZMORE

[1942]

If you have ever been to the beautiful city of Los Angeles, you will know that Pershing Square, a palm-shaded spot in the center of downtown, is the mecca of the motley. Here, a short walk up from "Skid Row," on the green-painted benches flanking the crisscrossed sidewalks, is haven for men of all races, all creeds, all nationalities, and of all stages of deterioration—drifters and hop-heads and tb's and beggars and bums and bindle-stiffs and big sisters, clipped and clippers, fraternizing with the tired business men from nearby offices, with students from various universities, with the strutting Filipinos, the sharp-cat Mexican youths in their ultra drapes, with the colored guys from out South Central way.

It is here the old men come to meditate in the warm midday sun, and watch the hustle and bustle of the passing younger world; here the job seekers with packed bags wait to be singled out for work; here the hunters relax and the hunted keep vigil. It is here you will find your man, for a game of pool, for a game of murder.

Along the Hill Street side buses going west line up one behind the other to take you out to Wilshire, to Beverly Hills, to Hollywood, to Santa Monica, to Westwood, to the Valley; and the red cars and the yellow cars fill the street with clatter and clang. On the Fifth Street side a pale pink skyscraper overlooks a lesser structure of aquamarine, southern California architecture on the pastel side; and along Sixth Street there are various shops and perhaps an office building which you would not notice unless you had business there.

But you would notice the Ritzmore, swankiest of West Coast hotels, standing in solid distinction along the Olive Street side, particularly if you were hungry in Pershing Square. You would watch footmen opening doors of limousines and doormen escorting patrons underneath the marquee across the width of sidewalk to the brass and mahogany doorway, and you would see hands of other doormen extended from within to hold wide the glass doors so that the patrons could make an unhampered entrance. And after that, if your views leaned a little to the Left, which they likely would if you were hungry in Pershing Square, you would spit on the sidewalk and resume your discussion, your boisterous and heated and surprisingly-often very well-versed discussion, on defense, or on the army, or the navy, or that "rat" Hitler, or "them Japs," or the F.B.I., or the "so and so" owners of Lockheed, or that (unprintable) Aimee Semple McPherson; on history and geography, on life and death; and you would just ignore the "fat sonsaguns" who entered the Ritzmore.

On this particular day, a discussion which had begun on the Soviet Union had developed into an argument on discrimination against Negroes, and a young University of Southern California student from Vermont stated flatly that he did not believe Negroes were discriminated against at all.

"If you would draw your conclusions from investigation instead of from agitation, you would find that most of the discrimination against Negroes exists only in communistic literature distributed by the Communist Party for organizational purposes," he went on. "As a matter of plain and simple fact, I have yet to visit a place where Negroes could not go. In fact, I think I've seen Negroes in every place I've ever been—hotels, theatres, concerts, operas . . ."

"Yass, and I bet they were working there, too," another young fellow, a drifter from Chicago, argued. "Listen, boy, I'm telling you, and I'm telling you straight, Negroes are out in this country. They can't get no work and they can't go nowhere, and that's a dirty shame for there're a lot of good Negroes, a lot of Negroes just as good as you and me."

Surveying the drifter from head to foot, his unshaven face, his shabby unpressed suit, his run-over, unpolished shoes, the student replied, "Frankly, that wouldn't make them any super race."

"Huh?"

"However, that is beside the point," the student continued, smiling. "The point is that most of what you term discrimination is simply a matter of taste, of personal likes and dislikes. For instance, if I don't like you, should I have to put up with your presence? No, why should I? But this agitation about Negroes being

discriminated against by the Army and Navy and defense industries and being refused service by hotels and restaurants is just so
much bosh."

"Are you kidding me, fellow?" the drifter asked suspiciously,
giving the student a sharp look, "Or are you just plain dumb? Say,
listen—" and then he spied a Negro at the edge of the group. "Say,
here's a colored fellow now; I suppose he knows whether he's being
discriminated against or not."

"Not necessarily," the student murmured.

Ignoring him, the drifter called, "Hey, mister, you mind settling
a little argument for us."

The Negro, a young brown-skinned fellow of medium build with
regular features and a small mustache, pushed to the center of
the group. He wore a pair of corduroy trousers and a slip-over
sweater with a sport shirt underneath.

"Say, mister, I been tryna tell this schoolboy—" the drifter began, but the Negro interrupted him, "I know, I heard you."

Turning to the student, he said, "I don't know whether you're
kidding or not, fellow, but it ain't no kidding matter with me.
Here I am, a mechanic, a good mechanic, and they're supposed to
be needing mechanics everywhere. But can I get a job—no! I gotta
stand down here and listen to guys like you make a joke out of it
while the government is crying for mechanics in defense."

"I'm not making a joke out of it," the student stated. "If what
you say is true, I'm truly sorry, mister; it's just hard for me to believe it."

"Listen, schoolboy," the drifter said, "I'll tell you what I'll do
with you; I'll just bet you a dollar this boy—this man—can't eat in
any of these restaurants downtown. I'll just bet you a dollar."

Now that a bet had been offered, the ten or twelve fellows
crowded about who had remained silent out of respect for the
Negro's feelings, egged it on, "All right, schoolboy, put up or shut
up!"

"Well, if it's all right with you, mister," the student addressed
the Negro, "I'll just take this young man up on that bet. But how
are we going to determine?"

They went into a huddle and after a moment decided to let the
Negro enter any restaurant of his choice, and if he should be refused service the student would pay off the bet and treat the three

of them to dinners on Central Avenue; but should he be served, the check would be on the drifter.

So the three of them, the student, the Negro, and the drifter, started down Hill Street in search of a restaurant. The ten or twelve others of the original group fell in behind, and shortly fellows in other groups about the square looked up and saw the procession, and thinking someone was giving away something somewhere, hurried to get in line. Before they had progressed half the length of the block, more than a hundred of the raggedy bums of Pershing Square were following them.

The pedestrians stopped to see what the commotion was all about, adding to the congestion; and then the motorists noticed and slowed their cars. Soon almost a thousand people had congregated on the sidewalk and a jam of alarming proportions had halted traffic for several blocks. In time the policeman at the corner of Sixth and Hill awakened, and becoming aware of the mob, rushed forth to investigate. When he saw the long procession from the square, he charged the three in front who seemed to be the leaders, and shouted,

"Starting a riot, eh! Communist rally, eh! Where do you think you're going?"

"We're going to lunch," the student replied congenially.

For an instant the policeman was startled out of his wits. "Lunch?" His face went slack and his mouth hung open. Then he got himself under control. "Lunch! What is this? I suppose all of you are going to lunch," he added sarcastically.

The student looked about at the crowd, then looked back. "I don't know," he confessed. "I'm only speaking for the three of us."

Shoving back among the others, the policeman snarled, "Now don't tell me that you're going to lunch, too?"

A big, raw-boned fellow in overalls spat a stream of tobacco juice on the grass, and replied, "That's right."

Red-faced and inarticulate, the policeman took off his hat and scratched his head. Never in the six years since he had been directing traffic at Sixth and Hill had he seen anyone leave Pershing Square for lunch. In fact, it had never occurred to him that they ate lunch. It sounded incredible. He wanted to do something. He felt that it was his duty to do something. But what? He was in a dilemma. He could not hinder them from going to lunch, if indeed they were going to lunch. Nor could he order them to move on, as they were already moving on. There was nothing for him to do but follow. So he fell in and followed.

The Negro, however, could not make up his mind. On Sixth Street, midway between Hill and Olive, he came to a halt. "Listen," he pointed out, "these guys are used to seeing colored people down here. All the domestic workers who work out in Hollywood and Beverly and all out there get off the U car and come down here and catch their buses. It ain't like if it was somewhere on the West Side where they ain't used to seeing them."

"What has that got to do with it?" the student asked.

"Naw, what I mean is this," he explained. "They're liable to serve me around here. And then you're going to think it's like that all over the city. And I know it ain't." Pausing for an instant, he added another point, "And besides, if I walk in there with you two guys, they're liable to serve me anyway. For all they know you guys might be some rich guys and I might be working for you; and if they refuse to serve me they might get in dutch with you. It ain't like some place in Hollywood where they wouldn't care."

When they had stopped, the procession behind them which by then reached around the corner down Hill Street had also stopped. This was the chance for which the policeman had been waiting. "Move on!" he shouted. "Don't block the sidewalk! What d'ya think this is?"

They all returned to the square and took up the argument where they had dropped it. Only now, it was just one big mob in the center of the square, waiting for the Negro to make up his mind.

"You see, he doesn't want to do it," the student was pointing out. "That proves my point. They won't go into these places, but yet they say they're being discriminated against."

Suddenly, the drifter was inspired. "All right, I'll tell you, let's go to the Ritzmore."

A hundred startled glances leveled on him, then lifted to the face of the brick and granite edifice across the street which seemed impregnated in rock-like respectability. The very audacity of the suggestion appealed to them. "That's the place, let's go there," they chimed.

"That's nonsense," the student snapped angrily. "He can't eat at the Ritzmore; he's not dressed correctly."

"Can *you* eat there?" the Negro challenged. "I mean just as you're dressed."

The student was also clad in a sweater and trousers, although his were of a better quality and in better condition than the Negro's. For a moment he considered the question, then replied, "To be fair, I don't know whether they would serve me or not. They might in the grill—"

"In the main dining room?" the drifter pressed.

Shaking his head, the student stated, "I really don't know, but if they will serve any of us they will serve him."

"Come on," the drifter barked, taking the Negro by the arm, and they set forth for the Ritzmore, followed by every man in Pershing Square—the bindle stiffs and the beggars and the bums and the big sisters, the clipped and the clippers, the old men who liked to sit in the midday sun and meditate.

Seeing them on the move again, the policeman hastened from his post to follow.

They crossed Olive Street, a ragged procession of gaunt, unshaven, unwashed humanity, led by two young white men and one young Negro, passed the two doormen, who, seeing the policeman among them, thought they were all being taken to the clink. They approached the brass and mahogany doorway unchallenged, pushed open the glass doors, and entered the classical splendor of the Ritzmore's main lounge.

Imagine the consternation among the well-bred, superbly clad, highly-heeled patrons; imagine the indignity of the room clerk as he pounded on his bell and yelled frantically, "Front! Front! Front!" Had the furniture been animate, it would have fled in terror; and the fine Oriental rugs would have been humiliated unendurably.

Outraged, the house officer rushed to halt this smelly mob, but seeing among them the policeman, who by now had lost all capacity for speech, stood with his mouth gaped open, wondering if perhaps it wasn't just the effects of that last brandy he had enjoyed in "217," after all. Stupidly, he reached out his hand to touch them to make certain they were real.

But before he could get his reflexes together, those in front had strolled past him and entered the main dining room, while, what seemed to him like thousands of others, pushed in from the street.

The student and the Negro and the drifter, along with ten or twelve others, took seats at three vacant tables. In unison the diners turned one horrified stare in their direction, and arose in post-haste, only to be blocked at the doorway by a shoving mass of men, struggling for a ringside view.

From all over the dining room the waiters ran stumbling toward the rear, and went into a quick, alarmed huddle, turning every now and then to stare at the group and then going into another huddle. The head waiter rushed from the kitchen and joined the huddle; and then the *maitre de hotel* appeared and took his place. One by one the cooks, the first cook and the second cook and the third cook and the fourth cook on down to what seemed like the twenty-fourth cook (although some of them must have been dishwashers), stuck their heads through the pantry doorway and stared for a moment and then retired.

Finally, two waiters timidly advanced toward the tables and took their orders. Menus were passed about. "You order first," the student said to the Negro. However, as the menus were composed mostly of French words, the Negro could not identify anything but apple pie. So he ordered apple pie.

"I'll take apple pie, too," the student said; and the drifter muttered, "Make mine the same."

Every one ordered apple pie.

One of the fellows standing in the doorway called back to those in the lobby who could not see,

"They served him."

"Did they serve him?"

"Yeah, they served him."

"What did they serve him?"

"Apple pie."

And it was thus proved by the gentlemen of Pershing Square that no discrimination exists in the beautiful city of Los Angeles. However, it so happened that the drifter was without funds, and the student found himself in the peculiar situation of having to pay off a bet which he had won.

They sat in the front room of a tiny cottage located on a side street off Central Avenue—three Communists; one a Negro, the others white.

The Negro, Calvin Scott, a tall, dark young man in his middle twenties, built along Henry Fonda lines, sat hunched forward on the green davenport facing the others; talking; weaving a spell of emotionalism with all the ardor of a thinning evangelist: "He doesn't hate you, Andy; it's not you he hates." His feet were toed tensely in the cheap rug as those of a sprinter waiting for the starting gun; and the concave curve of his body seemed taut to the snapping point. Turning to the woman, he repeated the words: "He doesn't hate you, either, Carol; it's not you he hates." Now his voice, timbred with a quality of raw intensity, encompassed them both: "You're his friends; you see him almost every day; you buy him steaks and come here and cook them for him. You've danced with him, and teased him, and gone out with him. He *knows* you're his friends. But when he got that letter, all of a sudden there were two sides and there was an awful gap, an awful wall in between you—one side was black and the other side was white. He was on one side and you were on the other. And all of a sudden, he hates everybody on that other side—that white side. He can't help it; he can't keep from."

In the spill of light from the lamp on the window ledge, his dark face, topped by its mat of unkempt, kinky hair, contained an expression unearthly in its power to demonstrate his suffering, as if, at some point in his twenty-five years, his social-conscious protestations of hurt had leapt the bounds of amateur sincerity and had indeed become a thing of skill, of even professionalism, in the perfect symmetry of its tears.

"He can't help it. He doesn't want to hate you; but he can't help it," he continued, becoming overwhelmed, it seemed, by his own heartbreaking performance, so that now genuine raw emotion overflowed from the fill of his voice and tears streamed from his eyes, and his suffering, too great for his body and soul to contain, went out from him into the room to be absorbed by the other two, intensifying and swelling and bloating their self-conscious sympathy and intellectual misery into a queer mixture of over-powering, tear-washed, vocal, physical, sensual agony and straight-slashing, geometrical exacerbation, causing the white man to cry out against his will, "Oh, Cal, don't!"

Andy Kyser, unlike Cal who was born in Harlem and educated at City College, had been born in Georgia and raised and edu-cated in Los Angeles; and ofttimes his saccharine sympathy for blacks, sexual in its development, which had led him, despite his heritage of condescension and the jeopardy to his own good job with the state welfare, to join in the Communist movement, was not sufficient to withstand Cal's onslaughts, which, to his reac-tionary background, were contrary both to precedent and logic. But these flashes of rebellion against the cause were only momen-tary, creating their aftermaths of shame which clogged him with a feeling of self-betrayal and inspired him to impulses of rashness.

Now, sitting well forward in his chair, his slight form grotesque in a position of uncomfortableness as if he sought a kindredship of misery; tortured by an emotional hurt which slowly, under Cal's crying, pleading insistence, had become physical in its intensity; his finely chiseled features, topped by a thatch of blond hair, quiv-ering between impulse and restraint; his hands clasping and un-clasping in his lap—he wanted by some word or act, unequivocally, once and for all, to align himself openly and aboveboard with the progressive movement; to embrace all races and creeds in one great sensuous, onrushing surge toward the revolution which would make them for all time equal and brothers and a whole, economically, socially, spiritually. But the cold sense of reason whispered, "What could you, one insignificant person, do, aside from destroying your-self, which would not only make you unfit for the cause, but of no good to yourself . . ." Finally, lamely, he begged, "Let me go in and talk to him, Cal."

Cal shook his head. "It wouldn't do any good, Andy. He doesn't hate you. He's just hurt; he's hurt deep inside. He'd only do like he did before." He raised his arms, hunching his body into a greater concavity, shrinking away as from an object of horror, in demonstrative pantomime. "He'd only draw up and shrink away from you. He'd say, 'Hello, Andy,' but there wouldn't be any feeling in his voice. It ain't that he hates *you*, Andy. He just can't find any words for you. You're on the other side of that gap; on the other side of that wall. You're white—can't you see? White people hurt him and he hates them." Tears came into Andy's eyes and flowed down his face as he suffered vicariously, the whole great crucifixion of black skin in white America.

Silent until now, the white girl, sitting on the rust-colored chair across from him, her stockinged feet drawn up beneath her, whispered pleadingly, "I can talk to him, Cal. I've got to talk to him."

"Honestly, it wouldn't do any good, Carol," Cal said, the edges of his voice lacerated by the manifestation of his emotion. Spreading his hands, he said again, "He doesn't hate you. That's what you've got to deal with; that's what you've got to understand. It's not you as an individual he hates; it's that great white world beyond the gap, on the other side of the wall. He—"

The girl sprang to her feet in a sudden outburst of pent-up torture; her hands flew ceilingward in a gesture of unbearable frustration. "My God, I love him!" she cried in a high soprano voice. "I love him as much as my brother! I love him more than I do my own brother! Why can't I talk to him?"

She might have been the personification of peasant motherhood, but for her face, as delicately sculptured as a fine old cameo, now luminous with a quality of suffering which, unlike both Cal's and Andy's, was neither repetitious nor negative, but positive in its honesty and dauntless in its courage.

The daughter of a successful businessman, she was primarily suited, both physically and emotionally, for motherhood; but somewhere along the road to maturity a love of people had sidetracked her into a fervor of self-sacrifice for the masses. She had flung herself recklessly into the movement, giving all that she had, associating with blacks in their most intimate lives as if to prove by self-demonstration that the black would not rub off; and was exalted in her zeal. It was as if, in the place of her own children, she would mother the entire black race; or if not that, give birth from her own deep love to an entire new social order.

Now when she spoke, her voice was no longer the white-hot flame that it had been before, but a feminine thing, begging of a man a favor: "Let me go in and talk to him, Cal. I love that kid."

And because of it, Cal hesitated before he replied, for he was not certain that his feelings for this girl were wholly encompassed in the ideology which they advocated, or that before hurting her, he would not hurt all the others. He looked beyond her, into the bedroom, where the person of whom they were speaking, James "Sonny" Wilson, a black youth of about twenty with a smooth, brown, unsmiling face and a heavy mop of hair, sat at a tiny table in a cone of light and stolidly studied an art lesson.

Although Sonny had heard every word which had been spoken, and was aware that the three of them had now turned to look at him, he did not glance up nor give any sign that he had heard. In his face, molded in pleasant, almost babyish lines, was a bitterness not contained in the faces of the three.

It was the bitterness in Sonny's face, a terrible thing in one so young, against which he wished to shield the girl, feeling that she, being white, would never understand, but would be inspired by it to greater acts of sacrifice that he desired she make, which finally decided Cal. "You can't help him, Carol," he said. "I can't help him either. Andy can't help him. No one can help him—not by talking to him. He's hurt deep inside. So what? So we got a job to do. And he's got a job to do. He's got to get over it by himself. He's got to be tough. He had to be hurt. He had to learn it sooner or later. He came all the way across the country from New York State to learn it. But he could have stayed in New York and learned that he was black. And now he'll have to learn to be tough."

Instilled in the raw intensity of his voice was a depressing quality, something of the feeling of an admission of handicap. It lingered in the room, this quality, like a tangible force, breaking into reluctant futility the glowing ardor of self-immolation which had flamed in Carol, garroting with sadistic glee Andy's fine sympathy for the underdog.

"He's going to write a letter to the President," Cal continued. "I could help him write it. He's written a copy already and it's childish and confused. I could help him write it. But I'm not. That wouldn't help him. He's hurt. So he's got to be tough. He's got to write the President by himself. He's got to fight this dirty discrimination. He's got to learn to fight. It's his generation, Andy, you've got to look to. It's him. I could help him write it. But he's not my problem. He's not my problem, Andy." Here he paused and pointed dramatically at the white man. "He's your problem, Andy." He shook his head and two tears trickled down his black, lit face. "Not mine, Andy—*yours*."

Again a protest burst involuntarily from Andy's reactionary background: "What do you want me to do, Cal? I can't make him white." And quickly he added, "I'll throw some bombs if that will help. I'll bomb the shop if you think that will get him a job. By God, I'll start the revolution if you think—"

"That's not what you're to do, Andy," Cal replied; and suddenly, as if his words had released them from the spell of emotionalism, both Andy and Carol became intellectual again, and Carol said, "No, that's not the way, Andy. We're dealing with a nation; and to solve the problem of one Negro is to solve the problem of the entire Negro nation—*but I get so mad* . . ."

"Listen," Cal said. "For three months Sonny studied at night preparing for those tests. For three months he studied at the N.Y.A. defense school. During that time he worked all day and went to school at night. He never got enough sleep for one day during those three months. He lost weight. Several times I started to make him quit. I couldn't promise him a job; all I could do was tell him when he could take the test. I didn't want to take the responsibility. I wanted to make him stop. But I didn't. He had to learn, see. He had to learn for himself. I could no more tell him to stop than I could encourage him to go on. For three months he studied night and day. And then he took the tests. He passed." Pausing, he said, "Today he received a letter from the plant. It stated that his application had been considered and that they could not give him any encouragement of employment by that aircraft company now or at any time in the future." He raised his gaze to look at the youth in the other room. "And now his heart is broken."

"What reason did they give?" Andy asked, struggling to keep the conversation rational, although he knew the question would fall in the room with the plop of inanity.

Cal spread his hands: "You know, Andy."

"Before the war the letters used to state that they employed only white," Carol remarked.

"He's not my problem, Andy," Cal said in that too raw voice. "He's not my problem. None of it's my problem. I'm black. Sure.

But I can make it. I can revert. I can go raggedy and sit in the park. Somebody will have to take care of me. I can walk down the street and whistle. I can stop in front of a joint where the juke-box's playing and cut a step of off-time boogie and listen to the white folks say, 'Look at that nigger dance.' Before I'd work for what some of these black men have to work for, that's what I'd do. I'd walk the streets and sit in the parks and let the country go to hell. I'd knock on back doors in Hollywood and Beverly Hills and beg white women for a handout. Listen, I can make it. Cal can make it. It's not my problem, Andy. It's yours."

"I know that," Andy admitted. "I know it is. And I'm not trying to shirk it. But what must I do? Sometimes I want to chuck up my job and get a gang of col— er Negro men and picket these plants."

"That's not the way," Carol said. "It's education for the masses that's needed first. It's to break down the prejudices."

"There's that gap, Andy," Cal said. "There's that gap between the races. In the South they've filled up a lot of it. Starvation did it. The black sharecropper said to the white sharecropper, 'Look, buddy, what are we fighting each other for, we're both starving; let's get together and fight the *man*.' Out here it's different. Look— Sunday you went out swimming. You went down to Manhattan Beach. You took Sonny along. You brought him a swimming suit . . .

"You know how that beach is—reactionary as Texas. The white people stared. But nobody said anything. That's the difference. He came back saying, 'I sure did have a good time, Cal. You know, Andy and Carol are sure swell.' "

It was a pleasant thought and for a moment they all relaxed quietly in a satisfying feeling of progress, of accomplishment. But Andy's intellectual insistence for the truth could not desert him for long. As if against his will he pointed out, "But in aircraft it's different."

In the exhaustion of their emotions a sudden surge of futility overwhelmed them, and they withdrew into themselves, each troubled with private thoughts. Then Carol got up and refilled their glasses with wine.

The revolution had never seemed so far away.

HEAVEN HAS CHANGED

[1943]

A Negro soldier heard the order to charge and with his company hurled himself against the enemy and was shot and killed. The next thing he knew he was in a hot, fertile country, walking down a dusty road between two fields of blossoming cotton stretching to the horizons.

He walked and wiped his brow and looked from side to side and saw thousands of Negro men, women, and children picking cotton and singing a spiritual. They sang loudly and defiantly and even a little rebelliously.

He walked on through the dust, listening to the chorus of loud, defiant, rebellious voices, and he came to a funeral procession. A casket was being carried to church in an old, rickety wagon, and a score or so of very old and gray-haired Negro men and women were following it, their new shoes kicking up the dust. They were singing also, but a different spiritual, one more resigned, less defiant: *"Swing low sweet chariot, comin' for to carry me home . . ."*

The soldier stopped and asked one of them who was dead, and was told, "Po Uncle Tom is dead."

The workers in the field had also seen the funeral procession and when the soldier passed they called to him and asked, "Who's dead?" and he told them, "Po Uncle Tom is dead."

They asked, "You kill 'im?"

He said, "Naw, I din kill 'im. Guess his time just come."

They stopped working and began shouting and singing and dancing and they yelled back and forth to each other, "Uncle Tom is dead! Uncle Tom is dead!"

A tall, thin, sour-faced, white man, the only white man whom the soldier had seen, came to them and asked what was the trouble that they have stopped work to dance and sing.

They told him, "Mistah Crow, Uncle Tom is dead." And they

asked permission to attend the funeral, because Mistah Crow is the "Little Boss Man" and they can't go anywhere unless Mistah Crow lets them.

But Mr. Crow said they couldn't go. "What you wanna go to Tom's funeral for?" he asked them. "You never did like him."

They told Mr. Crow they wanted to go so they could shout; and when Mr. Crow asked them what they wanted to shout about, one big, strapping, young fellow said, "Ain't this heav'n; ain't we s'posed to shout all over God's heaven?"

Mr. Crow ordered them back to work, but the big, strapping fellow argued that he ought to be allowed to go because he was Uncle Tom's son.

But Mr. Crow still said no. There was nothing Mr. Crow liked better than to say no.

Uncle Tom's son turned to the others and said, "Les go anyhow. Ain't we all Uncle Tom's chillun?"

So they threw down their sacks and started off to the funeral.

But when they got to the church they were barred at the door by a huge monster, neither man nor beast, who was bound in iron and held a big club in each hand.

"Soldier, you can enter," said the monster, but the others he pushed away.

"But Mistah Tradition, we are Uncle Tom's chillun," contended Uncle Tom's son.

"You can't shout at a funeral," declared Tradition adamantly. "It just ain't being done."

So Uncle Tom's children stood outside and shouted.

Inside the church, the soldier sat and listened to the service, every now and then wiping away the blood from his wounds.

The Little God preached the sermon. He was not little in stature, only in importance. In stature he was immense with a big body and a huge belly and a bristling, iron-gray beard. His voice was a rolling, booming, pleading, crying, shouting, fantastic thing which inspired the elderly people sitting in the church to jump and shout, "Amen! Glory to the Lawd! Halleluah!" He was black.

However, the Big God who lived over across the fields where the tall spires of white marble castles arose was white. In stature, He was little.

The Little God praised the virtues of Uncle Tom. He said Uncle Tom had been a good servant and the Big God had been pleased with him. He lamented the fact that Uncle Tom's children were not like their father; and he condemned their sinfulness in shouting at their father's funeral. He threatened to report them to the Big God.

Outside, Uncle Tom's children listened with expressions of trepidation. If he told the Big God on them, no telling what would happen, 'cause the Big God's people were a wild and vicious people who fought each other and killed each other and were never content to be peaceful and happy. They did not want any trouble with the Big God's people.

So after Uncle Tom was buried, Uncle Tom's son went among the children and tried to persuade them to elect a new god.

"We want a young god," he told them. "One who will protect and guide us and won't always be running to the Big God to have us chastised."

But Uncle Tom's children were scared and cautious and said that God would strike them dead long before they could elect a new god.

Uncle Tom's son became angry and disgusted and denounced them as cowards and sheep and disclaimed them and said he would have no more to do with them; and he cast his eyes at maidens in an effort to forget.

He saw a beautiful, lucious lass with breasts like smoky mountains and eyes like ripe muscadines and he fell in love with her and he walked with her in the cool of the evening and picked cotton in the row next to hers and slyly helped her fill her bag and when it was too heavy he carried it for her.

The Little God noticed and berated him for his sin.

"How can it be sinful to love when the Bible says to love?" Uncle Tom's son asked.

"The Bible mean to love thy neighbor," the Little God said.

"Well, ain't she my neighbor?" Uncle Tom's son argued.

But the Little God threatened to punish him if he persisted.

Uncle Tom's son became sullen and defiant and did not reply and that night he slipped out with the lass and they whistled a boogie beat in the woods and danced to their own music. But the Little God had followed them and spied upon them and he ran up to them and turned the maiden into grass and walked upon it. Uncle Tom's son raised his hand as if to strike the Little God, and the Little God became frightened and walked away with as much dignity as he could command. And Uncle Tom's son ran back to his cabin and drew up a petition, asking for an election of a new god.

The petition was passed around at night and read by candle light and signed with crude pens; and secret meetings were held. Finally, when enough signatures had been secured, Uncle Tom's son presented the petition to Mr. Crow.

But Mr. Crow said no; he refused to hold an election. "Whoever heard of Uncle Tom's children voting?"

The next day at work Uncle Tom's son told the children what Mr. Crow had said; and he told them, "Old Jim Crow has got to go!"

Back and forth they whispered to one another, "Old Jim Crow has got to go!"

Led by Uncle Tom's son, they threw down their sacks and rebelled and organized a great procession and marched toward the big manor house where the Big God lived. And they shouted, "OLD JIM CROW HAS GOT TO GO!"

The Big God came out to meet them and He asked them what was the trouble; and they told Him they wanted to hold an election for a god, but that Jim Crow wouldn't let them.

The Big God asked them to give Him a few days to think it over and in the meantime ordered them back to work.

In the meantime the Little God heard of their rebellion and he went to the Big God and said, "Ain't I been a good god? Ain't I kept the people from rebelling all these years? You can't get rid of me now, just because they rebelled one time."

But the Big God said, "I don't know; now take dying, if you die one time you're dead forever. You gods have got to have the confidence of the people or they'll get a new god and I won't even know nothing about it. And that might cause all kind of trouble here in heaven, because if I ain't got a god out there working for me, I can't stay here two minutes."

So He decided to let them hold their election. But He told them He couldn't let old Jim Crow go.

"Things would seem mighty strange around here without old Jim Crow," He ruminated.

The people held a big meeting to determine who to run against the Little God. There were many people in heaven who were not

Uncle Tom's children; but were his other relatives; brothers, sisters, cousins, and in-laws; and these, along with a few of Uncle Tom's children wished to retain the incumbent Little God. So they withdrew from the meeting and held another meeting of their own; and they called themselves the "Old" and the others called themselves the "New".

At their meeting, the New nominated Uncle Tom's son to run against the incumbent Little God. Uncle Tom's son began his campaign by promising first of all to get rid of old Jim Crow if he was elected a god. And besides which, he promised to ask the Big God for forty acres and a tractor and a home for everybody; and above all the right for everybody to pursue happiness.

Dancers and singers campaigned for him and a big dance was held for the young jitterbugs. But during the dance, the Little God entered and threatened to call down fire and brimstone upon their heads.

"There'll be no jitterbugging in heaven as long as I'm a god," he said.

They stopped because he was a god.

And then he began his campaign by cautioning the people against trying to force reforms. He told them they must be patient and wait and the good things would come to them. He told them that he also wanted his worshippers to own property and enjoy happiness and that he had been trying to get old Jim Crow to go for three-quarters of a century; but that violence and rebellion were not the ways of the Lord, and he has been waiting for old Jim Crow to just get up and go of his own accord some day.

The New were piqued because the Little God had forbidden them to dance and they sought him out and argued that there was no more sin in swinging it and jitterbugging than there was in singing the spirituals. And to prove it, they offered to hold a contest between swing and the spirituals to see which made the people happiest.

Uncle Tom's son suggested that they hold the contest instead of the election; and they could settle both issues with one vote.

The Little God consented, and for several days both sides prepared for the contest.

The contest was finally held, and the swing bands came out first and blew themselves dizzy and the beating of the drums was like drumbeating never heard on land or sea; and the jitterbugs went into delirium and jumped like grasshoppers with seven-league boots (man, you shoulda seen them cats). When they had passed out from sheer exhaustion, the choirs took the stage and began singing the fine old spirituals with an enthusiasm hard to imagine and the listeners became ecstatic and their gazes became transfixed and their lips began to move and they began to sing with the choirs with so much joy and abundance they could be heard all over heaven; and the Big God, busy at His work, stopped for a moment to listen.

When the vote was held, the spirituals won. But there were many among the New who were not satisfied with the result and claimed that the Old had stuffed the ballot box.

The dispute became so violent that the Big God was called upon to arbitrate; and He came among them and spoke to them. He told them that He had Little Gods for all of the people on earth and in heaven and that He was sorry they seemed dissatisfied with their Little God. He had been wondering for some time just what He ought to do about it, He said.

Then He talked to the Little God; and He told him that times had changed and that in order to be a good god, a god had to change with the times—that only gods who could keep up with the demands of their worshippers could remain gods.

Therefore, He proposed a plan. He would retain the Little God because the Little God, being old, was wise in the ways of men, and wisdom was needed. But He would appoint Uncle Tom's son the Little God's assistant, because Uncle Tom's son was young and spirited and courageous, and courage was also needed. In that way the young could balance the old and the old the young, and that would help everybody to be happy.

Now, happiness and joy reign in heaven. Old Jim Crow is gone to hell where he belongs. And the people dance and sing. They sing spirituals and the swing bands blow their toppers and the young folks jitterbug and no one thinks it is sinful anymore. And the maiden whom the Little God turned into grass has been made into a maiden once more. Peace grows and flourishes on the peoples' forty acres and they harvest it with their new tractors and sweep their homes with new brooms and dress their children in pretty clothes.

Well, it happens that one night the soldier returns to earth and he sees the soldiers in his regiment preparing to advance into battle. They are glum and morose and when he tries to cheer them up, telling them to be brave and fight valiantly and not to be afraid of death because dying ain't nothing, they say to him that they are not afraid to die but that they do not want to go to heaven because from all they have heard of it, it must be really a drag.

But the soldier tells them, "You guys don't know nothing, heaven has changed."

We was at the Creole Breakfast Club knockin' ourselves out when this icky, George Brown, butts in. Ain't nobody called him and I hardly knew the man, just seen him four or five times 'round the poolroom where I works. He takes a seat at our table and grabs my glass of licker and asts, "Is you mad at anybody?"

I was getting mad but I didn't tell him. "Me?" I laughed, tryna be a good fellow. "Only at the man wanna put me in the army."

The bugler caught a spot for a riff in "Don't Cry Baby" and blew my ear off. All down the time the cats latched on, shoulders rocked, heads bobbed, the joint jumped. My queen 'gan bouncin' out her twelve-dollar dress.

George waited for the bugler to blow out of breath. "Thass what I mean. You ain't mad at nobody, yet you gotta go to war. Thass 'cause you's a fool."

I didn't mind the man drinkin' my licker so much, nor even him callin' me a fool. But when I see my queen, Beulah, give him the eye and then get prissy as a sissy, I figured I better get him gone. 'Cause this George Brown was strictly an icky, drape-shaped in a fine brown zoot with a pancho conk slicker'n mine. So I said, "State yo' plan, Charlie Chan—then scram!"

"Don't rush me, don't rush me," he said. "You needs me, I don't need you. If'n you was to die tomorrow wouldn't mean nothing to me. Pour me some mo' of that licker."

He come on so fast I done took out my half-pint bottle and poured him a shot under the table 'fore I knew what I was doin'. Then I got mad. "This ain't no river, man," I said.

"Thass what I mean," he said. "Here you is strainin' yo'self to keep up a front. You works in the poolroom all day and you makes 'bout ten bucks. Then comes night and you takes out yo' queen. You pays two bucks to get in this joint, fo' bucks for a half-pint grog, two bucks for a coke setup. If'n you get anything to eat you got to fight the man 'bout the bill. For ten bucks a day you drinkin' yo'self in the grave on cheap licker—"

"You calls fo' bucks a half pint cheap?" I snarled.

He kept drivin' like he didn't hear me. "Then what happen. They put you in 1-A and say you gotta fight. You don't wanna fight 'cause you ain't mad at nobody—not even at the man what charge you fo' bucks for a half-pint grog. Ain't got sense 'nough to be mad. So what does you do?"

"What does I do?" I just looked at that icky.

"Well, what *does* you do?" That's my queen talkin'. She's a strictly fine queen, fine as wine. Slender, tender, and tall. But she ain't got brain the first.

"I does what everybody else do," I gritted. "I gets ready an' go."

"Thass what I mean," George Brown said. "Thass 'cause you's a fool. I know guys makin' twice as much as you is, workin' half as hard. And does they have to fight? They is deferred 'cause what they doin' means more to Uncle Sam than them in there fightin'."

"Well, tell High C 'bout it." That's my queen again. "I sho' don't want him to go to no war. And he may's well be makin' more money. Li'l 'nough he's makin' in that poolroom."

That's a queen for you; just last week she was talkin' 'bout how rich us was gettin'.

"Money! Make so much money he can't count it," he said to her. They done left me outen it altogether; I'se just the man what gonna make the money. "W'y in less than no time at all this cat can come back an' drape yo' fine shape in silver foxes and buy you a Packard Clipper to drive up and down the avenue. All he gotta do is go up to Bakersfield and pick a li'l cotton—"

I jumped up. "What's your story, morning glory? Me pickin' cotton. I ain't never seen no cotton, don't know what cotton is—"

"All he got to do," he went on talkin' to my queen, "to knock down his double sawbuck is pick a coupla thousand pounds. After that the day is his own."

"Why come he got to stop in the middle of the day?" my queen ast. "Who do he think he is, Rockefeller or somebody?"

"Thass what I been tryna tell you," George said. "He don't. He keep right on an' pick 'nother ton. Make forty flags. And does you have to worry 'bout him goin' to the army? You can go to bed ev'y night and dream 'bout them silver foxes."

I had to get them people straight and get 'em straightened fast. "Yo' mouth may drool, fool, and yo' gums may flop, pop—" but my queen cut me off.

"Listen to the man!" she shouts. "Don't you want me to have no silver foxes?"

"Ain't like what he thinks," he said. "Lotta hustlers up there. Cats say they's goin' east—slip up there and make them layers; show up in a Clipper. Cats here all wonder where they got their scratch." He turned to me. "I bet you bin wonderin'—"

"Not me!" I said. "All I'se wonderin' is how come you pick on me? I ain't that man. 'Fore I pick anybody's cotton I'll—"

So there I was the next mornin' waitin' for the bus to take me up to Bakersfield. Done give this icky twenty-five bucks to get me the job and all I got is a slip of paper with his name on it I'm supposed to give to the man when I get there. My queen done took what scratch I had left sayin' I wouldn't need nothin' 'cause George said everything I could want would be given to me for nothin'. All I had was the four bits she let me keep.

By then it had me too. Done gone money mad as her. At first I was thinkin' in the C's; knock seven or eight hundred then jump down. But by the time I got to Bakersfield I was way up in the G's; I seen myself with pockets full of thousand-dollar bills.

After knockin' the natives cold in my forty-inch frock and my cream-colored drapes I looked 'round for the cat George said gonna meet me. Here come a big Uncle Tomish lookin' cat in starched overalls astin' me is I "High C."

"What you wanna know for, is you the police?" I came back at him.

"Dey calls me Poke Chops," he said. "I'se de cook at de plantation. I come tuh pick y'all up."

"Well bless my soul if you ain't Mr. Cotton Boll," I chirped, givin' him the paper George gimme. Then I ast him, "Is that you parked across the street?"

He looked at the green Lincoln Zephyr and then he looked back at me. "Dass me on dis side," he mumbled, pointin' at a battered Model A Ford truck.

Well now, that made me mad, them sendin' that jalopy for me. But I was so high off'n them dreams I let it pass. I could take my twenty G's and buy me a Sherman tank to ride in if'n I wanted;

warn't like I just had to ride in that jalopy. So I climb in beside old Chops and he driv off.

After we'd gone along a ways he come astin' me, "'Bout how much ken y'all pick, shawty?"

"Don't worry 'bout me, Chops," I told him. "I'll knock out my coupla thousand all ricky. Then if'n I ain't too tired I'll knock out a deuce mo'."

"Coupla thousand." He turned in his seat and looked at me. "Dass uh tun."

"Well now, take yo' diploma," I said.

"Wun't tek us long tuh whup de enemy at dat rate," was all he said.

'Bout an hour later we pulled in at a shanty. I got out and went inside. On both sides there were rows of bunks and in the middle a big long wooden trestle table with benches. Looked like a prison camp where I done six months. I was mad now sure 'nough. "I ain't gonna stay in this dump," I snarled.

"Whatcha gunna do den?" he wanted to know. "Build yo'self a house?"

I'da cut out right then and there but the loot had me. I'm a hip-cat from way back and I don't get so mad I don't know how I'm gettin' down. If'n them other hustlers could put up with it, so could I. So when old Chops gimme a bunk down in the corner I didn't want him to know I was mad. I flipped my last half buck at him. "Take good care of me, Chops," I said.

He didn't bat an eye; he caught the half and stashed it. "Yassuh," he said.

At sundown the pickers came in, threw their sacks on their bunks, and made for the table. If there was any hustlers there, they musta been some mighty hard hustlers 'cause them was some rugged-looking stiffs. Them stiffs talked loud as Count Basie's brass and walked hard as Old Man Mose. By the time I got to the table wasn't nothin' left but one lone po'k chop bone.

Then when us got through eatin' here comes Chops from the kitchen. "Folkses, I wants y'all tuh meet High C. High C is a pool shark. He pick uh tun uh cotton ev'y day. Den if'n he ain't tahd he pick unother'n."

I got up and give 'em the old prize fighter shake. But them stiffs just froze. I never seen nothin' like it. Ain't nobody said nothin', not one word.

That night Bayou Dad and Uncle Toliver come down to my bunk. "Whar'd y'all evah pick cotton befor', son?" Bayou Dad ast me.

"Don't start me to lyin', you'll have me cryin'," I said. "I done picked all over. From 'Bama to Maine."

Uncle Toliver puffed at his pipe. "Dat Maine cotton is uh killer as de younguns say."

"You ain't just sayin' it," I said.

Somebody shook me in the middle of the night and I thought the joint was on fire and jumped up and run outside. By the time I find they was gettin' up for breakfast all the breakfast was gone but a spoon of grits. And the next thing I know there we is out in a cotton patch blacker'n me.

"What's this, a blackout?" I wanted to know.

But warn't nobody sayin' nothin' that early in the day. Big stiff on the right of me called Thousand Pound Red. 'Nother'n on the left called Long Row Willie. Stiffs shaped up like Jack Johnson. I hitched up the strap over my shoulder like I seen them do and threw the long tail out behind me.

"Well, we're off said the rabbit to the snails," I chirped jolly-like, rollin' up the bottoms of my drapes.

An' I warn't lyin' neither. When I looked up them two stiffs was gone. Let me tell you, them stiffs was grabbin' that cotton so fast you couldn't see the motion of their arms. I looked 'round and seen all the other stiffs in the patch watchin' me.

"W'y these stiffs call theyselves racin'," I said to myself. "W'y I'll pick these stiffs blind deaf and cripple."

I hauled off and started workin' my arms and grabbed at the first cotton I saw. Somp'n jumped out and bit me on the finger and I jumped six feet. Thought sure I was snakebit. When I found out it was just the sharp joint of the cotton boll I felt like a plugged slug. Next time I snuck up on it, got aholt, and heaved. Didn't stop fallin' 'til I was in the next row. Then I got mad. I 'gan grabbin' that cotton with both hands.

In 'bout an hour looked like I'd been in the rain. Hands ain't never been so bruised, look like every boll musta bit 'em. When I tried to straighten up my straightener wouldn't work. I looked at my bag. The mouth was full but when I shook it the cotton disappeared. Then I thought 'bout the money; forty bucks a day, maybe fifty since I'd done begun in the middle of the night. Money'll make a man eat kine pepper. I started off again.

By the time I got halfway through my row I couldn't hear nobody. I raised my neck and skinned my glims. Warn't nobody in the whole patch but a man at the end of my row. Thought the rest of them stiffs musta gone for water so I 'cided to hurry up and finish my row while they was gone and be ahead of 'em.

I'd gone ten yards through the weeds pickin' thistledown from dried weeds 'fore it come to me I was at the end of my row.

"Whew!" I blew and wiped the sweat out my eyes. An' then I saw the walkin' boss. "Howma doin', poppa," I crowed. "Didn't quit when them other stiffs did; thought I'd knock out my row 'fore I went for a drink."

"You did?" He sounded kinda funny but I didn't think nothin' of it.

"That's my story, Mister Glory; never get my Clipper stoppin' every few minutes for a drink." I shifted my weight and got groovy. "I ain't like a lotta stiffs what swear they won't hit a lick at a snake then slip up here and cop this slave sayin' they goin' east an' come back all lush. I don't care who knows I'm slavin' long as I get my proper layers. Now take when this icky, George Brown, sprung this jive; I got a piece of slave in a poolroom and figure I'm settin' solid—"

"This ain't no poolroom and the others ain't gone for no water," the man cut in. "They finished out their rows and went over the hump."

"Well, run into me!" I said. "Finished!" But I couldn't see how them stiffs got finished that quick. "Maybe they didn't have as much to pick as me," I pointed out.

The man stood there looking at me and not sayin' a mumblin' word. Made me nervous just standin' there. I picked up my sack and sorta sashayed off. "Which way they go, man?"

"Come back here, you!" he yelled.

"All right, I can hear you, man," I muttered.

"Take a look at that row." He pointed at the row I'd just finished.

I looked. It was white as rice. "Well look at that jive!" I said. "What's that stuff, man?"

"It's cotton," he said. "You know what cotton is, don't you? You heard of it somewhere, ain't you?"

I stepped over and looked down the other rows. They were bare as Mama Hubbard's cubbard. I came back and looked at my row again. "Say, man, where did all that cotton come from?" I wanted to know.

"It grew," he said.

"You mean since I picked it? You kiddin', man?"

He didn't say nothin'.

"Well then, how come it grew on my row and didn't grow nowhere else?" I pressed him.

He leaned toward me and put his chops in my face, then he bellowed, "Pick it! You hear me, pick it! Don't stand there looking at me, you—you grasshopper! Pick it! And pick every boll!"

I got out that man's way. "Well all root," I said quickly. "You don't have to do no Joe Louis."

That's where I learned 'bout cotton; I found out what it was all 'bout, you hear me. I shook them stalks down like the FBI shakin' down a slacker. I beat them bolls to a solid pulp. As I dragged that heavy sack I thought, Lord, this cotton must weigh a ton—a halfa ton anyway. But when I looked at the sack didn't look like nothin' was in it. Just a li'l ol' knot at the bottom. Lord, cotton sure is heavy, I thought.

Then it come to me all of a sudden I must be blowin' my lid. Here I is gettin' paid by the pound and beefin' 'cause the stuff is heavy. The more it weigh the more I earn. Couldn't get too heavy. I knowed I'd done picked a thousand pounds if'n I'd picked a ounce. At that rate I could pick at least four thousand 'fore sundown. Maybe five! Fifty flags in the bag! "Club Alabam, here to you I scram," I rhymed just to pass the time. Them cotton bolls turned into gin fizzes.

At the end of the row I straightened up and looked into the eyes of the man. "Fifty flags a day would be solid kicks, please believe me," I said. "I could knock me that Clipper and live on Central Avenue." I sat down on my thousand pounds of cotton and relaxed. "There I was last Friday, just dropped a trey of balls to Thirty No-count, and it seemed like I could smell salty pork fryin'. Man, it sure smelt good."

"Turn around," the man said.

I screwed 'round, thinkin' he was gonna tell me what a good job I done.

"Look down that row."

I looked. That was some row. Beat as Mussolini. Limp as Joe Limpy. Leaves stripped from stalks. Stalks tromped into the ground. The ground tromped 'round and 'round. And just as many bolls of cotton as when I first got started. I got mad then sure 'nough. "Lookahere, man," I snarled. "You goin' 'long behind me fillin' up them bolls?"

The man rubbed his hand over his face. He pulled a weed and bit off the root. Then he blew on the button of his sleeve and polished it on his shirt. He laughed like a crazy man. "Ice cream and fried salt pork shore would taste good ridin' down Central Avenue in a Clipper. Look, shorty, it's noon. Twelve o'clock. F' stay? Ice cream—" He shook himself. "Listen, go weigh in and go eat. Eat all the fried ice cream and salty clippers you can stand. Then come back and pick this row clean if it takes you all week."

"Well all root, man," I said. "Don't get on your elbows."

I dragged my sack to the scales. Them other stiffs stopped to watch. I waved at them, then threw my sack on the scales. I stood back. "What does she scan, Charlie Chan?"

"Fifty-five!" the weigher called.

"Fifty-five," I said. "Don't gimme no jive." I started toward the shanty walkin' on air. Fifty-five smackeroos and the day just half gone. Then I heard somebody laugh. I stopped, batted my eyes. I wheeled 'round. "Fifty-five!" I shouted. "Fifty-five what?"

"Pounds," the weigher said.

I started to assault the man. But first I jumped for the scale. "Lemme see this thing," I snarled.

The weigher got out my way. I weighed the cotton myself. It weighed fifty-five pounds. I swallowed. I went over and sat down. It was all I could do to keep from cryin'. Central Avenue had never seemed so far away. Right then and there I got suspicious of that icky, George Brown. Then I got mad at my queen. I couldn't wait to get back to L.A. to tell her what a lain she was. I could see my queen on this George Brown. My queen ain't so bright but when she gets mad look out.

When them stiffs went in for dinner I found the man and said, "I'm quittin'."

"Quit then," he said.

"I is," I said. "Gimme my pay."

"You ain't got none coming," he said.

I couldn't whip the man, he was big as Turkey Thompson. An'

I couldn't cut him 'cause I didn't have no knife. So I found Poke Chops and said, "I wanna send a tellygraph to my queen in L.A."

"Go 'head an' send it den," he said.

"I want you to go in town an' send it for me," I said.

He said, "Yassuh. Cost you two bucks."

"I ain't got no scratch," I pointed out. "That's what I wanna get."

" 'Tis?" he said. "Dass too bad."

All I could do was go back and look them bolls in the face. At sundown I staggered in, beat as down-home steak. I didn't even argue with the weigher when he weighed my thirty-five pounds. Then I got left for scoff. Old Chops yelled, "Cum 'n' get it!" and nine stiffs run right over me.

After supper I was gonna wash my face but when I seen my conk was ruint and my hair was standin' on end like burnt grass I just fell in the bed. There I lay wringin' and twistin'. Dreamt I was jitterbuggin' with a cotton boll. But that boll was some ickeroo 'cause it was doin' some steps I ain't never seen and I'm a 'gator from way back.

Next day I found myself with a row twixt two old men. Been demoted. But I figured surely I could beat them old stiffs. One was a-moanin': "*Cotton is tall, cotton is shawt, Lawd, Lawd, cotton is tall, cotton is shawt . . . How y'all comin' dare, son? . . . Lawd, Lawd, cotton is tall, cotton is shawt . . .*" The other'n a-wailin': "*Ah'm gonna pick heah, pick heah a few days longah, 'n' den go home. Lawd, Lawd, 'n' den go home . . .*"

Singin' them down-home songs. I knew I could beat them old stiffs. But pretty soon they left me. When I come to the end of my row and seen the man I just turned 'round and started back. Warn't no need 'f argyin'.

All next day I picked twixt them ancient stiffs. An' they left me at the post. I caught myself singin': "*Cotton is tall, cotton is shawt*" an' when I seen the man at the end of my row I changed to: "*Cotton is where it ain't.*"

That night I got a letter from my fine queen in L.A. I felt just like hollerin' like a mountain Jack. Here I is wringin' an' twistin' like a solid fool, I told myself, an' I got a fine queen waitin' for me to come back to her ever-lovin' heart. A good soft slave in the pool-room. An' some scratch stashed away. What is I got to worry 'bout?

Then I read the letter.

Dear High C daddy mine:

I know you is up there making all that money and aint hardly thinkin none about poor little me I bet but just the same I is your sweet little sugar pie and you better not forget to mail me your check Saturday. But dont you think I is jealous cause I aint. I hates a jealous woman worsen anything I know of. You just go head and have fun and I will go head and have mine.

I promised him I wouldnt say nothing to you bout him but he just stay on my mind. Didnt you think he was awful sweet the way he thought bout me wanting some silver foxes. Mr Brown I mean. And it was so nice of him getting you that fine job where you can improve your health and keep out the army at the same time. And then you can make all that money.

He been awful nice to me since you been gone. I just dont know rightly how to thank him. He been taking care of everything for you so nice. He wont let me worry none at all bout you being away up there mong all those fine fellows and me being here all by my lonely self. He say you must be gained five pounds already cause you getting plenty fresh air and exercise and is eating and sleeping regular. He say I the one what need taking care of (aint he cute). He been taking me out to keep me from getting so lonesome and when I get after him bout spening all his time with me he say dont I to worry none cause youd want me to have a little fun too (smile). Here he come now so I wont take up no more of your time.

I know this will be a happy surprise hearing from me this way when I dont even write to my own folks in Texas.

xxxxxxxxxxxxxxxxxxxxxxxx *them is kisses*
Your everloving sugar pie

Beulah

P.S. Georgie say for me to send you his love (smile) and to tell you not to make all the money. Save him some.

There I was splittin' my sides, rollin' on the ground, laffin' myself to death. I'se so happy. Havin' my fun. Makin' plenty money, just too much money. With tears in my eyes as big as dill pickles. I couldn't hardly wait to get my pay. Just wait 'til I roll into L.A. an' tell her how much fun I been havin'.

Then come Sat-day night. There we was all gathered in the shanty and the man callin' names. When he call mine everybody got quiet but I didn't think nothin' of it. I went up and said, "Well, that's a good deal. Just press the flesh with the cash."

But the man give my money to old Chops an' Chops start to figurin'. "Now lemme see, y'all owes me thirteen dollars. Uh dollah fuh haulin' yuh from de depo'. Nine dollahs fuh board countin' suppah. Three dollahs fuh sleepin'." He counted the money. He counted it again. "Is dis all dat boy is earned?" he ast the man.

The man said, "That's all."

"Does y'all mean tuh say dat dis wut y'all give George Brown twenty-five dollahs fuh sending up heah fuh help?"

The man rubbed his chin. "We got to take the bad ones with the good ones. George has sent us some mighty good boys."

My eyes bucked out like skinned bananas. Sellin' me like a slave! Slicin' me off both ends. Wait 'til my queen hears 'bout this, I thought. Then I yelled at Chops, "Gimme my scratch. I gotta throat to cut!"

Chops put his fists on his hips and looked at me. "Wut is y'all reachin' fuh?" he ast. "Now jes tell me, wut is y'all reachin' fuh?"

"Lookahere, man—" I began.

But he cut me off. "Whar is mah nine dollahs? All y'all is got heah is three dollahs 'n' ninety-nine cents."

"Say, don't play no games, Jessie James," I snarled. "If'n I ain't got no more dough 'n that—"

But 'fore I could get through he'd done grabbed me by the pants an' heaved me out the door. "An' doan y'all come back 'till y'all git mah nine dollahs t'gethah," he shouted.

I knew right then and there is where I shoulda fit. But a man with all on his mind what I had on mine just don't feel like fightin'. All he feels like doin' is layin' down an' grievin'. But he gotta have someplace to lay and all I got is the hard cold ground.

A old stiff took pity on me and give me some writin' paper an' I writ my queen an' he say he take it to church with him next day and get the preacher to mail it. That night and the next I slept on the ground. Some other old stiffs brung me some grub from the table or I'da starved.

Come Monday I found myself 'mongst the old queens an' the chillun. They men work in the mill and they pick a li'l now an' then. I know I'da beat them six-year-olds if'n I hadn't got so stiffened sleepin' on the ground. But I couldn't even stand up straight no more. I had to crawl down the row an' tree the cotton like a cotton dog. I was beat, please believe me. But I warn't worried none. I'd got word to my queen an' looked any minute to get a money tellygraph.

'Stead I got a letter come Wednesday. Couldn't hardly wait to open it.

> High C:
> I is as mad as mad can be. I been setting here waiting for your check and all I get is a letter from somebody signing your name and writing in your handwriting to send them some money and talking all bad bout that nice man Mr Brown. You better tell those hustlers up there that I aint nobodys lain.
> Georgie say he cant understand it you must of got paid Saturday. If you think I is the kind of girl you can hold out on you better get your thinking cap on cause aint no man going to hold out on this fine queen.
>
> > Your mad sugar pie
> >
> > Beulah
>
> P.S. Georgie bought a Clipper yesterday. We been driving up and down the Avenue. I been hoping you hurry up and come on home and buy me one just like hisn.

"Lord, what is I done?" I moaned. "If'n I done sompn I don't know of please forgive me, Lord. I'd forgive you if you was in my shape."

The first thing I did was found that old stiff and got some more writin' paper. I had to get that queen straight.

> Dear Sugar pie:
> You doesn understand. I aint made dollar the first. Cotton aint what you think. Ifn you got any cotton dresses burn them. I is stranded without funds. Does you understand that? Aint got one white quarter not even a blip. That was me writing in my handwriting. George Brown is a lowdown dog. I is cold and hungry. Aint got no place to stay. When I get back

I going to carve out his heart. Ifn you ever loved your ever-
loving papa send me ten bucks (dollars) by tellygraph.
Lots of love and kisses. I can hardly wait.

Your stranded papa

High C

Come Friday I ain't got no tellygraph. Come Sat-day I ain't got none neither. The man say I earned five dollars an' eighty-three cents an' Chops kept that. Come Sunday, Monday, Tuesday, Wednesday, I ain't got word one.

I is desperate, so help me. I said to myself, I gotta beat this rap, more ways to skin a cat than grabbling to his tail. So I got to thinkin'.

At night after everybody weighed in an' the weigher left, lots of them stiffs went back to the field and picked some more cotton so they'd have a head start next day. They kept it in their bags overnight. But them stiffs slept on them bags for pillows.

Well I figured a stiff what done picked all day an' then pick half the night just got to sleep sound. So Thursday night I slipped into the shanty after everybody gone to sleep an' stole them stiffs' cotton. Warn't hard. I just lifted their heads, tuk out their bags an' emptied 'em into mine an' put the empty bags back. Next day at noon I weighed in three hundred pounds.

Ain't got no word that night. But I got sompn else. When I slipped into the shanty an' lifted one of them stiffs' head he rolled over an' grabbed me. Them other stiffs jumped up and I got the worse beatin' I ever got.

Come Sat'day I couldn't walk atall. Old Chops taken pity on me an' let me come back on my bunk. There I lay a-moanin' an' a-groanin' when the letter come. It was a big fat letter an' I figured it sure must be filled with one-dollar bills. But when I opened it all dropped out was 'nother letter. I didn't look at it then, I read hers'n first.

High C:
I believe now its been you writing me all these funny letters
in your handwriting. So thats the kind of a fellow you turned
out to be. Aint man enough to come out in the open. Got to
make out like you broke. You the kind of a man let a little

*money go to his head. But that dont worry me none cause
I done put you down first.*

*Me and George Brown is getting married. He bought me
a fur coat yesterday. Aint no silver foxes but it bettern you
done and it cost $79.99. So you just hang onto your little
money and see ifn you can find another queen as fine as me.*

Your used to be sugar pie

Beulah

*P.S. Here is your induction papers come to your room while
you been gone. I hope the army likes you bettern I does.*

That's how I got back to L.A. The man bought me a ticket when
he seen the army wanted me. But I warn't the same cat what left
tryna dodge the draft. Done lost my queen, lost my soft slave, and
the man done got me. Now why they start all this cutting and
shooting in the first place, you tell me. 'Cause I ain't mad at them
people. They ain't done nothing to me. Who I is mad at is just
cotton. That old mother, cotton, is gonna kill me yet.

FOUR ESSAYS WRITTEN
DURING THE SECOND
WORLD WAR

NOW IS THE TIME!
HERE IS THE PLACE!

[1942]

Let it first be stated that the character of this writer is vulnerable, open to attack, easy to be smeared; that the strength of this writer is questionable, his person inconsequential, insignificant; that the name of this writer will soon be forgotten. But this is not the voice of this writer; he is only an instrument.

This is the voice of Negro heroes, dead on American fronts throughout all American history; the voice of Negro martyrs, dead, hung from American trees; the voice of the centuries of Negro oppression in the unmarked graves of Negro slaves who prayed to God for freedom from birth to death; the voice of the centuries of contained waiting, repressed hoping, stained with the tears of bitterness that saw death before light; the voice that comes out of a bruised and beaten past, out of a confused and shadowed present, an obscure future—like a clarion it comes, loud, clear, positive; if you are a Negro American, you cannot fail to hear this voice: *Now, in the year 1942, is the time; here, in the United States of America, is the place for 13,000,000 Negro Americans to make their fight for freedom in the land in which they were born and where they will die. Now is the time and here is the place to engage and overcome our most persistent enemies: Our native American fascists.*

At this time, we 13,000,000 Negro Americans are united with all Americans of all races, colors, and creeds, and with their allies, the Chinese Republic, the Soviet Union, the white ruler races of the British Empire, and other nations, races, and groups which comprise the United Nations, in a war to defeat and destroy nazism, fascism, and imperialism originating in Germany, Italy, and Japan. The governments of the United Nations are at full realization that the axis ideology, as embodied in nazism, is the most dangerous and destructive force ever to be pitted against the freedom of mankind throughout the history of the world.

Upon the face of abstract logic, it would seem that each of the nations of the United Nations is fighting primarily for *status quo* —to retain its interpretation of freedom as embodied in its statutes and administered by its government, the boundaries of its domain, and the resources thereof. It would seem that we, of the United States of America, are fighting for continuation of our form of democracy and our right to administer it as we see fit.

It is bitter knowledge that in the more than a century and a half of its existence, the government of the United States and its ruler races have not seen fit to liberate the American Negro from his contemptuous inferior position, nor to any comparable degree grant him his heritage of equal participation in government and equal benefit from national resources. The voice of the Negro American crying for justice has been ignored, and the footprints of the Negro American in our national history have been disclaimed. We, whose ancestors were on this continent, helping in the development of its great wealth, in the molding of its great government, before the ancestors of ninety percent of all other inhabitants; we, descendants of human beings who fought in every battle, bled in every river, labored and lived and died from end to end, from top to bottom, of this great nation, have not yet, in this more than a century and one-half, enjoyed even a fair semblance of the rights and privileges, the opportunities, "Life, Liberty and the pursuit of happiness," which they so valiantly aided in winning.

Shall the *status quo* remain unchanged? Shall this, then, be the outcome of this present war? If so, upon the face of abstract logic, the Negro American will be the loser in this war in any event. But we cannot form our judgments or formulate our aims from abstract logic, which will prove that all people lose in all wars. We must concern ourselves with the character of this war.

And what is this character—that by which an historical movement is known?

The leaders of the governments of the United Nations are giving us assurances that the character, the intrinsic nature, the full meaning, the very soul of this fight is for the freedom of all the peoples of all the world. Is there any question of this?

Within this nation, 13,000,000 Negro Americans are the vital, imperative question which must be answered to all minority groups, all subject races, the world over. For we must know, all minority groups and subject races, whether freedom exists in phrases, assurances, promises, or in the actual state of living twenty-four hours each day? Whether, within a nation, a race can live Jim Crow, and the nation be free? Whether, within an empire, can be contained ruler and subject races, ruler and subject nations, and the character of freedom exist?

These questions must be answered. *Now,* while the assurances are being given, while all our aims are the same, *is the time;* and *here,* where our destiny lies, where all of 13,000,000 Negro Americans were born, where all must live, and where all but those who fall on foreign battle fields fighting for a freedom which they never shared must die, where their children must be born, and their children's children, *is the place for us to open a second front for freedom.* This must be a contemporaneous, a concurrent effort, this fight of the Negro Americans for freedom at home; for is not this the very essence of the fight for freedom of all the peoples of all the world?

It is even realized by our native fascists, who would exclude us from everything but dying, that we must participate in the greater war without reservation. For if the United Nations are defeated, if the United States of America is conquered and her government destroyed, our fate is merciless slavery and eventual death.

No matter how we feel about it, no matter what emotional upheaval churns in our breasts, what protests gnaw at our minds, what abuses are heaped upon our persons, what degradations our spirits must wear for garments; no matter what denials, discriminations, ostracisms, contempt we must suffer; no matter the awful despair seeping into our souls, the oft-denied feeling of inferiority which in time comes to all oppressed—*we must enter full-bodied and wholehearted into this great war waged by the United Nations to stamp out nazism, fascism, and imperialism for all time to come.*

But how can we participate in this greater war without giving the same effort to our home fight against our native enemies? What pride will there be to urge us on? What ideal for which to fight? What love of country to inspire us with patriotic ardor? We know only too well that victory at home without victory abroad is impossible. But to us Negro Americans, is not victory abroad without victory at home a sham, empty, and with no meaning, leaving us no more free than before?

In the greater war, the world-wide fight for the freedom of all the peoples of all the world, we will be a small part of a great force; we will be with others and we will learn of the peoples' will, the great spiritual power of peoples united in a single cause, the magnificent inspiration of fraternal fellowship, of knowing we are not alone; and this will make us strong beyond all dreams, for people united are always strong.

Nor will we be less strong or more alone in our fight for freedom at home. From our government and its leaders, from the governments and leaders of all the United Nations, those who assure us that this is a fight for freedom, from every sincere, honest believer in the justice of law and the equality of man, will come encouragement, inspiration, concrete assistance. Can it be otherwise? Can a person own slaves and believe in freedom?

And even though it be otherwise; even though the assurances that this is a war for the freedom of all the peoples of all the world are lies conjured up to fire the people to fight a private war; even though all the people of all the world desert us. Even though we are denounced by the causists who are intolerant of causes other than their own, baited by the capitalists whose very existence depends on the disunity of the people, viciously, violently, underhandedly opposed by our powerful native fascists; even though we be lynched by mobs, murdered by law-enforcement officers, cursed and spat upon by those who by virtue of complexion claim superiority—*we will not be alone!*

For with us will be our millions dead who will march with us to victory. We will not be weak, nor frightened, nor despairing. Out of our past, the blood of our fathers and the tears of our mothers, out of the bootings and the lynchings and the jim-crowings, the grave of Odell Waller and the story of Bigger Thomas, out of all the martyred Negroes whose spirits have been crushed, whose souls have been tortured and ambitions humbled, dead, but yet living on, never dead in our memories, will come our strength, our courage, our motivation. Out of the years of bondage, discrimination, abuse, will come our determination; our fears will make us brave; and our shadows will light the way. *For we must win!* Not only for ourselves, our souls, our beliefs in democracy and the equality of mankind, not only so that we, ourselves, may be free in a world which may be free; but for the freedom of all generations born black, for the posterity of all minorities of all races, creeds, and nationalities the world over.

If you have never been enslaved, mentally, spiritually, in ambitions, dreams, and desires; if you have never lived Jim Crow, you might not understand. We Negro Americans do not have a choice. We have to win on *both* fronts—and at the same time.

There is no question of the Negro Americans' loyalty. We are loyal by any standard of comparison—more, we are the standard of comparison of loyalty—to the government and the nation of the United States of America. Here, in the land of our fathers, we fight for what is ours. Democracy is the Negroes'. Is not the blood of Crispus Attucks, who fired the first shot and gave the first life for its creation inalienable proof of this? Did not the red blood of black soldiers which has colored every American battlefield win us this democracy? Was the blood of the American heroes of other races a different blood? Did they spill more of it? Did they all die twice?

Does not, also, the nation of the United States of America, in a comparable degree, belong to the Negro American by right of creation, by right of development, by right of occupation? Are not these the inalienable rights by which peoples claim nations? What question can there possibly be of the Negro Americans' loyalty? This is our native land, our country; our participation in the war effort is a fight for what is ours. Our fight at home is simply for the possession of it.

And yet, in this peculiar paradox which finds this nation of Negro Americans within this great nation of the United States of America forced into a fight for freedom at home so as to give meaning to its participation in the fight of the United Nations for the freedom of all the world, there are those who would say that this is disunity, subversive. Then freedom itself is subversive, and democracy disunity. And so why are we, of the United Nations, fighting at all. For freedom? Or to defeat Germany, Italy, and Japan? The Negro American must fight to win for either cause. But let us get it straight. What *are* we fighting for?

In the broader view, the Negro Americans' fight for freedom is more than racial. It is a fight for justice, for an ideal, for a form of government in which people will be bound together, neither by race, nor creed, nor descent, but by common objectives and aims for the benefit of all. It is a fight to preserve in living force the spirit of the Declaration of Independence; a fight for the effective administration of the rights, privileges, and regulations of the Constitution of the United States. No American of any race, true to the ideals of Americanism, can refuse to participate in the Negro Americans' fight and on their side, for that for which we fight is the only true Americanism—that of our founders and of our Constitution and of all our laws, rights, privileges, and guarantees of our form of government.

Who can deny that these laws, rights, privileges, and guarantees extend to Negro Americans? Was the Declaration of Independence intended as a precept of aryanism? Is the Constitution jim-crowed? Is freedom for white only? Have not the Negro Americans, by rights of the justice of our own national laws, a legitimate claim to share in this essence of community self-determination, which is the spirit of democratic government?

One of the unfortunate aspects of the Negro Americans' fight for freedom at home is the discovery that many organizations, humanitarian ideologists, and realistic political groups, Americans who have long been in the front ranks of the Negro Americans' slow march toward equality, are now deserting them, advocating that this fight be set aside until the greater fight for freedom is won. Only by so doing, they state, will it be possible to achieve the national unity necessary to win the war. But what a travesty it would be, that when the United Nations win their fight for the freedom of all the people of all the world, we 13,000,000 Negro Americans remain in virtual bondage.

Therefore, the question now presents itself: Can these persons believe that this war, waged by the United Nations against the Axis Nations, is a war for the freedom of the people? Or is it presumed by them that this present conflict is only the beginning of a world-wide social upheaval in which all the impurities of society will be purged and the world emerge in a new splendor of equality of mankind? The latter is a precept difficult of normal rationalization. With above average intelligence it may be understood and maintained. But the self-application required to imbue the average person with the ardor to fight to preserve and make strong a form of government which will never serve the purpose for which one fights, and as a consequence, after the victory for its continuance is attained, must be overthrown and replaced by another form of government—the utter acceptance of this line of progression—is well-nigh impossible for average intelligence.

There is no question concerning the reality of this precept—be it real or unreal. The question concerns the acceptance of the logic of the sameness of two apparently conflicting objectives. Not that the objectives are actually conflicting; nor that the logic is false. *Simply that at this time it is not the point.*

The point is the Negro Americans' fight for freedom and equality in this present structure of American Democracy.

So let us first fight to achieve this end, *now*, in the year 1942, while the leveling influences of common peril and common objectives are breaking down the walls of intolerance, race hatred, discrimination; *now*, while peoples of all races, creeds, and colors are uniting in equality of sacrifice and effort, uniting in pride and love and glory in an ideal; *now*, while the spirit of mankind is returning to the fount of eternal justice for the strength to fight and win, while the only understandable ideology is to be found in the purpose of all creation which placed men of all races, colors, and creeds together in common environment to work out a common destiny for the benefit of all. *Now*, while the determination of mankind's choice of life is in the stages of creation for generations to come; and *here*, in the United States of America, where for those generations, we 13,000,000 Negro Americans, and our children, and our children's children, must live.

I suppose you have been reading about the birth of the storm troopers in Los Angeles, the reincarnation, or rather I should say, the *continuation* of the vigilantes, the uniformed Klansmen; and all about the great battle which took place on Main street and points east wherein the combined forces of the United States navy, army, and marine corps, contacted and defeated a handful of youths with darker skins. Yes, we have now defeated the "zoot-suiters"; all we have to do now is to defeat Germany, Italy, and Japan; or rather Japan, Germany, and Italy; since Japan is the most formidable foe and therefore should come first in any listing of our enemies.

Perhaps you don't know what it is all about. If you are a Negro, you should know. But if you are one of those Negroes who profess not to know (and no doubt there are plenty of you), I will be only too happy to inform you.

I understand it was a white manufacturer who designed the zoot suit and projected it upon an unsuspecting public. However that may be, all honest historians will record the fact that white American youths were first seen wearing them. As with all other aspects of our native culture, Negroes were soon to imitate; and since we, as a people, possess vivid imagination, the true artist's soul, and a penchant for personal adornment, we improved the zoot suit to its present sartorial splendor. When this mania reached the west coast, Mexican youths took it and went.

Pachuo is a Mexican expression which originally meant "bandit" but has degenerated by usage into a description of a juvenile delinquent, a species of youth common in America in all races. In Mexican districts in the county of Los Angeles, small bands of pachuos have organized into gangs to fight each other, to take each other's girl friends, to steal automobile parts and loot fruit stores, or just to have a gang. We Americans should understand this; we are strictly a gang-minded people. However, we are a little more deadly in our gangs; we lynch Negroes, rob banks, kidnap babies, extort merchants, beat strikers, etc.

Negro youths in Los Angeles county are not organized into gangs, nor do they belong to the Mexican pachuo gangs.

Now, only a very small percentage of Mexican youths are pachuos. And all pachuos do not wear zoot suits. Certainly, all zoot suit wearers, including many movie stars, are not pachuos.

This is the way it began in Los Angeles. Army, navy, and marine corps staffs seemed to have chosen Los Angeles as the ideal place in which to give white southerners leave. Whether this is intentional or not, only they can say. But we find huge numbers of uniformed southerners in the city. Most of them have no friends and know no girls.

Mexican girls and young women are very pretty on the whole. They are olive-skinned with big black eyes and thick, curly black hair. They have the warm disposition usually attributed to Latins. Like American white girls and women, they are hero worshipers. They might not trample each other to death and turn a city upside down to see a Lindbergh returning from a non-stop flight across the sea, but they have other ways of showing their adoration. They have very expressive eyes.

Now in the beginning, until they learned better, Mexican girls—a few of them, a very few—might have thought that all American white youths in uniform were heroes. A few of them might have flirted.

There is some rare and inexplicable (not only inexplicable but incomprehensible) ego in the average southern white man which makes him believe he can have an affair with any dark-skinned woman anywhere on earth—Los Angeles being no exception. And when these southern whites see these pretty Mexican girls, they become excited—they are not used to girls so pretty.

Adventuresome servicemen go out in the Mexican districts, patronize the bars, roam the streets, trying to pick up these girls or take them away from their boy friends. They actually believe that this is not only a very simple thing to do, but right, for what else could pretty Mexican girls be for other than to satisfy white men?

Maybe a few of the girls do make eyes. Maybe the Mexican boys who are used to pretty girls do not make over them enough. Maybe a uniform looks more impressive than a zoot suit. Maybe the Mexican girls feel in their hearts that white servicemen have as much respect for them as for the "Aryan" girls out in Beverly. After all, California state law specifically declares that Mexican people are white.

However, Mexican boys do not like the idea of Mexican girls being picked up by white servicemen. Neither do Negro boys like for Negro girls to be picked up by white servicemen. Perhaps because they, the Mexican and Negro boys, cannot go out in Hollywood and pick up white girls.

So, on occasion, a white serviceman in a Mexican bar in a Mexican district, trying to pick up, or having already picked up, a Mexican girl, might have been set upon by pachuos and slapped. We hate to think of what might have happened to a darker-skinned Mexican in a white bar in a white district, trying to pick up, or having already picked up, a white girl.

I'll give you an illustration, and this wasn't in a bar. Three drunken white sailors were on a Red car coming from Watts. They were nice looking boys. Evidently they had returned from one of the Pacific skirmishes for they were boasting of how they had whipped the Japs. That is what we are supposed to do, anyway, since we are fighting them; but it seems always to give a white man a wonderful feeling when he whips a Jap.

One of the boys, a blond, was saying in loud, whiskey-thickened voice, "Ah'm tellin' yuh, Ah fought lak a white man! Din Ah fight lak a white man, boy?"

At this point, a couple of Mexican kids, about nineteen or twenty, boarded the car, and seeing the seat vacant across from the three sailors, took it. The Mexican boy was very nice looking, gentlemanly, and possessed of the odd, old-fashioned chivalry found in most Mexicans. But the girl was beautiful; she was on the gorgeous side.

When this blond sailor saw her, he began saying in his loud, whiskey-thickened voice, "Boy, did those native gals go fuh us. Boy, uh white man can git any gal he wants. Can't he, boy, can't he git 'em if he wants 'em?" And then he went on to elaborate how he fought like a white man, trying all the time to get this Mexican girl's eye.

Many of the white people on the car saw the play and appeared rather disgusted, because this was even too strong for them. But the white boy continued, growing bolder as he went along.

Suddenly, the Mexican youth stood up and said to the girl, "Let's move down front."

Perhaps the girl realized that she had attracted the sailors' attention, and perhaps it flattered her. Anyway, she said, "Oh, why do you want to move? We're going to get off in a few minutes."

The Mexican boy sat down. The white sailors laughed.

But at the next stop, the Mexican boy suddenly jumped up and pulled the cord and dashed from the car, leaving the girl sitting there. She followed at the next stop.

Now, what should the Mexican boy have done? Or what should any Mexican or Negro youth do when walking down the public streets of Los Angeles with his wife or sweetheart to have a group of white servicemen look her over and wink or say, "Boy, Ah ought to change mah luck." Should he go back and hit them in the mouth? The best he could expect from such a procedure, attempted alone, would be a whipping by the gang of servicemen, a whipping by the Los Angeles police, and then a charge in the Los Angeles courts of inciting a riot.

You have no doubt read that white women are accosted, insulted, and molested by pachucos, and that this was primarily the cause of the subsequent riots. Any white woman or girl living in a Mexican neighborhood, or any who have to pass through such a neighborhood day or night, will gladly tell you that Mexican men, both young and old, do not accost, insult, or molest white women. They do not even look at them. They do not desire them. They do not admire them. This attitude of Mexicans is very noticeable, and perhaps a little strange.

I live in City Terrace, which is north of Belvedere, where much of the rioting occurred. Belvedere is inhabited by native whites and Mexicans with a sprinkling of Jews overflowing from Boyle's Heights. Coming home, I take the "P" car and come out First street to Rowan, the heart of Belvedere. There I wait for a cab which takes me up the hill into City Terrace for twenty-five cents. I have been on this corner, and other corners in this large Mexican district, at all hours of the day and night. I have seen white women of all ages pass these corners at all hours of day and night. I have never seen one molested or accosted by a Mexican. I have never even seen a Mexican look at one. Pachucos will meddle with passing white men, but if they meddle with passing white women, it is very rare. White women, of course, expect it, and the Mexicans seem to take delight in disappointing them.

However, I cannot say the same of a Negro district. Negro youths will crack at anyone of any race who is nice looking. They will say, "A fine queen . . . a reet cheet . . ." They might go further.

But they will never go as far as white men toward Negro women in a white district. A lone Negro woman, if she is young and nice looking, in a white neighborhood, will get a purely commercial proposal from every third unescorted white man or group of white men. When I first came to Los Angeles in the fall of 1940, an unescorted Negro woman could not walk down any part of Central avenue, or Vernon avenue between Central and Main, without having ten, fifteen, or twenty cars pull up to the curb beside her and some leering white man beckoning.

So now we have the riots. Your guess is as good as mine on how they began. It is my belief that some Los Angeles policeman or group of policemen suggested to some sailor or group of sailors that they get together and sap up on the zoot-suiters. Every one knows that it has been a long and bitter complaint of Los Angeles policemen that they were not allowed to beat up the zoot-suiters themselves. So perhaps they got the sailors to do it for them.

This we know: That during the first two nights of the rioting, no policemen were in evidence until the gangs of sailors, outnumbering the pachuos two-three-four to one, had sapped up on the pachuos with belt buckles and knotted ropes. When the sailors departed in their cars, trucks, and taxi-cabs, furnished them no doubt by the nazi-minded citizenry, the police appeared as if they had been waiting around the corner and arrested the Mexican youths who had been knocked out, stunned, or too frightened to run. We know that gangs of servicemen boarded streetcars and glared at women and insulted men at will, with no police in evidence. In fact, during the first three nights, by which time all manner of servicemen had joined the storm troopers, it seemed as if there were no civil officers at all in Los Angeles.

As long as the servicemen were getting the best of the fight, attacking and stripping, beating and molesting, all dark-skinned people who wore zoot suits or what might have been taken for zoot suits, regardless of whether they were pachuos, war workers, juveniles, or invalids, everyone seemed happy. The papers of Los Angeles crowed. "It was a gob job," they said. They rooted and cheered. What could make the white people more happy than to see their uniformed sons sapping up some dark-skinned people? It proved beyond all doubt the bravery of white servicemen, their gallantry. Los Angeles was at last being made safe for white people— to do as they damned well pleased.

There will, of course, be repercussions—serious repercussions. The Mexican government has made representations. There are, of course, repercussions when a Negro is lynched.

"But, by God, it was worth it, wasn't it, Mr. Jones. By God, we put 'em in their place. I bet they'll think twice now before they jump on one of our boys . . . Oh yes, that's right, or molest one of our women . . ."

But the outcome is simply that the South has won Los Angeles.

IF YOU'RE SCARED, GO HOME!

[1944]

I have no way of knowing whether the Negro race, as defined in the U.S., is inferior to other races or not. It has never occurred to me to give it any serious thought. All of my life I have believed in the equality of all people. It's my belief; I'm stuck with it. I don't have to do anything for it. I don't have to wake it up in the morning. I don't have to feed it sugar all day. I am a Negro and this is my belief. I don't know why I believe it. Maybe my parents taught me. It's just never occurred to me to believe otherwise.

Just as I have always believed in the equality of all people many people in the U.S. have always believed in the inequalities of peoples of different races and religions. The point I am trying to make is that there is no point. It is the same as arguing the merits of various breeds of milk cows. Nobody is ever convinced of anything and if they were it would make no difference. This business of belief in equalities or inequalities serves only to sidetrack the thinking of the public away from the only issue.

The only issue is whether a democracy provides for the inclusion of peoples of all races and religions. We will soon be discovering that we cannot cure anti-Semitism by proving that there is no physical difference between Jews and Gentiles. It has been proved. It is a fact. It has always been a fact. We all know it. We have always known it. In the United States most Jews are white. Most Gentiles are white. But anti-Semitism rolls tragically along.

Our history is that a group of idealists back at the beginning of our Republic created an ideology of democracy based on the premise that all men are created equal. That is the same as creating a form of mathematics based on certain tables of addition, multiplication, and subtraction. These are stated as truths, against which there is no argument or the system will not work. The same holds true with both democracy and mathematics. No problem in mathematics can be solved if we change these tables. Nor will democracy work when we attempt to change the premise that all men are created equal. The assumption that white men are superior to black men, or Gentiles superior to Jews, will cause the same error in the working of democracy as the assumption that two times two equals five will cause in solving a problem in mathematics.

In our democracy people are not equal by processes of anthropology nor by genealogy. They are not equal by similarity; nor are they equal in intellectual capacities, wealth, or station in life. People in the United States of America are equal for only one reason. They are equal because we made them equal. We made them equal by stating that all people are created equal. We stated they were equal so we could create an ideology based on this equality.

At the time our national fathers came up with this democracy, Negroes were owned as slaves. Negroes were chattel. Therefore the original premise that all men are created equal did not apply to human beings owned as chattel.

But the time came in our history when the majority of the people of the United States decided to make our Negro residents equal. Previous to this Negroes had been freed from slavery by a proclamation issued by President Lincoln during the fighting of the Civil War. But it was by the calm and considered acts of the voters of the United States who ratified the Thirteenth, Fourteenth, and Fifteenth Amendments to the Constitution that Negroes were made equal. They were made equal by the majority of the voters of the United States. They were made equal by the same process which made the Colonials equal following the Revolutionary War. Negroes were made equal as whites were made equal— by the will of the majority of the people.

For purposes of conducting a democracy it is not necessary that the people be proved equal. It is only necessary that they maintain equality by common assent.

Therefore, and quite obviously, the basic issue does not concern Negroes as a race, but is concerned only with the question whether democracy is an acceptable ideology to the majority of citizens. This dominant group is responsible for the creation of democracy. It may be said that persons of other races and religions gave to the world such ideologies as Communism, Shintoism, Buddhism, Fascism, Nazism. But democracy was created by the white Gentiles of the United States of America. It was not brought here by the slaves, nor by religious or political refugees, unless in the form of desires in their hearts to be free and equal. But the words and statements, the premise and tables of this ideology of democracy were created by the "majority"—the white Gentiles of the newly formed Republic.

The problem now is as it was then—the problem of the white Gentile majority. The Negro with twenty thousand dollars with which to buy a house is not bothered with a problem of democracy. He believes in democracy. He's bothered with restrictive covenants, discrimination, race hate; but his only problem is housing. He is not bothered with the problem of inferiority. He does not believe he is inferior; he believes he is equal. Any man with twenty thousand dollars with which to buy a house is not inferior by financial standards, certainly. The problem is the problem of the white people who do not want a Negro to live in their neighborhood. The problem is whether they are willing to accept the ideology of democracy based on equality. No other problem exists.

No other problem exists in any of the circumstances of our national life which has to do with peoples of minority races and religions.

So when we tend to think in terms of Negro accomplishment as a basis for equality, when we tend to base our convictions on how Negroes act, how they look, what they think, we are either inadvertently or deliberately confusing the basic issue. When white Americans begin to feel good because Jackie Robinson, a Negro, a competent ballplayer, has succeeded with distinction in holding down the position of first base on the Brooklyn Dodgers baseball team—when they begin to feel good because they have let a Negro do this well—then democracy is in a very sad state. It would be in a much better state if the people thought, "Well, what of it? He's a baseball player, isn't he? A hell of a good one. Why shouldn't he be playing first base for the Dodgers? Or for the Yanks? Or for whatever team can pay him the most money?"

By the same token, when white Americans begin to pat themselves on the back for their racial tolerance, they are getting farther away from the ideology of democracy. Tolerance is one of the finest of human virtues. There is no question. The more tolerant people become the more advanced will be the way of life of mankind. Let us have and practice tolerance to the highest degree. But let us do it quietly and from the heart. After all, tolerance is not a noisy virtue. Tolerance is the disposition to tolerate beliefs, practices, habits, and peoples of appearances differing from one's own. Let us have all of tolerance. It is by tolerance that the ideology of democracy may be made to work. But let us not substitute tolerance for democracy. Democracy is not tolerance. Democracy is a prescribed way of life erected on the premise that all men are created equal. And though it depends on tolerance to function, it is the democracy and not the tolerance which maintains that all men are created equal. So let us have tolerance, quietly and in our hearts. But not tolerance simply for the *poor Negro* lest by such tolerance we define him as a *poor Negro*—a poor benighted inferior. Let us have tolerance, and while we are having it, let us all have tolerance for ourselves.

A democracy is a way of life that people want for themselves. It is to be shared, not bestowed. The impulse to share it must come from a deep belief in the ideology itself. Those who believe must be brave. We must be willing to speak out for it. As our forefathers, we must be willing to fight and die for it. Now is the time.

Martyrs are needed to create incidents. Incidents are needed to create revolutions. Revolutions are needed to create progress.

These are the tactics devised by the peoples of the world who wanted freedom. No one has ever proved or denied that these are the best tactics to employ for the attainment of this end; it has been proved that these are the *only* tactics to bring about such attainment.

The American Colonials were not the first to recognize the singularity of these tactics, but they were the first to use them effectively for the benefit of a large number of people. Since the American Revolution they have become the ABC's of political advancement throughout the world. The first and fundamental convictions of the political tactician fighting for the human rights of the people are: (1) Progress can be brought about only by revolution; (2) Revolutions can only be started by incidents; (3) Incidents can be created only by martyrs.

Of all the oppressed groups of people in the world today, racial, religious, and political, the thirteen million Negro Americans are the only group who have not yet employed these tactics in some manner or other in their quest for democratic equality. This is one of the strangest conditions of history. No serious unbiased scholar will deny that the Negro Americans have been the most oppressed minority group in the world for the past three hundred and twenty-three years. But yet no intelligent politician will deny that there is *no other manner* in which Negro Americans can release themselves from this oppression.

Let us consider then what a Negro American revolution will be and what it will do.

First I must point out the possible ways of existence for all people. There are only three:

(1) *Wherein every one is free.* As of today, citizens of the com-

munist-dominated socialist state of the U.S.S.R. have come closest to this goal. However, it does not matter whether the structure of the government is communistic, socialistic, or democratic; this is the most preferable way of existence for the majority of the people of the world.

(2) *Wherein a ruling class or race is free.* This is the point to which citizens of the United States of America and of the British Empire have advanced. Outwardly, this would seem preferable to the ruling class or race. But the fallacy of that is that this is not a fixed stage of existence; *it is a pivot of change.* The ruling class or race must share their freedom with every one in order to preserve it; or they must give it up.

(3) *Wherein no one is free.* Loosely we may say that this comprises dictatorships and imperialistic nations, especially if they are at this time our enemies. It is generally agreed that less than one-tenth of one per cent of the people of the world prefer this way of existence; so we may state for point of argument that no one prefers it.

AIM OF REVOLUTION

There can be only one (I repeat: *Only one*) aim of a revolution by Negro Americans: That is *the enforcement of the Constitution of the United States.* At this writing no one has yet devised a better way of existence than contained in the Constitution. *Therefore Negro Americans could not revolt for any other reason.* This is what a Negro American revolution will be: A revolution by a racial minority for the enforcement of the democratic laws already in existence.

What will a revolution by Negro Americans do:

(1) Bring about the overthrow of our present form of government and the creation of a communistic state. A communist organization of immense proportions already exists in this nation. "I therefore defined," Engels wrote, "the objects of Communists in this way: (1) To achieve the interests of the proletariat in opposition to those of the bourgeoisie; (2) To do this through the abolition of private property and its replacement by community of goods; (3) To recognize no means of carrying out these objects other than a democratic revolution by force."[1]

---

[1] *Marx-Engels Selected Correspondence*, pp. 1–2.

It is obvious that the Communist Party of America will attempt to direct any revolution, whether by Negro Americans or any other group, to the accomplishment of these aims. It is equally obvious that in any nation where great numbers of people are oppressed the communists have fair chances of success.

(2) Bring about the overthrow of our present form of government and the creation of a dictatorship.

The first reaction of the people who are endeavoring to continue the existence of white supremacy in all its vicious destructiveness will be to stamp out this revolution with a maximum of violence and a minimum of mercy. Many Negroes will be shot. Many will be imprisoned. The remainder will be literally enslaved. *If these people are successful.*

But what is more to be feared in the historic progress of the human race: *At this pivot of change where we now exist we will cease to go forward and go back.* Law, order, decency, all the democratic principles which we have so far developed in this nation will be destroyed. The white race will become barbarians. The darker races slaves.

When people become barbarians they can no longer govern themselves. They respect only might. The strongest, the most deadly, most vicious, most cunning, most murderous, will become the ruler. He will rule as long as he is feared.

(3) It may be successful and bring about the enforcement of the Constitution, democratic equality, and the acceptance of the democratic way of existence by all of the citizens of our nation.

For this to happen it will be necessary that the majority of the people of the United States believe in democracy and will join with us in bringing about its establishment. In this event a Negro American revolution will cease to be a revolution and become a movement of the people to stamp out injustices, inequalities, and violations of our laws. The people who would try to prohibit the people from so doing would become rebels, traitors, secessionists, and would be dealt with accordingly.

If the majority of the people of the United States do not believe in democracy as the best way of existence, we will not achieve democratic equality in any event. So we are forced to begin our thinking here; we have no other point from which to begin.

MARTYRS NEEDED

At this point Negro martyrs are needed. The martyr to create the incident which will mobilize the forces of justice and carry us forward from the pivot of change to a way of existence wherein every one is free.

It is obvious that we can not stay here; we've got to go somewhere. If we can not of our own accord go forward, we will against our will be pushed backward.

The first step backward is riots. Riots are not revolutions. In the best sense revolutions are the renunciation of the existing evils of government by the governed. Revolutions are not necessarily brought about by force of arms. *They may be successfully accomplished by the manifest will of the people.* In the event of a Negro American revolution it is to be hoped there will be no shooting.

Riots are tumultuous disturbances of the public peace by unlawful assemblies of three or more persons in the execution of private objects—such as race hatreds. No matter who passes the first blow or fires the first shot, riots between white and black occur for only one reason: *Negro Americans are firmly convinced that they have no access to any physical protection which they do not provide for themselves.* It is a well-known and established fact that this conviction is rooted in history: *Negroes in fact do not have any protection from physical injury inflicted by whites other than that which they provide themselves.*

It is a rather deadly joke among Negroes (especially since the Detroit riots) that the first thing to do in case of a race riot is not to call the police but to shoot them. . . . "Man, what you mean call the police; them the people gonna kill you. . . ."

White citizens who believe in democracy (and white citizens who do not believe in democracy but do not want to have race riots) can stop race riots whenever and wherever they occur by simply appearing on the scene and making it apparent to the white persons thus engaged that they do not approve. The reason for this is obvious: White persons who incite and engage in race riots are in a minority, but *they are firmly convinced that the majority of white people morally support their actions.* As a consequence most Negro Americans clearly realize that the white citizens who stay at home and remain quiet during riots are morally as guilty as those who wield the clubs and fire the guns.

Negro martyrs are needed to assemble these white citizens who believe in democracy and stay at home; and to inspire them to fight for their beliefs.

MARTYRS RARE

It is necessary that such a Negro martyr be a person of integrity who loves freedom enough to make any sacrifice to attain it. Preferably, he should be a Negro leader, a person reasonably intelligent by the accepted standards, one who is well-known to Negro and White Americans alike and who can not be ignored by either white or Negro media of news distribution. He must be a Negro who will not compromise, and who does not mind embarrassing his white liberal friends who believe sincerely that "adaptation" or "evolution" is the best policy for Negroes to follow. And, of course, he must be a Negro who will not sell out. Therefore we must get our lanterns.

He must be solidly supported by the Negro middle class for there is no Negro leader solidly supported by the Negro lower class. Not only should he be solidly supported by this group, but so identified with them as to make it impossible for them to abandon him.

It is apparent that the Negro middle class must be out in front in any Negro American revolution, so this must be fixed in mind, and further reasoning must go forward from it. *The Negro middle class must accept the responsibility for the successful culmination of any Negro attempt for democratic equality.*

Therefore it is of singular importance that members of this group be able to recognize democratic equality when it comes, and not confuse it with social acceptance by members of other groups or races. We have not achieved equality by week-ending with our white friends and drinking their liquor or flirting with their wives. In fact, many of us who are Negro Americans wish to retain the right to choose our house guests and paramours as much as any white American.

The incident, of course, must be a denial of some rights guaranteed to every citizen of the United States by the Constitution, such as the right of any decent, honest person to live wherever he chooses, or the right of a citizen to vote or serve on juries. Incidents such as an unjust accusation of rape serve no primary purpose other than to agitate or inflame and fix no constructive precedent for progress.

The martyr must make the stand and refuse to yield. The Negro middle class must come to his assistance, also refusing to yield, and must influence the Negro lower classes to follow.

What is of utmost importance is the stand. All of us Negro Americans must make the stand. And after we have made it, we must not give on any point. We must not compromise a breath. *After all, we have nothing to lose, except our lives, and one preferable change to win: Democratic equality.*

EIGHT SHORT STORIES

ALL GOD'S CHILLUN GOT PRIDE

[1944]

He was twenty-five in 1940 and she was twenty-three, and they had been married since the summer of 1937; and in all that time he had only kept one secret from her. That was a thing he could not tell her; if he had ever told her that, they would have both been lost. Because the way had been rocky; dark and rocky. And the only thing that had kept them going was his posed belligerance, his air of bravado, disdain, even arrogance.

As the white girl, Helen, said in 1938, when employed by the W.P.A. he had been promoted from labor to research and assigned to work in the public library, "When I first saw you, I said to myself, 'What's this guy doing on his muscle? What have we done to him?'"

But don't condemn him from the start. Because he needed it; he needed being on his muscle, he needed his tight-faced scowl, his high-shouldered air of disdain, his hot, challenging stare, his manner of pushing into a pleasant room and upsetting everyone's disposition with the problem that he rolled in front of him, as big and as vicious and as alive as if it were a monster on a chain; he needed all of his crazy, un-called-for and out-of-place defiance, his lack of civility and rudeness; he needed every line of the role he assumed in the morning upon arising and played throughout the day, not even letting down when alone with his wife, the role of swaggering, undaunted, and unafraid, even ruthlessly through the ever-coming days, through the hard-hurried crush of white supremacy, through the realization of odd identity, through the ever-present knowledge that if he lost the ball no one would pick it up and give it to him, if he ever fell down he'd be trampled, unmercifully, indifferently, without even being thought of, that he was alone and would always be alone without defense or appeal; he needed every ungracious thing he ever did.

Because every morning that he lived, he awakened scared. Scared that this day, maybe, toleration of him would cease; scared that this day, maybe, he would just give up and quit the struggle —what was the use, anyway? What could he hope for? He was tired, so terribly tired; he doubted if he could get through the day; scared not only of his giving up but of his crushing out, scared of saying to himself, "I'm gonna break out of here, I'm gonna crush out this existence of being a black beast in white America; I'm gonna take a running head start and butt a hole through this wall, no matter how thick it is, or I'm gonna splatter my brains from end to end of Euclid." Scared of just being black—that was it. One of the ancient librarians who avoided him as if he were diseased, who refused to hear when he addressed them directly, who were vitriolic when finally replying, who let him stand unattended before their desks while they carried on thirty-minute conversations over the telephone concerning everything under God's sun and would then arise and walk away, who made it as tough as they possibly could, would some day say to him, "Why in heaven's name can't you colored people be patient?" and he would snarl at her right off the very top of his muscle, "Why you-you, why go to hell, you beatup biddy!" And he would be out of a job. All of the Negroes who ever hoped to work in the library project of the W.P.A. in Cleveland, Ohio, would be out of jobs; the whole race would feel it and he would be a traitor not only to himself but to twelve million other people who didn't have a thing to do with it. He'd have to go home and tell Clara that he blew up and lost his job; and God knows they couldn't go hungry anymore. He hated to think of what might happen, because they couldn't take another period of that hungry hopelessness. Or he would go into a store and raise cain because the white clerks would not wait on him and the police would come and he would tell them he was a citizen and they would laugh and take him down to central station and beat his head into a bloody pulp; and the only thing he could do would be just to fight back physically as long as he could. Scared of walking down the street and being challenged because some one might think he walked too proudly. Scared of asking for a white man's job; just scared to do it, that's all. Not scared because he might not be able to do the job, because he might turn out to be the very best. Nor scared so much of being refused, because being refused was something that he always expected; being black and being refused were synonymous. Being refused had its own particular sensation; not so much scare, not even anger so much—just a dead heavy weight that he must carry, just an eternal pressure, almost too much, but not quite, to bear, impossible to ignore, but too tightly smothering to rebel, too opaque, too constant, too much a part of the identification of color; it was impossible to realize what it would mean not being refused, impossible to visualize the mind outside of this restriction, impossible to rationalize acceptance. Why, good Lord! To cut him loose from the anchoring chains of refusal, he'd go running, jumping mad. As mad as Thomas Jefferson when he wrote, "All men are created equal . . ." As mad as all those crazy, freezing men who crossed the Delaware, fighting for the right to starve— and be independent. As mad as all the other running, jumping, insane people who shoulder through the world as if they owned it, as the women who flounce down Broadway with silver foxes dragging, knowing they are accepted. Mad! He'd go stark, raving mad! Mad as all free people. . . . Just scared to walk in and ask; scared of the act. Why? Why are little children scared to cross the street. Surely they are not scared of what's on the street. Because they have been taught not to; because they know they will get a whipping if they do. And although he tried to get outside this teaching of America; it was inside of him, making him scared. Scared to talk to a white girl, to laugh with her and tell her she was beautiful. Not of being rebuffed; he was a handsome chap and the chances were against his being rebuffed by any woman. Not of being lynched; this was Cleveland, Ohio. They don't hang Negroes in the north; they have other and more subtle ways of killing them. Just scared of talking to her, of the act.

He could not tell this to anyone; especially not to Clara. She was scared, herself; and she couldn't tell him. No Negro can tell another, not even wife, mother, or child, how scared he is. They might discover that they are all scared, and it might get out. And if it ever got out then they wouldn't have but two choices; one would be to quit, and the other would be to die. Whereas now they have three; they have self-delusion. If he told Clara, they wouldn't have had a chance; because what kept her going was thinking he wasn't scared.

So each day, of a necessity, in order to live and breathe, he did as many of these things of which he was scared to do as he could do short of self-destruction. He did them to prove he wasn't scared so the next day he would be able to get up and live and breathe and go down to the library and work as a research assistant with a group of white people.

The necessity of his continuing to live and breathe troubled him to some extent because he could not really understand it. Having been educated in America, he had learned of course that living and breathing, unaccompanied by certain other inalienable rights, such as liberty, and the pursuit of happiness, were of small consequence; but he had learned, also, that this ideology did not apply to him. He never really sat down and thought about it for any length of time; because he knew that if he ever did, living in America would become impossible. That if he ever made an honest crusade into abstract truth and viewed Negroes and whites in physical, spiritual, mental comparison, detached from false ideologies and vicious, man-made traditions, dwelling only on those attributes which made of what he saw a man, and not of what his forebears might have been nor what he claimed to be by race, he would see, aside from pigmentation of skin and quality of hair, little difference in anatomy, mentality, and less difference in soul. He would see the same flesh, the same bones, the same blood, the same ability to walk upright, differentiating them all from other, and supposedly lower species of animals, the same organs of reproduction; he would see the same false convictions, taught by the same teachers and learned in the same way; the same capacity for good and evil, for viciousness and generosity, for lust and philanthropy, he would see the passions in both compelling them to rape, steal, maim, murder, he would see the impelling urge for wealth, the destructive desires for power, the seeds of untold lies and the skeletons of deceits, he would see the same knowledge gleaned from the same founts; and when he looked into their souls and saw all the rotted falseness of ideologies imposed upon them all so that the few of any race could live and fatten from the blood, sweat, and tears of the many of all races, all the corruption of religions and philosophies and laws by which they all chained themselves to spiritual and physical slavery, and dedicated their offsprings for untold generations to ever-recurring horrors, for the life of him, God be his solemn judge, he could not have told the black from the white.

And after that, after he had seen the truth sheared of all the

falseness of tradition and ideology, there would have been nothing to have done with that "nigger" but to have taken him out
and shot him.

But he did not ever seek the conviction of this truth—or its
strength; he let it remain vague and unexplored in the fastness of
his mind like some hidden, vicious monster that would destroy
him once it was released. He never once opened *that* door, although he opened many others. Simply because he was scared;
that was all—just scared.

His name was Keith Richards, but people called him "Dick." He
was about five-nine, weighed between one-fifty-five and one-sixty,
and walked with a stiff-backed swagger. He had never had more
than two good suits of clothes and one good pair of shoes since
he had been grown, but he always managed to look well-groomed,
perhaps because he was handsome. His complexion was black
and he had features like an African prince, and when he forgot
his scowl and accidentally laughed, he came on like bright lights.

Women could have loved him if he had given them a chance,
but illness and poverty had thrown him mostly into contact with
white women and he had always been on his muscle. He seldom
relaxed enough for them to get to know him.

He had often wondered why Clara Street had married him; she
was a really beautiful girl. She could have married any one of a
number of handsome and very well-to-do men of all races; and
why she chose to string along with him, a rebel more or less who
had been kicked out of college in his sophomore year and who
didn't know how to do anything at all but starve, he never knew.
He could sketch a little and he dabbled in water colors and occa-
sionally he wrote a feature article for one of the weekly newspapers;
but this did not make him extraordinary—there are a million
Negro youths with that much talent on the ball.

So he was a little scared of this, also. Some day some crazy impulse would prompt him to touch it, to prod into it to see if it
was real, to search for its dimensions and perspective, to see if it
was another practical joke the white people were playing on him,
and he would discover that Clara was not there at all, and that
Negroes were even denied the emotion of love and the holy state
of matrimony.

At first their marriage had been a series of shabby rooms, somehow anchoring their sordid struggle for existence—for bare ex-

istence; room rent when it was due and enough food for each meal coming up. Not once during all that time did they buy any salt, nor sugar either until each landlady learned to keep hers put away. Just a dark-brown-toned plane of nothingness no deeper than sex relationship on which they lay as darker silhouettes while time pushed them on, not as individuals, separate identities, but as an infinitesimal part of universal change.

At times they got drunk together and imagined things. This was the best, the highest they could reach in the dark-brown-toned pattern—this imagining. It was something burnished—almost silver, almost gold; really it was brass. When they both caught it at the same time, it was beautiful in a way. All the pageantry and excitement and luxuriousness of rich white life in white capitalism was there—the rainbow Room and the Metropolitan Opera, Miami and Monte Carlo, deluxe liners and flights by night. And doing things, noble, heroic, beautiful things for her—"Because I love you." . . . Things he had been taught to desire from birth—denied him before he was born.

Because I love you. . . . If I really loved you, baby, I would blow out your brains. Right now! Because all you can ever look forward to, baby, is never having anything you ever dreamed about. Low lights and soft music, luxury and ease, travel and pleasure—*acceptance!* Not for you, baby, not for us. We got dipped in the wrong river, baby, we got dipped in the mud. Your soul might be white as snow; but the color of your soul doesn't count in America, baby.

However, all that was before he got on WPA. He wasn't born on WPA as in after years white industrialists seemed to think when he applied for work. During the first year of their married life he had several jobs—busboy in a hotel dining room, porter in a drug store; he even tried writing policy, but the players didn't like him. He couldn't shop the proper degree of sympathy when some one played 341 and 342 came out. It was a dirty clip racket as far as he could see and he felt sorry for them. And that just didn't do. The pickup man took his book one day, and he told Clara, "We should have been on the other end."

The best job he had was one at the Country Club in the spring of 1939. He was serving drinks in the tap room. But it was hard to take. When the members got in their cups, all their white su-

premacy came out. They were very, very white when they got
drunk.

He could have borne their disgustingness, for after all that didn't
prove their racial superiority. They were no more disgusting when
drunk than the Negroes down on Scovil avenue in the prostitution
area. He could even had put up with their "mammies"; their dear
old "black mammies" who raised them, and in later years gave
cause to, and proof of, the fact that all white people love Negroes.
He came to feel that a white person without a "black mammy"
just didn't count. And the exhibitions of odd and unusual sex
presented by some of the members in their stages of drunkenness
did not shock him, nor even disturb him—he could see this coming up and dodge.

But what finally got him and drove him away from a really good
job; a job where all he had to do to earn his ten and fifteen dollars in tips every night was just to be a nigger; what finally gnawed
him down to a jittery wreck was the fear that he might take
a drink of Scotch some day and it would go to his head and make
"that nigger crazy" and he would pull Mr. John Sutter Smythe
out from under the table and ask him, "Look, Mr. Smythe, just
what makes you think you are so superior to me?"

He quit the night Mr. Hanson told the joke about an old
"black mammy," her daughter, and the white traveling salesman.
If Mr. Hanson's wife and daughter had not been present, and a
number of other members and their wives, he would never have
repeated it a year later to white women on WPA who insisted
that white men treat Negro women with the greatest respect and
chivalry—because it was really a dirty story.

"You understand, Miss Wilson," he apologized at the end, "I
would not have dared tell you such a story if I had not heard a
respectable white gentleman tell it in the presence of a number
of respectable white gentlewomen . . ."

Miss Wilson got up and walked away.

But he had not told her the most important part. The most
important part was simply that after having listened to the joke,
after having remained until it was too late to leave, having allowed
himself to be maneuvered into a position where he had either to
be a fool or a coward, he turned and went inside the office and
quit.

He could have stepped over to the table, picked up some

"blunt instrument," as the prosecution says, and knocked Mr. Hanson unconscious. But that would have given him three beatings and a sentence of one to twenty years for assault with intent to kill; and he would have not been released under the twenty years unless Mr. Hanson had relented, and that was to say the least, unlikely.

On the other hand it was also a matter of the value of his pride. It was problematical from the first whether his pride was worth all of those beatings and twenty years to boot. Or if it was worth it, whether he was prepared to spend that much to keep it.

Now the value of pride is something that either goes up or down with the passing of years.

Keith's went up. Some time during his wearing of the proud uniform of a soldier in the Army of the United States it went priceless.

Keith is in the guard-house now.

"Now if you're a good little girl and sleep sound so the Sandman won't have to throw sand in your eyes, Santa Claus will bring you something nice for Christmas," Norma Stevens told her five-year-old daughter as she undressed her for bed.

"I want my daddy," Lucy replied, her brown, long-lashed eyes as wide as saucers. "I want my daddy for Christmas."

Norma sat on the side of the bed and helped Lucy into her sleepers, her rough, work-stiffened hands fumbling slightly as she buttoned them down the front.

"There now," she said, giving Lucy a pat. "Hand mother the comb and brush."

She sat watching Lucy cross the rag rug barefooted to fetch the comb and brush, a little awed as always by the delicate beauty of the child she had borne—she had her father's eyes and mouth, and her nose and chin, the best features of each, and—

"Mummy, Mummy, will Daddy be here tomorrow?" Lucy asked, handing her mother the comb and brush. "'Morrow's Christmas, Mummy. Will Daddy be here for Christmas, Mummy?"

"Perhaps," Norma said wistfully, then noting the sudden shadow come to Lucy's eyes, hastily added, "If God is willing he'll be here. Now turn around, dear."

She began combing and brushing her daughter's long black hair . . . Oh, God, it would be wonderful if Johnny did get home for Christmas, she thought with a sudden incontrollable surge of hope. His last letter, received three weeks ago, had sounded as if he were coming home. Or was she just making it up to support her sudden hope? After she'd put Lucy to bed she'd have to get his letter and read it over. He had a way of saying things to get them past the censors that only the two of them could understand. He had said something about "dig the long white whiskers and spread the mat . . ."

"Mummy, Mummy, if I ask God do you think He'll let Daddy come home tomorrow?"

"Perhaps, darling, it wouldn't hurt to ask." Lord knows she had been asking Him every night herself . . .

"Does God know where Daddy is, Mummy?"

"Yes, darling, God knows everything."

"Does God know when Daddy is coming home, Mummy?"

"Yes, darling, God knows."

"Why don't *you* ask Him, Mummy, so He can tell you and you can tell me."

She laid the comb and brush aside and began braiding Lucy's hair.

"God doesn't tell us such things, darling. We must wait and find them out for ourselves."

"Why, Mummy? Is it a secret, Mummy? If God told us we wouldn't tell, would we, Mummy?"

"No we wouldn't, darling." She finished braiding Lucy's hair and stood quickly up. "There now."

Turning, she knelt on the rag rug beside the bed and pulled her daughter down beside her. "Come now, you must say your prayers."

While Lucy recited in her small, childish voice: *"Now I lay me down to sleep; I pray the Lord my soul to keep . . ."* Norma prayed with swift silent earnestness: Dear God, please send Johnny home for Christmas; it's been three years now, Lord, and the war is over and he's done his part and he hasn't seen his little girl in three years, Lord . . . *"If I should die before I wake; I pray the Lord my soul to take . . ."* Dear God, I don't want to be selfish; I know that every wife wants her husband home this Christmas; but Johnny had so little to fight for anyway and he's been there three long years and it's not like it was last Christmas when I was working 'cause I'm out of a job this Christmas and probably never will be able to get anything else to do but go back to Mrs. Calhoun's kitchen and I wouldn't even mind that, God, if only Johnny was home . . . *"God, please bless Daddy and send him home for Christmas; and I'll remember, God, and I'll always love You, and I won't never forget . . . Amen."*

Shocked, Norma turned to reprimand her daughter, but catching sight of Lucy's small brown face, tight with earnestness, and her wide-open eyes, star-bright with hope, she didn't have the heart. Blinking to keep back tears, she suddenly stood and turned back the covers.

"In you go," she said, lifting Lucy and swinging her into bed. She bent, pulling the covers over her, and kissed her.

"Good night; sleep tight . . ."

"And don't let the jiggers bite," Lucy completed their nightly ritual, snuggling down beneath the covers.

Norma picked up the comb and brush and returned them to the small unpainted dresser, thinking, I'll get some paint and paint this dresser the first thing after Christmas.

"I want Santa to bring me a bicycle, too, Mummy," Lucy said.

"Maybe Santa'll bring you one next year," Norma replied, giving a last look to see that her daughter was comfortable.

"I love you, Mummy," Lucy said, her eyes already beginning to dim with sleep.

"Mummy loves you too, darling." Norma threw her a kiss.

She turned from the room, leaving the door cracked slightly, went quickly across her own room to lie face downward across the bed, crying quietly, thinking to herself at the time that she was beginning to cry too easily; that it wasn't really that bad even with being out of work in Mississippi and with Johnny away from home.

II

The train didn't even stop; it just slowed enough for Johnny Stevens to jump to the station platform. The brakeman signaled with his lantern, swung aboard, and it picked up again.

For a moment Johnny stood watching the train out of sight, feeling a sudden sinking sensation of being cut off from civilization; a cold hollow fear of himself, of his inability to take it any longer. Then he shrugged it out of his mind, changed the cheap light suitcase from his left to his right hand, and started around the station.

Hell, he'd taken it all of his life—before he'd enlisted and all the while he was in the army; had taken as much of it in the army as he had in Mississippi—he could take it a little longer. If not for himself, at least for Norm and his little baby, Lucybelle. It wouldn't be long now; he was cutting out of Mississippi, going north—Chicago, or maybe New York. Just as soon as the holidays were over; as soon as they could pack what they wanted to take and sell the rest. He wasn't gonna have Lucy brought up to work in no white woman's kitchen . . .

"Halt, boy!"

The hard cracker voice jarred him to a stop, raked him with an almost unbearable antagonism.

"Where tha hell you think you goin' at three o'clock in the mawnin'?"

His tight hot gaze searched the shadows where the voice had come from, made out the dim outline of a tall, stooped figure in a wide-brimmed hat. No doubt Tim Prentiss, one of the sheriff's deputies, the ornery son of a bitch, he thought, debating whether to tell him to go to hell or answer civilly.

"Answer when you're spoke to, nigger! Is you forgot how tuh talk tuh a white man?"

The second voice, more youthful than the first, but just as hard, came from the shadows at the other side of the path, where two oak trees blotted out the moon.

"I'm goin' home," Johnny replied in a low controlled voice, inwardly raging. "I just got off the special when it slowed just now."

Two men converged from the shadows, took shape in front of him. Tim, just as he had suspected, and a big hulking youngster whom after a moment he recognized as Slobby Simmons, the sheriff's nephew, grown up since he'd last seen him.

"Put some light on this sojer boy," Tim said. "You know I can't see a nigger in the dark."

Slobby flashed a light in Johnny's face. "W'y, by God, it's the Stevens nigger!" He kept the light on Johnny, running it up and down. "Lookit them things this nigger got stuck on him—stripes and medals. W'ut you git them fur, Johnny, cleanin' out latrines?" He suddenly broke out laughing.

A little hammer began tapping Johnny at the base of the brain, but he kept his body under control, his voice under wraps. "I got 'em for killin' the enemy—" he caught himself just before he added, "—like you."

Slobby's laugh came to an abrupt stop. "Say *suh* w'en you talk tuh me, you yellah bastard!"

The light blinded Johnny so he couldn't see either of the men, but he could imagine the sudden hard hatred in their faces. He said deep from his stomach, his rage showing in the edges of his voice:

"You got the wrong feller, ain'tcha? That's what you've been callin' the Japs."

"Put out the light," Prentiss hissed in a deadly voice.

The light went off, abruptly encasing Johnny in complete blackness; then he felt the blow across his face, a searing sheet of flame. The suitcase dropped from his grasp as he clinched someone in the darkness.

"Hit 'im 'cross the head," he heard a voice pant.

He wheeled with the body he was grappling; raised it from the ground. The second blow caught him flat across the base of his skull. His grip went suddenly slack as he pitched into the body and sunk slowly to the ground. He didn't feel it when they kept beating him across his head with their gun butts; he didn't feel it when they stood over his inert body and kicked him until they became leg-weary; he didn't feel it when he died.

III

Lucy was up tugging at her mother at the break of day.

"Mummy, Mummy, let's go see what Santa Claus has brought me."

Coming suddenly awake, Norma rolled over and pulled Lucy into bed with her.

"Lie here with mother for a while."

"Can I guess, Mummy?" Lucy asked, snuggling up close to her mother. "Can I guess what Santa Claus brought me, Mummy?"

Her eyes were so bright with excitement Norma felt her forehead to see if she was ill.

"Not *can* I, darling, but *may* I."

"May I, Mummy? May I?"

"Well—"

"A bicycle?"

Norma shook her head.

"A pair of roller skates?"

Again Norma shook her head.

"I bet you don't know yourself, Mummy," Lucy said, jumping from the bed and tugging at her mother.

"Come on, Mummy, let's go see."

"All right, darling," Norma replied, swinging her feet over the side of the bed to feel for her mules. "Mummy's coming with you to see what Santa Claus has left."

[1945]

Ward was walking down the sidewalk in Rome, Georgia, when he came to a white woman and two white men; so he stepped off the sidewalk to let them pass.

But the white man bumped into him anyway, and then turned and said, "What's the matter with you, nigger, you want all the street?"

"Now, look, white folks—" Ward began, but the white man pushed him: "Go on, beat it, nigger, 'fore you get in trouble."

"All right, Mr. Hitler," Ward mumbled and started off, but the white man wheeled and grabbed him and spun him about: "What was that last crack, nigger?"

"I din say nothing," Ward replied. "Just cussin' old Hitler."

"You're a damn lie!" the white man snarled. "You called me Hitler, and I'll not take that from anybody!"

So he hit Ward on the side of the head. Ward hit the white man back. The other white man ran up, and Ward drew his knife. The woman screamed, and Ward cut the white man on the arm. The other white man grabbed him from behind and Ward doubled forward and wheeled, swinging him off. The first white man kicked Ward in the stomach and Ward stabbed him in the neck. The woman kept screaming until some other white people came running and overpowered Ward.

A policeman came up finally, but by then the mob was too big to handle, so he did the best he could. He said, "Don't lynch him here, take him out in the country."

But the people didn't want to lynch him. He hadn't cut the man so bad, so all they wanted to do was teach him a lesson. A man with a C card furnished some gasoline and they soaked his feet, tied his arms behind him, set his feet on fire, and turned him aloose. He ran through the streets with his feet flaming until his shoes had burned off and his feet had swelled twice their normal size with black blisters; then he found an ice wagon and crawled in it and stuck his feet on the ice and fainted.

All up and down the street, the people laughed.

Two weeks later a doctor came out to the city jail where Ward was serving ninety days for assault with a deadly weapon—a very lenient sentence, the judge had declared—and cut off both his feet.

Ward had a brother in the navy and one in the army and a brother-in-law working in a defense plant in Chicago. They got together and sent him enough money to go to Chicago when he got out of jail.

When his ninety days were up, some church people gave him some crutches, and when he had learned how to use them a little, he caught the train and left. In Chicago, his sister gave him enough money to buy some leather knee pads and he got a job shining shoes and was doing all right.

He bought three $25 war bonds and was saving up money to buy a fourth.

The picture, *Bataan*, was showing in a downtown theatre that week, so one night he took off early and went down to see it. He had heard them talking about this colored man, Mr. Spencer, playing the part of a soldier, and he wanted to see it for himself.

He sat next to the aisle so as not to disturb anybody passing over them, and shoved his crutches underneath his seat. It was a good picture, and he enjoyed it. Just shows what a colored man can do if he tries hard enough, he thought. Now there's that Mr. Spencer, actin' like a sho-nuff soldier, just like the white men in the picture.

But when the picture came to an end, a big, beautiful American flag appeared on the screen, and the stirring strains of the National Anthem were heard. The audience rose rapidly to their feet and applauded.

Ward did not arise.

A big, burly white man, standing behind him, reached down and thumped him on the head. "Stand up, fellow," he growled. "What's the matter with you? Don't you know the National Anthem when you hear it?"

"I can't stand up," Ward replied.

"Why can't you?" the white man snarled.

"I ain't got no feet," Ward told him.

For an instant the white man stood there in a sort of frustrated fury; and then he drew back and hit Ward on the side of the head. Ward fell forward, down between the rows of seats; and the white man turned and ran up the aisle toward the exit.

A policeman, who had been standing in the foyer, and had witnessed the incident, grabbed the white man as he came out of the aisle.

"You're under arrest," he said. "What's the trouble, anyway?"

"I just couldn't help it," the white man blubbered, tears running down his cheeks. "I doan understand you people in Chicago; I'm from Arkansas, myself. I just couldn't stand seein' that nigger sitting there while they played the National Anthem—even if he din have no feet!"

[1946]

When I got off work at the cannery, I went home and washed the slop off my hands and face and washed under my arms then changed from my overalls to a slack suit. I got my money out of the tin can back of the stove where I kept it hid and counted it. I had eighteen bucks and some change. I went out and walked up Long Beach to José's at the corner of 40th and bought a quart of beer.

José wiped the bar with a dirty rag, then wiped the sweat off his face with the same rag and said, "You owe me thirty-five cents from yesterday."

"Pay you munanner," I said.

"Always mañana, mañana!" he beefed and spit in the sink.

"Hey, don't spit in the sink where you wash the glasses," some paddy down the bar said.

José shrugged. "All the same," he said.

I beat at the flies and drank my beer. It made me sweat like a son of a gun.

"The Spanish kid," another paddy took it up. "Spit where you please, Spanish."

José wiped his face with the dirty rag and gave the paddy a side-wise look.

There was three paddies and a coupla Mexes and two other spooks scattered along the bar. Some pachuco kids were ganged about the juke box, talking in Mex and blowing weed; and a coupla beat-up colored mamas sat in the window booth waiting for chumps. In the next booth a big snuff-dipping mama had her two slaving studs in overalls; and the booth in back had a coupla Mexes from old Mexico drinking "Mus-I-Tell."

When I finished my second quart, I had to go. I went out in the alley at the side. Then I went back and said, "Gimme another quart, les fill 'er up again."

Two old beat-up high-yellow biddies came in with a big yellow stud called "Sweet Wine" who went for bad. They sat down beside me and Sweet Wine leaned on my shoulder and said, "Buy us some beer, Tar Baby."

I didn't like the stud, and I didn't like to be called "Tar Baby" —Brown is my name—but I didn't have my blade so I just said, "Here, you can have some of what I got," shoving him the bottle.

He picked it up and drank it dry and set it down.

"Now ain't dat sompin'," one of the old biddies said to the other. "Ain't offered you or me a drap." She turned to me, "You'll buy us a lil beer, won'tcha, mister?"

Sweet Wine said, "Sure, this nigger'll buy us a drink; he got everything, working at the cannery, making all that gold. Come on, Tar Baby, set us up."

I knew he was looking for trouble. "Four wines," I said to José.

I had to break a five to pay him. The biddy next to me leaned over and said, "Come on, les you 'n me have some fun."

The other old biddy giggled.

I said, "What's the matter with the fun you already got?"

"That nigger done gone," she said.

The other old biddy giggled again.

I looked around and sure 'nough, Sweet Wine had slipped out. I oughta known that old yellow hag didn't want nobody black as me, but I said anyway, "Come on down to my pad."

We hadn't no more than got outside by the alley, when she grabbed me from behind and Sweet Wine come out the alley and cold-cocked me. When I come to, the pachucos had me halfway up the alley, rolling me. I turned over, braced my hands against the ground, pushed to my knees. Then I got to my feet. My jaw felt numb. I fingered it lightly, moved it from side to side to see if it was broke.

Then I said to the pachucos, "Gimme back my dough."

One of them laughed. "Sweet Wine cleaned you 'fore he turned you loose."

"He sure clipped you," another said.

I fanned myself anyway, just to be sure, but I was bare. "Which-away they go?" I asked.

The pachucos shrugged. I started home to get my blade to look for 'em and run into a police cruiser down at Vernon.

"Hey!" I called. "Wait a minute; I been robbed."

The young cop driving backed over to the curb and said, "Cum-mere, boy."

I came over by the car, and he and the other cop, an older man with gray hair and a sergeant's stripes, looked me up and down.

"Who robbed you?" the young cop asked.

"A fellow they call Sweet Wine," I said. "He and some woman who was with him."

"Where'd they rob you?"

"Down by the alley right next to José's."

He sniffed my breath. "Drunk, eh? They rolled you, eh?"

"No sir. I was in José's drinking beer and wasn't bothering no-body when they come in and want me to buy 'em a drink. I bought 'em the drink just to keep from having no trouble, then Sweet Wine, he left. Then after a while me and the woman come out and—"

"Oh, you were with the woman?" he cut in.

"No sir. I just come out with her. Sweet Wine, he was *with* her. I just come out on the street with her. Then she grabbed me, and he cold-cocked me. When I come to—"

"What's your name, boy?" he cut in again.

"Brown," I said. "William Brown."

"What do they call you?"

"Well, some calls me Tar Baby, but most just calls me Brown by my name."

"You ain't the Tar Baby what stabbed that sailor up here a coupla nights ago, are you?" he asked.

"No sir. I ain't been up here a coupla nights ago. I work at the cannery," I told him.

The sergeant said, "I knew a dinge in Kansas City called Ruckus Fuckus."

"We picked up a boy the other night called White Baby," the young cop said. "He was black as my shoe."

They laughed a little. Then the young cop jumped out the car and shook me down. When he didn't find anything, he said, "Where's that knife, boy?"

"I don't carry no knife," I said.

He got back in the car and started the motor. The sergeant said, "Better go home, boy. We'll find Sweet Wine and get your money. How much was it you said he took?"

" 'Bout fifteen dollars."

I went home and got my knife and put it in my pocket and went back to José's. Sweet Wine and the woman hadn't come back. I walked down Long Beach to the Cove at 36th. They weren't there either. I cut across to Ascot, stopped in two or three joints along the way, then turned back out toward Vernon.

It was about eleven o'clock when I found them out at the Dew Drop Inn at 51st and Hooper. I saw the old hag sitting at the bar guzzling juice, but I didn't see Sweet Wine. Next to her a guy was drinking a quart of beer. The bar was filled, and all the booths along the wall was filled. There was a lot of people standing around.

I went in and picked up the quart bottle the guy had next to her and broke it across her head. She staggered up, snapped open a switchblade knife and slashed at me. I jumped back and popped open my blade and cut her on the arm. Sweet Wine come from somewhere behind me and hit me across the head with a chair.

I fell forward into her, butting her back into the Juke Box. I went down on my hands and knees but I turned and crawled between somebody's legs before she got herself set. People was running all around trying to get out the way so neither of us could get to the other. Sweet Wine got over to one side of me and reached around behind a guy and hit me with the chair again. Somebody kicked me on the side of the face trying to get out the way. I got between somebody's legs and cut Sweet Wine on the leg. I just reached around the fat part of his leg and pulled my shiv forward like I was chopping down sugar cane. He kicked me in the mouth, and I stabbed him in the thigh.

People was all running out into the street, screaming and cussing. The old hag run up and stabbed me in the back. I jumped to my feet and began slashing out right and left, cutting at everybody. What people was left, run over each other trying to get out of the way. I moved around, getting both her and Sweet Wine in front of me, then I jumped at 'em and slashed as fast as I could move my arm. I didn't cut neither one of 'em. The old hag ran toward me, slashing back and forth like I was. She didn't cut me, neither, but she made me back up. I kept on backing up until I backed into something, and I looked around and saw cases of pop bottles stacked against the wall.

I slashed at her real fast until she backed up a little; then I stuck my knife in my pocket and started chunking bottles. The first one popped Sweet Wine square in the forehead and bust the skin wide open; the next one caught him in the mouth and bust his lips. The woman was running around trying to get behind the bar to chunk some wine bottles and the bartender was trying to stop her. Her arm was bloody where I had cut her and she bled all over the floor. Sweet Wine turned and tried to run, but his leg was cut so bad all he could do was hobble. I bust him a couple of times in the back, but I was chunking bottles so fast I couldn't see where they was going.

Then all of a sudden I heard somebody scream, "He hit me with a bottle!" and I looked up and saw an old white woman standing in the door with blood coming out of her head.

Everybody knew her. She was an old wino used to come there every night and get juiced up. Lived somewhere close by.

But when we saw her standing there with the blood coming out her head everybody stopped and just gaped at her. We quit fighting and just stood there. I was scared maybe I had killed her and she a white woman, too.

She started cussing everybody out and then the police came. They were two young guys this time. They held all four of us there waiting for the ambulance and the paddy wagon and they kept gritting their teeth and looking at me.

"This the nigger what hit you, mam?" one of 'em asked the old white lady, grabbing me by the collar.

"That's the dirty black bastard!" she screamed. "Hitting me with a pop bottle!"

"I didn't go to hit you, lady," I said. I was scared as hell. "I wasn't chunking at you, lady. I was chunking at these people what rob—"

The cop drew back and hit me in the mouth. "Shut up, you black son of a bitch," he said. "Goddamn you, we kill niggers for hitting white women in Texas."

People was coming back into the joint and they was crowding all about looking at us but wasn't nobody saying nothing. They just stood there looking black and evil and wondering what the cops was going to do to me.

"I didn't go to hit her, cap," I said. "Hones' to God—"

"Well, goddamn you, you black bastard, what'd you hit her for?" the other cop asked.

"She just happen to come in, cap; you know I wasn't chunking at no white—"

"Goddamn you, don't you say nothing when you talk back to me!" he said.

"Yes sir."

"If I had you in Texas—" the first cop began.

About that time the ambulance drove up. They put the white woman in on the stretchers, and the other woman sat there in the back on a chair. Then they looked at me and Sweet Wine. They wrapped a string or something around Sweet Wine's leg and drew it tight and said it'd be all right to bring him down in the paddy wagon. When they started to look at me, one of the cops said, "We'll bring this nigger in, he ain't hurt!"

The other cop said, "Yet!"

"I'se stabbed in the back—" I began. The first cop hit me in the mouth again.

When the paddy wagon came they put Sweet Wine in it and drove off, then they took me out to the cruiser and put me in the back seat with one of the cops sitting beside me.

"Where y'll taking me, cap?" I asked. "Y'll ain't gonna beat me, are you, cap?"

"Shut up, you black son of a bitch!" the cop said, and hit me across the mouth with his pistol butt.

I didn't say no more. They turned up Vernon to Long Beach and kept downtown 'til they came to where the railroad tracks split off. Then they drove up a dark alley beside a scrap iron foundry and the cop told me to get out.

"Cap'n, you oughtn'ta whip me," I began. "I'se hurt, cap, I'se been—"

He grabbed me by the collar and jerked me out on the ground. I lay there just like I fell, scared to move. The other cop got out and came around the car. One of them shot me. My stomach went hollow and my chest seemed to cave in. I was so scared I couldn't hardly breathe. "Y'all ain't gonna shoot me, are you, cap?" I begged.

One of the cops laughed. "What's he think we're doing now."

"This is what we do with niggers in Texas," the other one said, and shot me square through the stomach.

"Cap'n, y'all ain't gonna kill me!" I cried.

They stood there looking down at me, grinning. One of them

spit on me. Then the whole sky began to spin around and around and the telegraph poles along Long Beach began shimmying like they was alive and then everything began to go away. I kept looking at the two cops, looking at their faces until they was just blurred and white and I couldn't hardly make 'em out at all.

I was begging 'em over and over again, "Cap'n, please don't kill me. Please, cap'n. I swear I'll never hit another white woman as long as I live, not even by mistake." I knew my lips were moving, but I couldn't even hear my own voice.

I heard the first cop say, "Let's get it over with."

Then I heard the sound of the shot and felt the bullet go right through my chest. I couldn't even see nothing at all. I felt myself leaking all inside. It was just like a kettle on the stove and begin running over. But I didn't hurt much. I was just going on away.

The last thing I heard was a whole lot of shots real fast and I could feel all the bullets going through me. But they didn't hurt at all. It was just like a guy sticking a fork in soft butter. Like a guy jabbing an icepick into a piece of fresh killed meat.

The last thing I thought as I lay there on the goddamned ground and died was, "It just ain't no goddamned sense in you white folks killing me."

[1946]

The dimly lit stairway was encased in mirrors. They saw several reflections of themselves at the same time. Their dark brown faces looked back in the gloom. Their expressions were serious and unsmiling, as if they were going to view the body of a friend. Bubber climbed jerkily. But the girl moved with a sinuous grace. Her body sang a melody but her face was carved in cold disdain. A white couple coming down the stairway looked at them and smiled, but at sight of their dark sullen scowls hurriedly looked away.

At the top an attendant met them. "Check your coat, sir."

Both immediately began taking off their coats.

"Over this way, please," the attendant said.

Dumbly they followed him to the checkroom. The checkroom girl looked startled when Bubber handed over his girl friend's coat. "Oh, you'd better keep yours," she said to the girl. The girl snatched her coat and gave the checkroom girl a cold, defiant look.

"Come on," Bubber whispered tensely, pulling her toward the entrance to the dining room.

The floor show had not started and couples were on the dance floor. The girl shook her shoulders in time with the music but her face did not relax. Bubber felt a sudden rush of nervous energy, a wild, crazy desire to laugh; he didn't know why.

"Two?" The headwaiter was suddenly before them, smiling mechanically.

Bubber slanted him a look, then suddenly he grinned, a white blossom of teeth in his smooth black face. "You kiddin'?"

The headwaiter led them down an aisle. At the back they crossed over and turned again at the far side, moving down the far aisle until they came to a vacant table in the corner behind one of the mirrored pillars. The headwaiter pulled out the table so they could squeeze into the wall seats and a waiter came and gave them menus. Bubber began tightening inside. He didn't like the table; he didn't want to sit there. He wanted to protest but he didn't want to start any trouble. He knew if he started any trouble and the man made him angry he'd get up and hit him. He didn't want to do that. He wouldn't look up. In silence he stared down at the menu, trying to control the wild, crazy frustration which surged through him. The waiter poised impatiently with pencil and pad.

"I should like to have a steak," the girl said. Her voice, usually softly melodic, was stilted to a sharpness now.

Bubber noticed the white people at the next table cast her a furtive look. "I'm gonna have fried chicken," he said defiantly.

"Anything to drink?" the waiter asked.

"I think I should like a pink lady," she said.

"Whiskey for me," Bubber said.

"Any special kind of whiskey?"

"Yeah, good whiskey." Abruptly he grinned again. The waiter looked startled, then grinned in return.

When the waiter left they tried to see the dancers. Half of the dance floor was obscured by the side wall of the pantry, the remainder by the mirrored pillar.

"Less dance," he said.

She turned to the white couple at the table beside her and said coldly, "Excuse me."

He lifted the table out into the aisle and they arose and he lifted it back. On the dance floor they did intricate steps to the solid beat of the Negro orchestra, looking away from each other with glazed eyes and frozen faces. When the dance ended they turned to go back. They had not said a word to each other.

"Excuse me," she said to the white couple again.

He lifted out the table; they sat down; he lifted it back. The lights were dimmed for the floor show as the waiter served their drinks. Neither of them could see anything at all of what took place in the show. Suddenly they heard a staccato voice. It came so quickly they did not understand the joke. A wave of laughter rolled over them. He gave a loud burst of laughter. A split second afterward she let out a brittle giggle. The laughter of the others had ceased and the staccato voice had begun again. Heads turned to look at them. He felt ashamed, embarrassed.

"Don't laugh so loud," she whispered tensely.

"Who laughing loud?"

"Hush up and listen to the man."

The next time the audience laughed he remained silent. Her laughter trilled out in time with the others but lasted an instant too long. He turned to look at her. She picked up her drink and sipped it.

Now they could hear the sound of tap dancing. He leaned one way then another trying to see the floor.

"Quit shoving me 'gainst these folks," she said in a tense whisper.

"Look at that ol' boy dancin'," he said loudly.

She gave him a push with her hip. Aloud she replied, "He surely can dance."

"He mos' good as ol' Bill was," he said.

"He's all right but he not that good," she said.

The tap dancing ended and the staccato voice introduced two comedians. Now the laughter came in sharp bursts and rolling waves. They tried to time their laughter with that of the others. But first he laughed too long; then she laughed too late. The jokes had little point without sight of the comedians and more often than not the words were drowned in the laughter. Bubber felt a sudden hatred for himself for having to pretend that he was amused. He hated her also; he knew that she was also pretending. He felt cringing and cowardly. The desire to be angry became stifling within him, but there was no one to be angry with but himself.

When the girl laughed again he turned on her furiously, "What you laughin' at?"

She looked at him in surprise. "At what he said; it was funny." She didn't know that he had stopped pretending; she didn't know what had happened to him.

"Wan't nobody else laughin'," he muttered.

"They got through laughin'."

"Then what you laughin' for after ev'ybody else done got through?"

"I laughs when I want to laugh."

"Shhhh—" he said.

The waiter approached with their order. During the remainder of the floor show they ate their dinner in silence. It was dark in the corner and they could barely see what they ate. It didn't make much difference anyway, the food was unseasoned and tasteless. They didn't discover the salt and pepper and condiments behind the bread basket until they had finished eating. The waiter had gone off and they could not summon him. The meal was wasted.

Just as they were finished the floor show ended and the lights were raised. The bus boy came over and cleared their table. The waiter approached. He gave Bubber a broad, friendly grin.

"Would you like dessert?"

Bubber looked sullen. He didn't return the waiter's grin. "Naw," he said.

"I don't think I do either," the girl said.

"It's free," the waiter said confidentially, leaning forward. "It goes with the meal."

"Naw, I don't want nothin'," Bubber maintained.

The waiter looked at the girl again. She looked away with cold disdain. The waiter motioned for the bus boy to fill their water glasses and went off to add up the check.

Next to them the couple was preparing to leave. Bubber looked around. The dining room was emptying rapidly. He made up his mind to get a better table and stay through the next show. Beckoning to the waiter, he got set to ask for another table. He was grinning. But just before he got out the words the waiter presented him with the check. Anger rushed over him in a blinding wave. *Hadn' seen nuthin'—food wan't no good—now the sonavabitch was throwin' them out!* he thought. He had to hold himself in hard.

"Like the show?" the waiter asked congenially.

Bubber swallowed. "Fine," he said loudly. "Great show, man." His voice sounded so jubilant the waiter looked suddenly happy.

Bubber tipped him two dollars and felt better than he had since his arrival. As he and the girl left, going down the stairway and standing outside on the sidewalk, waiting for a taxi, they kept talking about what a funny show it was. They laughed so loudly that people turned to look at them.

Now he was blotto.

He had been blotto for the past hour but no one knew it. Even Maria didn't know it. Later on, thinking of some of the things he had said, she would realize it. She would remember how he kept repeating: *I didn't think it could happen to me.* And she would become annoyed, a little angry. She would think, *What's the matter with me? why can't it happen to him? who does he think he is?* Then she would realize that he had been blotto all the time. It wouldn't make her any happier. When people were drunk they spoke their sober thoughts, she would think. But at the time the bar was filled, demanding her attention. She was too busy to wonder other than when he was going home.

The next day he would ask her: *What time did I leave last night?* And when she had told him he would want to know what he did. And then: *What did I say?*

Now he fiddled awhile with the empty glass, leaning his bare arms on the damp bar. When she stopped at the cash register across from him to ring up a sale he said, "Baby, I really love you." He smiled, trying to look soulful, and added, "I didn't think it could happen to me."

He tried to hold her with his smile. Actually, it was more a grimace than a smile. His face was twisted to one side and down-pulled with weariness. His skin was greasy; his eyes deep-sunk and haggard. There were harsh, deep lines pulling down the edges of his mouth. His age was showing in his face. At such times he looked a great deal like his father, a small, black man who had faded to a parchment-colored mummy in his old age. It was hard for him to realize that he looked so old. Even blotto, at five o'clock in the morning, he still felt youthful and good-looking. He tried to hold her attention long enough for her to notice that his glass was empty. But she smiled perfunctorily and moved down the bar. By now the night was telling on her also. Although she was twenty years younger than his forty-one, her eyes were pouching slightly and slowly glazing with sleepiness. And she still had a long way to go. She wanted him to leave so she could get her business straightened out. She didn't want him to know what she did after daylight. For all of his drunkenness she still retained a vague respect for him.

He slid from the tall red stool and stood up. She came up and leaned across the bar, smiling at him.

"I'm going home, baby," he said, weaving on his feet.

"Now don't go out there singing and get in Dutch again," she said, laughing a little.

He thought maybe she'd offer him a nightcap, but she didn't.

"I won't," he said. "I'm going to crawl in silent as a mouse."

But already, when she had failed to refill his empty glass, the song had begun forming in his cloudy mind.

"Now don't get involved with the trees," she said. She referred to the trees in the park. It was a joke they had. Once he had told her of how, as a youth, he had lost his virginity to a tree. Both of them began to laugh.

"Not even a little sixteen-year-old virgin tree?"

She raised her brows incredulously. "You mean to say there are some left?" They both started laughing again.

Then he said, "Baby, I really love you." But she had moved away before he could add: *I didn't think it could happen to me.*

It was the ninth time in two weeks that he had been blotto. During the past five years he had discovered he couldn't drink as much as he could when he was younger. Now, after a certain time he would go blotto, maybe two or three times in one day, coming to in snatches, so that afterward, when he tried to reconstruct his actions from memory, he would draw blanks, say from noon until three in the afternoon, and perhaps from eight o'clock until midnight.

The first time he'd learned that he had gone blotto it had frightened him. That had been eight years before in Los Angeles. He had been living with a group of hard-drinking young radicals. On that particular day the group had drunk several gallons of wine topped off with several quarts of whiskey and then some brandy eggnog. When their supply had run out at three o'clock in the morning he had grandly announced he knew a liquor store where they could get whiskey after hours.

The group of them had piled into Freddie's car and he had gotten behind the wheel. Afterward they told him that he'd driven them several miles out to this store where they had bought three bottles of whiskey. They said he'd driven at blinding speed all the way there and back. No one had realized that he was blotto. They'd seemed to think he was a very skillful driver.

It had frightened him on two counts: First, because, sober, he could not recall ever having heard of the store where he had taken them and bought the whiskey; and secondly, because he had no memory whatsoever of driving them there.

But now it didn't frighten him like that anymore. He knew now that he was as safe when he was blotto as he was when he was drunk but still in command of all his senses. What worried him now was what he might talk about when he was blotto. He was afraid someone might find out his thoughts.

Now already the song was singing itself inside of him . . . *da-da-dee . . . Old Jethro . . . Old Jethro Adams . . . da-da-dee . . . You are gone . . . You are really and truly gone . . . You didn't think this could happen to you, did you? . . . da-da-dee . . .*

Over beyond the bar against the wall the jukebox was blaring a bounce tune and one of the prostitutes was dancing with a John. But Jethro didn't hear it. The tune in his head had pushed out all other sound.

He staggered along the bar and groped with his hand against the wall, moving slowly toward the door. Slim, the proprietor, glanced up from the back of the room where he had a tonk game going, then crossed glances with Jack, his bouncer. Jethro staggered into the tiny foyer which held a pool table. Lucy, Maria's bosom friend, glanced up from her game. "Going?" she called. Jethro turned, clinging to the wall, trying to bring her into focus. "Isn't it time?" The three young fellows with whom she was playing looked at him and grinned. They tolerated him. He was a great man, a famous writer of two racial novels who was the guest of the celebrated artists' colony, Skiddoo. They thought of him as something a little inhuman—a celebrity.

Jack headed him off and unlocked the door for him. He went out into the dark stairwell and looked up the stairway toward the street. For a moment he paused, leaning against the stairwell wall, gathering his resources.

"Can you make it?" Jack asked.

da-da-dee . . . "Oh, sure." . . . *da-da-dee* . . .

Jack closed the door.

He was grateful for the darkness. Laboriously, step by step he mounted to the street. He traversed the short block of Federal Street back of the Union Hotel. At the corner of Congress Street was Jimmy's Bar & Grill where they began drinking each evening. The place from which he had just come was a dim, dirty joint underneath Jimmy's called The Hole. Maria worked there as a barmaid.

He went down Congress Street alongside the hotel toward Broadway. But the brick sidewalk was old and uneven, making progress difficult, so he moved out into the center of the street. Now, instead of staggering from side to side, he staggered from curb to curb. Later, he would not remember that he had begun to hurry so as to get back to Skiddoo before sunrise. But it was in his mind at the time. He didn't run, but his head jutted forward and he walked just fast enough behind it to keep from falling on his face.

He came to Broadway and crossed it diagonally, entering the park . . . *Old Jethro . . . Jethro Adams . . . You didn't think it could happen to you, did you? You didn't think it. You really and truly didn't think it* . . .

Suddenly, as he came underneath the light in front of the Casino, the first tentative notes of the song sounded aloud in the quiet night . . . *da-da-dee* . . . It was like a violinist tuning his instrument . . . *da-da-dee* . . . *You know now, don't you? You sure in the hell know now. You know. Yes sir. Old Jethro Adams* . . . *da-da-dee* . . . *You are beat, son. You had a good ride but they got you now. They really and truly got you now, son* . . . *da-da-dee* . . .

Across the park he mounted the steps and came out at the beginning of Union Street. It was a dark tunnel beneath the tall, stately elms, going down to the dark void of infinity. He chose the right-hand side and for a time, while he passed the first buildings of the girls' college, he was silent. The song went on silently in his head. He passed the library and came to the row of beautiful old homes that had been converted into dormitories. Here the elms shaded the street light and it was darker. Now he began to sing aloud again . . . *da-da-dee* . . . *da-da-dee* . . . Soon he was shouting at the top of his voice: *da-da-dee* . . . *da-da-daaaa-deeeee-deeeeeeee-deeeeeeee-da-dee-dee-do* . . .

He was very sad. He had the greatest sadness any man had ever known . . . *da-da-dee* . . . All of his life he had wanted to experience it—just this one, simple emotion—just to be in love. He'd searched for it; he'd been everywhere looking for it. And now when he was too old, disillusioned, broke, defeated, it had happened to him . . . *Old Jethro. You found it, boy. You really and truly got it now* . . . *da-da-dee* . . . *deeee-deeeeeeeeeeeeee-deeeeeeeeeeeeeeeeeeeeeeeeeeeEEEEEEEEEEEEEEEeeeeeeee-e-do-do-do* . . . *You have fallen in love with a twenty-one-year-old Negro barmaid and now you are so shocked by it that you are completely demoralized* . . . *da-da-dee* . . . *Hell, you are a nigger, too, Jethro, didn't you know it?* . . . *da-da-dee* . . .

It was not really a song but a series of sounds. It was melodic in a sense, such as certain passages of symphonies are melodic. Its underlying melody was something like that of a popular song called "I'll Get By—As Long As I Have You." But he had not yet discovered this, although he, along with all of the other guests at Skiddoo, was trying to discover its origin. By now it was quite an infamous song.

It went something like this: *da-da-dee* . . . *da-da-dee* . . . *da-da-da-deee-do* . . . *da-da-da-da-da-da-daaaaaa-daaaaa-daaaaaaaaa-daaaaaaaaaaaaaaaaaa-da-de-do-do* . . . *da-da-deee* . . . *da-da-dee-deeeee* . . . *da-di-dee-do* . . . *deee-deee-deee-deeeeeeeeeeeeeeeeeeeee-eeee-deeeeeeeeeeeeeeeeeEEEEEEEEEEEEEEEEEEEEEEEE-da-dee-do-do* . . . *do-do-do-dooooooooooooo-dooooooooooooooooooo-dooooooooooooOOOOOOOOOOOOOOOOOOOOOOOOOOO-OOO-do-do-do-de-do* . . .

On and on through the night.

Sometimes he hummed it, but most times it came out in loud, weird, desolate sounds. There were no two stanzas ever exactly alike, if you can define such sounds emitted between breathing as stanzas. Each time he prolonged the sound in loud wailing notes until he was breathless, or else he repeated the basic *da-da-dee* until he had caught his breath. The sounds were interlaced with silences and repetitious to the point of dreadful monotony. Yet, in a sense, it was the monotonous repetition that brought relief. It was a melodic wailing of pain as if he were being beaten to some vague rhythmic beat. It was as if the loud, wailing notes, themselves, relieved the pain.

It filled him with a great, overwhelming emotion. The nearest he ever came to defining the emotion was that it felt like crying. Not like a man crying in bitter surrender, but like a woman crying who has been defeated from the start. Not crying inside, breaking up with it, but letting it out, crying for everyone to hear, like a whore crying drunkenly in a dim and dingy joint three o'clock of a Sunday morning while a gin-drunk piano player taps out a melancholy blues.

Yet whatever turbulent thing it was boiling out of him in these wailing, melancholy sounds, it gave him strength. It gave him the strength that comes from conceding that whatever it is that you want and cannot have is not worth a goddam anyway. Without it he would have lain down on the side of the road and gone to sleep. But it carried him, drove him along even though he was blind drunk, completely blotto.

When he turned in between the old fieldstone pillars that flanked the entrance to the estate of Skiddoo he was going great. His voice rolled down the dark narrow lane and climbed the embankment to the buildings. Even though he was still a great distance from the mansion and its surrounding studios, already some of the guests had been awakened. By the time he reached the inner grounds practically all of them were awake and listening. They all knew that Jethro was coming in drunk again.

Sonny, the composer, who dabbled in psychiatry as a hobby, once more asked himself the question: *I wonder what it is?*

Without lowering his voice, Jethro opened the massive oak door of the West House where he lived and began climbing the carpeted stairs.

Rose, the young Jewish writer from London, became a little frightened as always. She slipped quickly from bed and turned the key in the lock of her door. Fay, the Greenwich Village painter, frowned in the darkness, experiencing her customary moment of annoyance. She just didn't believe that he was that drunk. She thought he was just being defiant. She didn't see why she had to put up with his nightly show of defiance. Dick, the Texas historian, turned on his back and folded his arms across his chest, letting his thoughts drift back to Negroes he had known **at** home. But there was nothing in his memory which was quite like this. The song—yes. The tone, the blue notes, the wailing—these he could place. But he could not conceive of them in the present circumstances. After all, Jethro had it fine. He had the master bedroom. Everyone was going out of his way to treat him nice. What more could he expect?

Jethro opened his door and went into his room. He began undressing in the dark. A shaft of moonlight lay across the table on which his typewriter sat . . . *A writer! Old Jethro. You're a writer all right* . . . He hadn't stopped singing but now his voice was lowered to a long, distant wail: *deeeeeeee-deeeeeeeeeeee-deeeeeeeeeeeeeeeee-deeeeeeeeeeeeeeEEEEEEEEEEEEEEEEEE* . . . *dee-dee-di-do* . . .

He had been invited there to work on a novel called *Stool Pigeon*. After having written sixty-odd pages he had quit in favor of an autobiographical book called *Yesterday Will Make You Cry*. But now he was filled to overflowing with a story which he intended to title *I Was Looking for a Street*. He had found it all right. He had found the street—Congress Street, a back street of black joints dropping down a hill to the main stem. Just an ordinary street of black life. He had lived on that street and become a part of it in a score of different cities. And yet it had taken him forty-one years to discover how much of the street was in himself and how much of himself was in the street. It was all there, right inside of his mind. Every single tear of it . . . *da-da-dee* . . . Every whisper. Every smell. Every tone. If he could just sit down and write it before he sobered up . . . *da-da-dee* . . .

I Was Looking for a Street . . . *Well, you found it, son. You found it. You really and truly found it.*

He dropped his clothes on the floor and stepped out of them and crawled naked into bed. Now he was silent . . . *Old Jethro. Yes sir. The genius kid. Jethro Adams. They taught you, didn't they, son? They really and truly taught you. When they started talking about how things could be you believed them, didn't you? Yes sir, you believed everything that everybody said. But you were the only one. Old Jethro. The great Mister Jethro Adams. The great fool. The great chiseler of drinks from a small-town whore. The great astonished lover. You didn't think it could hap-*

*pen to you, did you? Well, now you know. You know a whole lot
of things now. You are a smart boy now. You are really and truly
a smart boy now.*

He was humming and he could feel the sharp vibrations of the
sounds in his nostrils. It filled his head with a great melancholy.
He felt as if nothing would ever matter again one way or another.
He thought it was something Congress Street did to him. He experienced Congress Street like a man experiences home after a
shipwreck. It was like going back to Central Avenue, a street of
dives and whores, of which he had been a part at seventeen and
nothing mattered but the night. It was like putting behind him
everything that he had learned and experienced since and going
back to that year of vice and indifference. He was never meant to
be anything but a cheap, smiling gambler with a flashy front, he
told himself. He was a simple man. All he ever wanted was a street
that he could understand.

*Old Jethro Adams. It was too much for you, wasn't it, boy?
You could understand the whores; and you could understand the
gamblers; and you could understand the thieves. But what you
could never understand was why really great and important people
ever found it necessary to tell you blankfaced lies. Or what there
could be about your simple thoughts that could make so many
great and important people hate you . . .*

*Jethro Adams—author. If you could just make up your mind,
son, once and forgoddamever what it is you want from this
world . . .*

Soon he was asleep. But even in his sleep the song kept going
on in his mind . . . *da-da-dee* . . .

Tomorrow he would remember none of it.

MAMA'S MISSIONARY MONEY

[1949]

"You Lem-u-wellllll! You-u-uuuu Lem-u-wellllllLLLLLLLLL!"

Lemuel heard his ma call him. Always wanting him to go to the store. He squirmed back into the corner of the chicken house, out of sight of the yard. He felt damp where he had sat in some fresh chicken manure and he cursed.

Through a chink in the wall he saw his ma come out of the house, shading the sun from her eyes with her hand, looking for him. Let her find Ella, his little sister, or get somebody else. Tired of going to the store all the time. If it wasn't for his ma it was for Miss Mittybelle next door. Most every morning soon's he started out the house here she come to her door. "Lem-u-well, would you lak t' go t' the sto' for me lak a darlin' li'l boy?" Just as soon's he got his glove and started out to play. Why din she just say, "Here, go to the sto'." Why'd she have to come on with that old "would you lak t' go" stuff? She knew his ma 'ud beat the stuffin's outen him if he refused.

He watched his ma looking around for him. She didn't call anymore, trying to slip up on him. Old chicken came in the door and looked at him. "Goway, you old tattle tale," he thought, but he was scared to move, scared to breathe. His ma went on off, 'round the house; he saw her going down the picket fence by Miss Mittybelle's sun flowers, going on to the store herself.

He got up and peeped out the door, looked around. He felt like old Daniel Boone. Wasn't nobody in sight. He went out in the yard. The dust was deep where the hens had burrowed hollows. It oozed up twixt the toes of his bare feet and felt hot and soft as flour. His long dark feet were dust powdered to a tan color. The dust was thick on his ankles, thinning up his legs. There were numerous small scars on the black skin. He was always getting bruised or scratched or cut. There were scars on his hands too and on his long black arms.

He wondered where everybody was. Sonny done gone fishing with his pa. More like Bubber's ma kept him in 'cause he was feeling a little sick. From over toward Mulberry Street came sounds of yelling and screaming. He cocked his long egg-shaped head to listen; his narrow black face was stolid, black skin dusty dry in the noon day sun. Burrhead was getting a licking. Everybody knew everybody else's cry. He was trying to tell whether it was Burrhead's ma or pa beating him.

Old rooster walked by and looked at him. "Goan, old buzzard!" he whispered, kicking dust at it. The rooster scrambled back, ruffling up, ready to fight.

Lemuel went on to the house, opened and shut the screen door softly, and stood for a moment in the kitchen. His ma'd be gone about fifteen minutes. He wiped the dust off his feet with his hands and started going through the house, searching each room systematically, just looking to see what he could find. He went upstairs to his ma's and pa's room, sniffed around in the closet, feeling in the pockets of his pa's Sunday suit, then knelt down and looked underneath the bed. He stopped and peeped out the front window, cautiously pulling back the curtains. Old Mr. Diggers was out in his yard 'cross the street, fooling 'round his fence. His ma wasn't nowhere in sight.

He turned back into the room and pulled open the top dresser drawer. There was a big rusty black pocket book with a snap fastener back in the corner. He poked it with a finger. It felt hard. He lifted it up. It was heavy. He opened it. There was money inside, all kinds of money, nickels and dimes and quarters and paper dollars and even ten dollar bills. He closed it up, shoved it back into the corner, slammed shut the drawer, and ran and looked out the front window. Then he ran and looked out the back window. He ran downstairs and went from room to room looking out all the windows in the house. No one was in sight. Everybody stayed inside during the hot part of the day.

He ran back upstairs, opened the drawer and got to the pocket book. He opened it, took out a quarter, closed it, put it away, closed the drawer, ran downstairs and out the back door and across the vacant lot to Mulberry Street. He started downtown, walking fast as he could without running. When he came to the paved sidewalks they were hot on his feet and he walked half dancing, lifting his feet quickly from the pavement. At the Bijou he handed up his quarter, got a dime in change, and went into the small hot theatre to watch a gangster film. Pow! Pow! Pow! That was him shooting down the cops. Pow! Pow! Pow!

"Where you been all day, Lem-u-well?" his ma asked as she bustled 'round the kitchen fixing supper.

"Over tuh the bayou. Fishin'. Me 'n Bluebelly went."

His ma backhanded at him but he ducked out of range. "Told you t' call Francis by his name."

"Yas'm. Francis. Me 'n Francis."

His pa looked up from the hydrant where he was washing his hands and face. "Ummmmp?" he said. His pa seldom said more than "Ummmmp." It meant most everything. Now it meant did he catch any fish. "Nawsuh," Lemuel said.

His little sister, Ella, was setting the table. Lemuel washed his hands and sat down and his pa sat down and said the blessing while his ma stood bowed at the stove. It was very hot in the kitchen and the sun hadn't set. The reddish glow of the late sun came in through the windows and they sat in the hot kitchen and ate greens and side meat and rice and baked sweet potatoes and drank the potliquor with the corn bread and had molasses and corn bread for dessert. Afterwards Lemuel helped with the dishes and they went and sat on the porch in the late evening while the people passed and said hello.

Nothing was said about the quarter. Next day Lemuel took four dimes, three nickels and two half dollars. He went and found Burrhead. "What you got beat 'bout yes-diddy?"

"Nutton. Ma said I sassed her."

"I got some money." Lemuel took the coins from his pocket and showed them.

"Where you git it?" Burrhead's eyes were big as saucers.

"Ne you mind. I got it. Les go tuh the show."

" 'Gangster Guns' at the Bijou."

"I been there. Les go downtown tuh the Grand."

On the way they stopped in front of Zeke's Grill. It was too early for the show. Zeke was in his window turning flapjacks on the grill. They were big round flapjacks, golden brown on both sides, and he'd serve 'em up with butter gobbed between. Lemuel never had no flapjacks like that at home. Burrhead neither. They looked like the best tasting flapjacks in the world.

They went inside and had an order, then they stopped at Missus

Harris's and each got double icecream cones and a bag of peanut brittle. Now they were ready for the show. It was boiling hot way up in the balcony next to the projection room, but what'd they care. They crunched happily away at their brittle and laughed and carried on. . . . "Watch out, man, he slippin' up 'hind yuh."

Time to go home Lemuel had a quarter, two nickels and a dime left. He gave Burrhead the nickels and dime and kept the quarter. That night after supper his ma let him go over to the lot and play catch with Sonny, Bluebelly, and Burrhead. They kept on playing until it was so dark they couldn't see and they lost the ball over in the weeds by the bayou.

Next day Lemuel slipped up to his ma's dresser and went into the magic black pocket book again. He took enough to buy a real big league ball and enough for him and Burrhead to get some more flapjacks and icecream too. His ma hadn't said nothing yet.

As the hot summer days went by and didn't nobody say nothing at all he kept taking a little more each day. He and Burrhead ate flapjacks every day. He set up all the boys in the neighborhood to peanut brittle and icecream and rock candy and took them to the show. Sundays after he'd put his nickel in the pan he had coins left to jingle in his pocket although he didn't let his ma or pa hear him jingling them. All his gang knew he was stealing the money from somewhere. But nobody tattled on him and they made up lies at home so their parents wouldn't get suspicious. Lemuel bought gloves and balls and bats for the team and now they could play regular ball out on the lot all day.

His ma noticed the new mitt he brought home and asked him where he got it. He said they'd all been saving their money all summer and had bought the mitt and some balls. She looked at him suspiciously. "Doan you dast let me catch you stealin' nothin', boy!"

About this time he noticed the magic black bag was getting flat and empty. The money was going. He began getting scared. He wondered how long it was going to be before his ma found out. But he had gone this far so he wouldn't stop. He wouldn't think about what was going to happen when it was all gone. He was the king of the neighborhood. He had to keep on being king.

One night after supper he and his pa were sitting on the porch. Ella was playing with the cat 'round the side. He was sitting on the bottom step, wiggling his toes in the dust. He heard his ma come downstairs. He could tell something was wrong by the way she walked. She came out on the porch.

"Isaiah, somebody's tuk all my missionary money," she said. "Who you reckin it was?"

Lemuel held his breath. "Ummmmp!" his pa said.

"You reckin it were James?" He was her younger brother who came around sometimes.

"Ummmmp! Now doan you worry, Lu'belle. We find it."

Lemuel was too scared to look around. His pa didn't move. Nobody didn't say anything to him. After a while he got up. "I'm goin' tuh bed, ma," he said.

"Ummmmp!" his pa noticed.

Lemuel crawled into bed in the little room he had off the kitchen downstairs. But he couldn't sleep. Later he heard Doris Mae crying from way down the street. He just could barely hear her but he knew it was Doris Mae. Her ma was beating her. He thought Doris Mae's ma was always beating her. Later on he heard his ma and pa go up to bed. All that night he lay half awake waiting for his pa to come down. He was so scared he just lay there and trembled.

Old rooster crowed. The sun was just rising. Clump-clump-clump. He heard his pa's footsteps on the stairs. Clump-clump-clump. It was like the sound of doom. He wriggled down in the bed and pulled the sheet up over his head. He made like he was sleeping. Clump-clump-clump. He heard his pa come into the room. He held his breath. He felt his pa reach down and pull the sheet off him. He didn't wear no bottoms in the summer. His rear was like a bare tight knot. He screwed his eyes 'round and saw his pa standing tall in mudstained overalls beside the bed with the cord to his razor strop doubled over his wrist and the strop hanging poised at his side. His pa had on his reformer's look like he got on when he passed the dance hall over on Elm Street.

"Lem-u-well, I give you uh chance tuh tell the truth. What you do with yo' ma's missionary money?"

"I didn't take it, pa. I swear I didn', pa."

"Ummmmp!" his pa said.

Whack! The strap came down. Lemuel jumped off the bed and tried to crawl underneath it. His pa caught him by the arm. Whack! Whack! Whack! went the strap. The sound hurt Lemuel as much as the licks. "Owwwwwww-owwwwwwWWWW!" he began to bawl. All over the neighborhood folks knew that Lemuel was getting a beating. His buddies knew what for. The old folks didn't know yet but they'd know before the day was over.

"God doan lak thieves," his pa said, beating him across the back and legs.

Lemuel darted toward the door. His pa headed him off. He crawled between his pa's legs getting whacked as he went through. He ran out into the kitchen. His ma was waiting for him with a switch. He tried to crawl underneath the table. His head got caught in the legs of a chair. His ma started working on his rear with the switch.

"MURDER!" he yelled at the top of his voice. "HELP! POLICE! Please, ma, I ain't never gonna steal nothin' else, ma. If you jes let me off this time, ma. I swear, ma."

"I'm gonna beat the truth into you," his ma said. "Gonna beat out the devil."

He pulled out from underneath the table and danced up and down on the floor, trying to dodge the licks aimed at his leg.

"He gone, ma! Oh, he gone!" he yelled, dancing up and down. "Dat ol' devil gone, ma! I done tuk Christ Jesus to my heart!"

Well, being as he done seen the light she sighed and let him off. Her missionary money wasn't gone clean to waste nohow if it'd make him mend his stealin' ways. She guessed them heathens would just have to wait another year; as Isaiah always say, they done waited this long 'n it ain't kilt 'em.

The way Lemuel's backsides stung and burned he figured them ol' heathens was better off than they knew 'bout.

The police parade was headed north up the main street of the big city. Of the thirty thousand policemen employed by the big city, six thousand were in the parade. It had been billed as a parade of unity to demonstrate the capacity of law enforcement and reassure the "communities" during this time of suspicion and animosity between the races. No black policemen were parading for the simple reason that none had been asked to parade and none had requested the right to parade.

At no time had the races been so utterly divided despite the billing of unity given to the parade. Judging from the appearances of both the paraders and the viewers lining the street the word "unity" seemed more applicable than the diffident allusion to the "races," for only the white race was on view and it seemed perfectly unified. In fact the crowd of all-white faces seemed to deny that a black race existed.

The police commissioner and the chiefs of the various police departments under him led the parade. They were white. The captains of the precinct stations followed, and the lieutenants in charge of the precinct detective bureaus and the uniformed patrolmen followed them. They were all white. As were all of the plainclothes detectives and uniformed patrolmen who made up the bulk of the parade following. All white. As were the spectators behind the police cordons lining the main street of the big city. As were all the people employed on that street of the big city. As were all the people employed on that street in department stores and office buildings who crowded to doors and windows to watch the police parade pass.

There was only one black man along the entire length of the street at the time, and he wasn't in sight. He was standing in a small, unlighted chamber to the left of the entrance to the big city's big Catholic cathedral on the main street. As a rule this chamber held the poor box of the big cathedral from which the daily donations were collected by a preoccupied priest in the service of the cathedral at 6 P.M. each day. But now it was shortly past three o'clock and there were almost three hours before collection. The only light in the dark room came through two slots where the donations were made, one in the stone front wall opening onto the street and the other through the wooden door opening into the vestibule. The door was locked and the black man had the chamber to himself.

Chutes ran down from the slots into a closed coin box standing on legs. He had removed the chutes which restricted his movements and he now sat straddling the coin box. The slot in the stone front wall gave him a clear view of the empty street, flanked by crowds of white civilians, up which the policemen's parade would march. Beside him on the floor was a cold bottle of lemonade collecting beads of sweat in the hot humid air. In his arms he held a heavy-caliber blued steel automatic rifle of a foreign make.

The muzzle of the barrel rested on the inner edge of the slot in the stone wall and was invisible from without. He sat patiently, as though he had all the time in the world, waiting for the parade to come into sight. He had all of the remainder of his life. Subjectively, he had waited four hundred years for this moment and he was not in a hurry. The parade would come, he knew, and he would be waiting for it.

He knew his black people would suffer severely for this moment of his triumph. He was not an ignorant man. Although he mopped the floors and polished the pews of this white cathedral, he was not without intelligence. He knew the whites would kill him too. It was almost as though he were already dead. It required a mental effort to keep from making the sign of the cross, but he knew the God of this cathedral was white and would have no tolerance for him. And there was no black God nearby, if in fact there was one anywhere in the U.S. Now at the end of his life he would have to rely upon himself. He would have to assume the authority which controlled his life. He would have to direct his will which directed his brain which directed his finger to pull the trigger; he would have to do it alone, without comfort or encouragement, consoled only by the hope that it would make life safer for the blacks in the future. He would have to believe that the children of the blacks who would suffer now would benefit later. He would have to hope that the whites would have a second thought if it was their own blood being wasted. This decision he would have to take alone. He would have to control his thoughts to formulate what he wanted to think. There was no one to shape them for him. That is the way it should have been all along. To take the decisions, to think for himself, to die without application. And if his death was in vain and the whites would never accept the blacks as equal human beings, there would be nothing to live for anyway.

Through the slot in the stone front wall of the cathedral he saw the first row of the long police parade come into view. He could faintly hear the martial music of the band which was still out of sight. In the front row a tall, sallow-skinned man with gray hair, wearing a gray civilian suit, white shirt and black tie, walked in the center of four red-faced, gold-braided chief inspectors. The black man did not know enough about the police organization to identify the police departments from the uniforms of their chiefs, but he recognized the man in the civilian suit as the police commissioner from pictures he had seen in the newspapers. The commissioner wore highly polished spectacles with black frames which glinted in the rays of the afternoon sun, but the frosty blue eyes of the chief inspectors, squinting in the sun, were without aids.

The black man's muscles tightened, a tremor ran through his body. This was it. He lifted his rifle. But they had to march slightly farther before he could get them into his sights. He had waited this long, he could wait a few seconds longer.

The first burst, passing from left to right, made a row of entries in the faces of the five officers in the lead. The first officers were of the same height and holes appeared in their upper cheekbones just beneath the eyes and in the bridges of their noses. Snot mixed with blood exploded from their nostrils and their caps flew off behind, suddenly filled with fragments of their skulls and pasty gray brain matter streaked with capillaries like gobs of putty finely laced with red ink. The commissioner, who was slightly shorter, was hit in both temples and both eyes, and the bullets made star-shaped entries in both the lenses of his spectacles and the corneas of his eyeballs and a gelatinous substance heavily mixed with blood spurted from the rims of his eye sockets. He wore no hat to catch his brains and fragments of skull, and they exploded through the sunny atmosphere and splattered the spectators with goo, tufts of gray hair and splinters of bone. One skull fragment, larger than the others, struck a tall, well-dressed man on the cheek, cutting the skin and splashing brains against his face like a custard pie in a Mack Sennett comedy. The two chiefs on the far side, being a shade taller than the others, caught the bullets in their teeth. These latter suffered worse, if such a thing was possible. Bloodstained teeth flew through the air like exotic insects, a shattered denture was expelled forward from a shattered jaw like the puking of plastic food. Jawbones came unhinged and dangled from shattered mouths. But the ultimate damage was that the heads were cut off just above the bottom jaws, which swung grotesquely from headless bodies spouting blood like gory fountains.

What made the scene so eerie was that the gunshots could not be heard over the blasting of the band and the soundproof stone walls of the cathedral. Suddenly the heads of five men were shattered into bits without a sound and by no agent that was immediately visible. It was like the act of the devil; it was uncanny. No one knew which way to run from the unseen danger but everyone ran in every direction. Men, women and children dashed about, panic-stricken, screaming, their blue eyes popping or squinting, their mouths open or their teeth gritting, their faces paper white or lobster red.

The brave policemen in the lines behind their slaughtered commissioner and chiefs drew their pistols and rapped out orders. Captains and lieutenants were bellowing to the plainclothes detectives and uniformed patrolmen in the ranks at the rear to come forward and do their duty. And row after row of the captains and lieutenants were shot down with their service revolvers in their hands. After the first burst the black man had lowered his sights and was now shooting the captains in the abdomens, riddling hearts and lungs, livers and kidneys, bursting potbellies like paper sacks of water.

In a matter of seconds the streets were strewn with the carnage, nasty gray blobs of brains, hairy fragments of skull looking like sections of broken coconuts, bone splinters from jaws and facial bones, bloody, gristly bits of ears and noses, flying red and white teeth, a section of tongue; and slick and slimy with large purpling splashes and gouts of blood, squashy bits of exploded viscera, stuffed intestines bursting with half-chewed ham and cabbage and rice and gravy, were lying in the gutters like unfinished sausages before knotting. And scattered about in this bloody carnage were what remained of the bodies of policemen, still clad in blood-clotted blue uniforms.

Spectators were killed purely by accident, by being caught in the line of fire, by bullets that had already passed through the intended victims. It was revealing that most of these were clean, comely matrons snugly fitting into their smooth white skins and little girl children with long blond braids. Whether from reflex or design, most mature men and little boys had ducked for cover, flattening themselves to the pavement or rolling into doorways and underneath parked cars.

The black man behind the gun had not been seen nor had his hiding place been discovered. The front doors of the cathedral were closed and the stained glass windows high up in the front wall were sealed. The slot in the wall for donations to charity was barely visible from the street and then only if the gaze sought it out deliberately. And it was shaded by the architecture of the clerestory so that the dulled blued steel gun barrel didn't glint in the sun. As a consequence the brave policemen with their service revolvers in their hands were running helter-skelter with nothing to shoot at while being mown down by the black killer. The white spectators were fortunate that there were no blacks among them, despite the accidental casualties, for had these irate, nervous cops spied a black face in their midst there was no calculating the number of whites who would have been killed by them accidentally. But all were decided, police and spectators alike, that the sniper was a black man for no one else would slaughter whites so wantonly, slaughter them like a sadist stomping on an ant train. And in view of the history of all the assassinations and mass murders in the U.S., it was extraordinarily enlightening that all the thousands of whites caught in a deadly gunfire from an unseen assassin, white police and white civilians alike, would automatically agree that he must be black. Had they always experienced such foreboding? Was it a pathological portent? Was it inherited? Was it constant, like original sin? Was it a presentiment of the times? Who knows? The whites had always been as secretive of their fears and failings as had the blacks.

But it was the most gratifying episode of the black man's life.

He experienced spiritual ecstasy to see the brains flying from those white men's heads, to see the fat arrogant bodies of the whites shattered and broken apart, cast into death. Hate served his pleasure; he thought fleetingly and pleasurably of all the humiliations and hurts imposed on him and all blacks by whites; in less than a second the complete outrage of slavery flashed across his mind and he could see the whites with a strange, pure clarity eating the flesh of the blacks and he knew at last that they were the only real cannibals who had ever existed. Cordite fumes stung his eyes, seared his lungs, choking him.

When he saw the riot tank rushing up the wide main street from police headquarters to kill him, he felt only indifference. He was so far ahead they could never get even now, he thought. He drew in the barrel of his gun to keep his position from being revealed and waited for his death, choking and almost blinded. He was ready to die. By then he had killed seventy-three whites, forty-seven policemen and twenty-six men, women and children civilians, and had wounded an additional seventy-five, and although he was never to know this figure, he was satisfied. He felt like a gambler who has broken the bank. He knew they would kill him quickly, but that was satisfactory too.

But, astoundingly, there remained a few moments of macabre comedy before his death arrived. The riot tank didn't know where to look for him. Its telescoped eye at the muzzle of the 20-mm. cannon stared right and left, looking over the heads and among the white spectators, over the living white policemen hopping about the dead, up and down the rich main street with its impressive stores, and in its frustration at not seeing a black face to shoot at it rained explosive 20-mm. shells on the black plaster of Paris mannequins displaying a line of beachware in a department store window.

The concussion was devastating. Splintered plate glass filled the air like a sandstorm. Faces were split open and lacerated by flying glass splinters. One woman's head was cut completely off by a piece of flying glass as large as a guillotine. Vari-colored wigs flew from white heads like frightened long-haired birds taking flight. And many others, men, women and children, were stripped stark naked by the force of the concussion.

On seeing bits of the black mannequins sailing past, a rookie cop loosed a fusillade from his .38-caliber police special. With a reflex that appeared shockingly human, on hearing itself shot upon from the rear, the tank whirled about and blasted two 20-mm. shells into the already panic-stricken policemen, instantly blowing twenty-nine of them to bits and wounding another one hundred and seventeen with flying shrapnel.

By then the screaming had grown so loud that suddenly motion ceased, as though a valve in the heart had stopped, and with the cessation of motion the screaming petered out to silence like the falling of a pall. Springing out of this motionless silence, a teenage youth ran across the blood-wet street and pointed with his slender arm and delicate hand at the coin slot in the front of the cathedral. All heads pivoted in that direction as though on a common neck, and the tank turned to stare at the stone wall with its blind eye also. But no sign of life was visible against the blank stone wall and the heavy wooden doors studded with brass. The tank stared a moment as if in deep thought, then 20-mm. cannon shells began to rain upon the stone, and people fled from the flying rock. It did not take long for the cannon to reduce the stone face of the cathedral to a pile of rubbish. But it took all of the following day to unearth the twisted rifle and a few scraps of bloody black flesh to prove the black killer had existed.

In the wake of this bloody massacre the stock market crashed. The dollar fell on the world market. The very structure of capitalism began to crumble. Confidence in the capitalistic system had an almost fatal shock. All over the world millions of capitalists sought means to invest their wealth in the Communist East.

Good night.